D1083819

"HOW CELIA CHANGED HER MIND"

CHANGED HER MIND"

and Selected Stories

AMERICAN WOMEN

WRITERS SERIES

Series Editors

Joanne Dobson

Judith Fetterley

Elaine Showalter

"HOW CELIA CHANGED HER MIND"

and Selected Stories

ROSE TERRY COOKE

Edited and with an Introduction by

ELIZABETH AMMONS

RUTGERS UNIVERSITY PRESS

New Brunswick, New Jersey

Library of Congress Cataloging-in-Publication Data

Cooke, Rose Terry, 1827–1892.
"How Celia changed her mind" and selected stories.

(American women writers series)
Bibliography: p.
1. Ammons, Elizabeth.   II. Title.   III. Series
PS1391.A46   1986   813'.4   86-3684
ISBN 0-8135-1165-8
ISBN 0-8135-1166-6 (pbk.)

CONTENTS

Acknowledgments   *vii*

Introduction   *ix*

Selected Bibliography   *xxxvi*

A Note on the Text   *xxxix*

Maya, the Princess   *1*

My Visitation   *14*

The Ring Fetter   *32*

Freedom Wheeler's Controversy with Providence   *59*

Mrs. Flint's Married Experience   *93*

How Celia Changed Her Mind   *131*

Miss Lucinda   *151*

Dely's Cow   *182*

Miss Beulah's Bonnet   *196*

Contents

Too Late   214

Some Account of Thomas Tucker   234

Explanatory Notes   261

ACKNOWLEDGMENTS

I am grateful to Judith Fetterley for introducing me to the work of Rose Terry Cooke. I am also indebted to Katherine Kleitz for advice and excellent research assistance. Finally I wish to thank Tufts University for a Faculty Research Award, which aided me in the preparation of this anthology, and the Tufts University interlibrary loan staff which, as usual, was very helpful.

Rose Terry Cooke is unfamiliar today. That was not the case one hundred years ago when there seemed to be an abundance of women eager to pose as the popular New England regionalist. One such impersonator, a magnetic Christian zealot who dove into trances that provoked wild admiration, declared that it was she who had created all of the writer's stories, under the *nom de plume* "Rose Terry" (a name she claimed to have from a little cousin who died in childhood), and that every penny of the fortune she had amassed from her literary labors had gone to educate poor girls. The landlady of this flamboyant Rose Terry wrote in indignation to Harriet Beecher Stowe:

> "DEAR MADAM,—I call upon you to silence the base reports spread about here concerning a lovely Christian woman at present staying with me. A line from you, stating that she is the author of the works written under the signature of Rose Terry, will stop the rumors at once, and much oblige yours truly."

Stowe replied that she had known Rose Terry all her life, that the author did not live in Pennsylvania but Hartford, and that the good woman's boarder was an impostor.[1]

1. Unless otherwise indicated, all biographical information in this introduction comes from Harriet Prescott Spofford's two works on Rose Terry Cooke and from Jean Downey, "A Biographical and Critical Study of Rose Terry Cooke."

Introduction

Echoing the Pennsylvania hoax, a different woman, seated beside the sister of a friend of Cooke's on a railway car, quite coolly detailed the next book that she—the great author Rose Terry—planned to write, while two other pretenders surfaced in New York, one volunteering her services to a Sunday school (where she never showed up), the other trying to fool and impress a tourist by dropping the titles of stories and poems she had supposedly written. Still another operator, working the rails between Hartford and New York and posing as one of the author's intimates, not only took up with one of Cooke's friends, but also took off with the friend's pocketbook. But perhaps the most brash was the young woman who sat down on a train next to Cooke herself and proceeded to describe how she had composed this story or that and how she felt about all the praise and money that followed. (Cooke, a woman who could be caustically funny and outspoken when need be, reportedly remained silent, whether out of embarrassment or pity we do not know.)

Why these women impersonated Cooke is in some ways easy to understand. In the second half of the nineteenth century Rose Terry Cooke was a well-known author. She was a success. Women could look to her as an ideal.

When the new *Atlantic Monthly* came out in 1857, the lead story in the first great issue had been written by Rose Terry. One of only two women to have fiction appear in that historic number of the magazine, she went on to publish her sketches and stories regularly in the leading publications of the time: the *Atlantic*, *Harper's*, *Putnam's*, *Galaxy*. William Dean Howells, grouping her with Sarah Orne Jewett, Alice Brown, and Mary Wilkins Freeman, gave her work high praise, saying of Cooke's New England fiction that her "stories [were] always so good that I grieve to have them the least forgotten" (234). In this century Ima Honaker Herron has declared in *The Small Town in American Literature* that the "real pioneer of the New England school of realism was not Mrs. Stowe, who sentimentalized about the past, but a Connecticut villager . . . Rose Terry (later Mrs. Cooke)" (80). In *Harvests of Change* Jay Martin insists that "Mrs. Cooke's work has been unjustly ignored by historians of American literature. . . . More clearly and astutely than Mrs. Stowe and long before Garland or Howe, she treated the story of rural decline, the tragedies of heroic characters whose brand of heroism no longer has any function and so sours into incredible meanness. . . . Her analysis of the tragedy of New England character was shrewd and decisive, establishing the conventions to be followed by Sarah Orne Jewett, Mary E. Wilkins, and even Edwin Arlington Robinson and Robert Frost" (140–41). That various obscure women in the nineteenth century wished to trade places with this important writer reflects on Cooke's accomplishment in her own era. Perhaps by association an ordinary woman could feel what it was like to have visibility, recognition, respect.

Yet still we might ask why. Why did such a motley assortment of women—a religious zealot, a thief, a would-be Sunday school teacher, and a handful of frustrated artists—decide on Rose Terry Cooke as their heroine (or target, as the case may be)? The answer, I think, is that they saw themselves—twisted, disguised, transplanted—in her fiction. She seemed to understand them, so why shouldn't they, in turn, get inside of her? For Rose Terry Cooke was above all a teller of women's stories. Women's anger, dreams, fears, repressions, small pleasures, occasional triumphs, and countless defeats, these were Rose Terry Cooke's subject. Moreover, it is intriguing that, like the women who wanted to get inside her experience, she in turn, to tell the stories she found most compelling, sought to penetrate the lives of women at some distance from her, women in rural New England one and two generations before her own.

Like Hawthorne or Stowe, Cooke was fascinated by Calvinist New England. She did not always write about that subculture. One of her stories, "A Hard Lesson" (*The Continent*, 1884), dramatizes the evil of slavery and is set in the deep South part of the time; in others (two of which open this volume) it is the landscape of the psyche rather than of any specific geographical region that interests Cooke. But these are unusual. Most of her best and all of her most characteristic fictions examine life in rural New England during the late eighteenth and very early nineteenth centuries. In her lifetime, in addition to publishing poetry, stories for children (appearing principally in the *Christian Union* and *The Youth's Companion*), and a couple of undistinguished novels, *Happy Dodd* (1887) and *Steadfast* (1889), Cooke produced more than one hundred pieces of short fiction, many of which she collected into four anthologies: *Somebody's Neighbors* (1881), *Root-Bound* (1885), *The Sphinx's Children and Other People's* (1886), and *Huckleberries Gathered from New England Hills* (1892). In particular she rendered with a realism unprecedented in American fiction the lives of women trapped by poverty and male tyranny.

How much of this subject matter came from her own experience, individual and familial, is hard to determine. There is no full-length biography of Rose Terry Cooke, and the major published sources that do exist—Harriet Prescott Spofford's *Our Famous Women: Lives and Deeds of Distinguished American Women of Our Times* (1884) and *A Little Book of Friends* (1916)—are short and protective. Many questions that we might wish to raise we cannot answer on the basis of existing published biographical material. Who were the models for the cruel father figures and husbands in Cooke? What was the character of the marriage of her sister (to whom she was very close)? Was it "happy," or was it a source for the many debilitating domestic arrangements we find in her fiction? And how do we understand the marriage of Cooke herself, a woman who remained single for forty-six years? Spofford describes it as a blissful match, but we know that it brought Cooke to financial ruin, forcing her to produce hackwork to keep her household running; and there can be little doubt that anxiety and pinched circumstances helped wear down her health and contributed to the pneumonia that killed her when she was sixty-five.

Yet despite these holes in our knowledge, and they are both large and deep at this point, sufficient information does exist to reconstruct the outline and some details of Rose Terry Cooke's life and career. In addition to Spofford, the excellent dissertation by Jean Downey includes valuable unpublished biographical information, and there are strong statements by the author herself published in *Sunday Afternoon* in January and August 1879, "A Letter to Mary Ann" and "One More Letter to Mary Ann," in which she talks candidly, even bitterly in spots, about her experience as a woman writer.

Rose Terry was her parents' first child. Born into comfortable circumstances in Wethersfield, Connecticut, on February 17, 1827, she spent her first three years in the country six miles west of Hartford. Her father, Henry Wadsworth Terry, described by Spofford as a warm-hearted man who loved the outdoors and was a "social favorite," descended on his mother's side from the same Wadsworth for whom Longfellow was named. What he did, if anything, to supplement the living he had as a member of an affluent middle-class family is uncertain. (One account names landscape gardening but most identify no occupation.) The child's mother, Anne Wright Hurlbut, was the daughter of the first New England shipbuilder to sail around the world, a man said to have lost his life as the result of nursing others during an epidemic. Left an orphan at nine, Cooke's mother matured into a dark, passionate woman who was sensitive and yet undemonstrative on principle, a woman, in the words of Spofford, with a "morbid conscience."

That Rose Terry adored her mother, at least consciously, seems clear from several anecdotes. In her short essay about being a woman writer, "A Letter to Mary Ann," Cooke avers: "For myself, I owe whatever power of expression I have to the patient care of my mother, who educated me chiefly herself, and made it a part of my daily drill that I should learn by heart a column of a fine print Walker's dictionary, and then write two sentences containing two of the words properly used. I have now the little book begun when I was six years old, written in a child's round hand, and filled with the day's occurrences. These quaint, priggish paragraphs with the long words underlined, were stiff and constrained enough at first, like the work of any one who handles new tools; but I recognize them now as of the greatest benefit to my future work." In "One More Letter to Mary Ann," published later that year, Cooke testifies further to the beneficial effects of her mother's stern discipline:

> I never shall forget my own childish tears and sulks over my sewing. My mother was a perfect fairy at her needle, and her rule was relentless; every long stitch was picked out and done over again, and neither tears nor entreaties availed to rid me of my task till it was properly done; every corner of a hem turned by the thread; stitching measured by two threads to a stitch; felling of absolutely regular width, and patching done invisibly; while fine darning was a sort of embroidery. I hated it then, but I have lived to bless that mother's patient persistence; and I am prouder to-day of the six patches in my small girl's school-dress which cannot be seen without searching than of any other handiwork—except perhaps my bread!

These lessons from her mother, good Calvinist schooling in patience and self-discipline, for which the author was consciously grateful as an adult, contain within them significant instruction in the repression of anger and rebellion. The little girl's victory over her own rage gives us some clue into the grown woman's extraordinary sympathy with children, as in "Miss Beulah's Bonnet" (reprinted here).

These childhood episodes also suggest where Cooke experienced at least some of the rage that she showed boiling within many of her women characters, sometimes to the point of explosion, but more often to the point, turned inward, of bitter depression and hopelessness. To be sure, Cooke's mother, teaching her daughter self-control, was simply doing her duty as a responsible Protestant parent in New England in the early nineteenth century, and doing it, from the evidence we have at least, with kindness in addition to sternness and determination. At the same time, however, something wild in both mother and child rebelled against this unbending Puritan ethic, with its calm, relentless emphasis on obedience to authority and suppression of emotion. Asked by Spofford where her mother, who looked Spanish, got her "tropic streak," Cooke responded with a memory from her childhood considerably different from the dictionary and sewing-lesson anecdotes shared with the readership of *Sunday Afternoon*.

Cooke told Spofford: "My mother was nursed by a gypsy, and in her were the oddest streaks. Severer in her Puritanism than ever I was, there was a favorable wildness about her, a passion for getting out of doors, and in just as little covering as possible. I have known her to go out in her garden, of a summer day, with only a scant skirt over her under-garment, and a hat on her head, and weed, risking interruption. The blood told. She struggled to be rugged and free and out of doors, though her habit was to be proper and shy and meek. It made her interesting, though alarming," Cooke recalled, "especially when young men used to be about of a summer's afternoon and Alice [Rose Terry's sister] and I spied her, stealing out among the young trees to the carnation bed. Poor little mother! 'Without were fightings, within were fears,' for her always." Cooke ended with the sad admission: "I dreamed, Sunday night, that she came for me to go home. I saw her as plainly as if I had been awake. But when I was awake, she did not come" (Spofford, *Book of Friends*, 155–56). In Anne Terry's mixture of orthodoxy and abandon—her struggle between fears and fightings—and in the daughter's yearning for this mother, the wild one with her passion for the out-of-doors and her disregard for authority, lies much of the energy of Rose Terry Cooke's most searching fiction. She understood repression and rebellion, at least in part, because both she and her mother wrestled with them.

A precocious child (she was able to read at three), Rose Terry moved at the age of six with her family, which now included her one-year-old sister Alice, to Hartford, where they took up residence in her paternal grandmother's brick mansion, built for her in 1799 by her father, Colonel Jeremiah Wadsworth. This house, with its abundant gardens and huge kitchen fireplace in which the children were permitted to roast apples and melt lumps of sugar, generated some of Rose Terry Cooke's happiest memories, as several stories about Thanksgiving in particular reflect. She spent hours watching and helping her grandmother as the old woman rolled out dough, filled pie shells, and transferred the brimming results to the oven without sloshing so much as a drop of filling onto the carefully fluted crusts. Described as "chill and steel" by her granddaughter, yet also as a necessary balance to her genial husband whose elegant Revolutionary War velvets the little girl liked to finger and dream over in the attic, this grandmother lingered in Rose Terry Cooke's imagination throughout her life as a model of faultless housekeeping and hospitality. She wrote to a friend in distress years later, when she had a home of her own: "'If you want to run away from every place that is haunted for you by memory or association, come here. Come any time, with or without warning, and feel as if you were coming home. There will at least be love and welcome for you here as long as I have a home'" (Spofford, *Book of Friends*, 148–49). This concept of "home" as a place that should be safe, warm, and beautiful (but too often was not)—a concept that permeates Cooke's fiction—surely had its roots in the author's fond memories of life in her grandmother's house.

But her childhood also had dark corners. She suffered a severe illness as a child which nearly killed her (leaving her delicate, this sickness had its bright side, ironically, since it prompted her father, like Sarah Orne Jewett's a generation later, to include the little girl on as many outdoor excursions as possible in order to build up her health); and she was afflicted even as a child with severe headaches which would recur throughout her life. Also as a small child she first experienced the intense fear of psychological tyranny which would show up again and again in her adult fiction.

She recalled for her friend Harriet Prescott Spofford how various household servants would tell her (at her request, no doubt) ghost and horror stories that so frightened her that, years later, she would creep out of bed in the dead of night to crouch on a top stair where she could see a little light beneath a door or hear some voices that might reassure her.

One teller of such tales stood out, a Greek boy named Athanasius who had escaped from the Turks and subsequently was employed by the little girl's family. One of his duties was to take three-year-old Rose for a walk each day, on which, as Spofford repeats the story, "he would regale her . . . with the most frightful recitals, threatening that if she ever told her father or mother he would murder her, a possibility which she fully believed of him." Spofford continues: "So thoroughly had secrecy been burned into her soul by fear that she never told of him till she was a grown woman, and had forgotten every word of his stories; but she never forgot, she has said, her horror when she chanced to meet his fierce black eyes at the table, and, thinking he might fulfill his threat on the supposition that she had betrayed him, would open her lips to cry out, 'O Athanasius! don't kill me! I haven't told!' when the thought that such an exclamation was truly betrayal and sudden death checked her." Spofford quite logically concludes from this information, "It is very possibly something of her own experience of this sort that has made her one of the most eloquent advocates of oppressed children" (*Famous Women*, 187).

It is also very possible that this anecdote about a man's sadism—conveniently displaced onto a "foreigner"—provides insight into the adult author's repeated dramatization of a man's power to terrify a dependent female into submission and silence. In the fiction, the men who victimize women as did the Athanasius of her childhood are not, except for the rare case such as "The Ring Fetter" (reprinted here), dark, sinister, foreign types. They are upright New England Calvinists. If, as no doubt was the case, a Greek servant did scare the little girl with horror stories and threats of violence lest she tell adults about their secret pastime, one must also wonder what other men—good powerful Calvinist fathers or uncles or grandfathers—were reinforcing that fear in much less exotic, more mundane ways? What other men closer to home, so to speak, were also sitting at the family table, sending lethally silent even if less dramatic threats in the little girl's direction? The experience she recorded in her fiction was the abuse of women by Calvinist New England fathers and husbands, which probably, although she did not choose to share it as she did the safer—because more distanced—Athanasius story, had its basis in fact as well.

Rose Terry completed her formal schooling at the Hartford Female Seminary, the respected women's institution founded by Catharine Beecher in the 1820s and attended by, among others, young Harriet Beecher. According to Cooke's obituary in the *New York Times* (July 19, 1892) she hurried her education, graduating at sixteen, because her father had suffered some financial reversals and it was necessary for her to begin earning her own living. (The obituary also volunteers, with how much accuracy it is hard to say, that the girl's father "held very frigid ideas in reference to her mingling in the society of young people, and the young woman was taught utterly to discourage the society and attentions of young men. The restrictions thus laid upon her life and development caused her to become diffident in society and almost prudish in manner, and she found her relief and companionship in books and in her own imagination.") At the same time that her formal schooling came to an end, Rose Terry officially joined the Congregational Church, and she remained an orthodox and serious Christian throughout her life. Although she often criticized Calvinism in her work, her critique was offered from inside, as it were, rather than outside the Christian fold. She taught in Hartford for a while after graduation and then decided to take a post in a Presbyterian church school in Burlington, New Jersey. After four years, during which time she became the governess for the clergyman's family, she returned to Hartford to be with her own family again.

Rose Terry's return to Hartford in 1847 began a period of combined domestic responsibilities and literary productivity which would last in one form or another until her death in the early 1890s. It was a point of pride with her that she supported herself all her life, a decision motivated by necessity but also by principle, as she makes clear in "A Letter to Mary Ann": "I have taken care of myself ever since I left school, and hope to do so as long as I live." Fulfilling this hope would not always be easy.

Rose Terry Cooke's first love as a writer was poetry, the most prestigious literary form of her era, and it was as a writer of verse that she hoped to make her way in the late 1840s and early 1850s. Although she never had major success as a poet (her verse for the most part is un-distinguished), she did publish her first poems in the *New York Tribune*, under the editorship of Charles Dana at the time (it speaks to her emo-tional investment in the enterprise that she chose her mother's initials— A. W. H.—as her pseudonym for these poems). She wrote verse for many years, collecting her poems in two volumes, the first published in 1861, the second in 1888. Some poems such as "The Two Villages" enjoyed wide circulation and remain effective today, and she did achieve recognition for her poetry, being honored for example by an invitation to read her verse at the Commencement Exercises of Smith College in 1881.

But it was as a fiction writer that Rose Terry Cooke was truly gifted and would manage, although sometimes just barely, to earn her own living. To the best of our present knowledge, she published her first story in *Putnam's Magazine* in 1855 (the story, which is about Mormons, forecasts later themes in its attack on husbands' unlimited power within marriage) and went on to build in the 1850s a solid magazine publishing record. Yet her situation was always precarious. She relates in "A Letter to Mary Ann": "If a man has a reputation as a writer, it does him great service; there are a few men in America who might write the wildest nonsense, and in their script and under their name no editor would dare to refuse it; but it is not so with women." She then tells how one of her best stories met with repeated refusals, which climaxed in an "elaborately polite letter" from one of the magazines "saying that the canons of taste forbade the editor to accept a story so sad in its motive; that it was a duty to brighten life for the public, not darken it with melancholy detail; so with much regret, etc., etc., it was returned." Yet, she continues, "in the next issue of that magazine there was a ghastly story by Turgenieff, beside which my simple detail of a common New England family was really hilarious; and also a dreary story of confused woe and despair from a popular American (male) author!" Cooke draws a resigned moral—"this is the sort of thing that befalls a woman who writes, and all she can do is to accept the situa-tion"—which attempts but fails to disguise the author's indignation at the inequity she was forced to live with. Likewise the double standard in pay angered Cooke, though, again and characteristically, her advice in "A

Letter to Mary Ann" was to live with it: "I only say that as a rule men are paid more than women. . . . It is the thing that is, and being a woman you will have to submit to it; therefore have the strength to do so quietly, for there is no help for you." When it came to prudery, however, she was merely amused: "I have had stories returned, one because there was a profane expression put into the mouth of a character, who was represented as surprised into that one oath and deeply penitent for it; one in which I had written 'stomach-ache,' came back marked, 'Say "a pain"'; and also 'for "big" say "large"'" ("A Letter to Mary Ann"). Disgusted rather than upset, Cooke, who was conventional when it came to matters of taste or even most moral issues, could only laugh at such squeamishness.

She could not laugh, however, at the economic worries that frequently pressed upon her. (Her impersonators' fantasies about her wealth must have seemed pitiful to her.) The habit of first-class magazines' not paying promptly for stories they accepted compelled her, to her regret, to seek publication in magazines that did not demand—indeed, did not desire—the sophistication that the *Atlantic* or *Harper's* assumed its audience capable of. It is indisputable that Cooke's published work is highly uneven; much of what she wrote is not good at all. Yet this occurred in part at least because she was forced to write much of the time under acute financial pressure.

That pressure grew worse when, on April 16, 1873, Rose Terry married Rollin H. Cooke, a widower sixteen years her junior. He was a bank clerk in Winsted, Connecticut, as well as an aspiring author of historical and genealogical works (some of which he published). In *A Little Book of Friends* Spofford explains that Rose Terry and Rollin Cooke met when both boarded in the same house in Connecticut, and that "his circumstances so excited her pity, that pity which is akin to love, that finally she yielded to his persuasion and became his wife" (146). Spofford describes Rollin Cooke as "a very attractive and lovable man, witty himself and the cause of wit in others, always interesting and always good-natured," and she states that "their relation was quite perfect." Full of admiration for her work and evidently unstinting in his emotional support, Rollin Cooke seems to have been devoted to his wife, and the union probably brought Rose Terry Cooke a great deal of happiness.

It also brought her desperate economic worries. Rollin Cooke was not a steady provider and soon after the marriage he and his father managed to run through all of Rose Terry Cooke's savings, which meant that she had to make a completely new start financially at a time in life when she might well have expected to be economically secure, even if not wealthy. A proud woman, she had to bring herself to wrangle about payments and word limits even more than usual. A year before her death she wrote to the editor of the *Atlantic*, Horace E. Scudder: "One reason why I have not written for the *Atlantic* has been their long delay in printing. In writing as I have from daily necessity you will understand that I had to write for papers and magazines that paid on acceptance. But I have always wanted to go back to the *Atlantic* for I was one of the two women who wrote for its first number and all my early successes were achieved in its columns. It is an old friend. So if you think you can print my story by June, I will not put a price on it, but will wait and be paid per page" (Downey, "*Atlantic* Friends," 133). This letter recalling her distinguished beginning with the magazine, such a far cry from present anxieties about words per page and payment timetables, could not have been easy to write, although it may be that the timely publication of the story in question, "A Town Mouse and a Country Mouse" (the letter was written in February and the story did appear in the June issue), made this particular haggle less depressing than some.

On July 18, 1892, Rose Terry Cooke died at home. She was by the time of her death a writer highly regarded by such old friends and admirers as Harriet Prescott Spofford and William Dean Howells, but rather rapidly forgotten by a new generation of readers and critics increasingly eager to dissociate themselves from all but a very few of their nineteenth-century forebears, especially if they were female.

Rose Terry Cooke exactly represents one type of nineteenth-century American woman writer that most twentieth-century literary criticism and history have been eager to dismiss as unimportant. She did not produce "a" great work. She left behind no solitary, monumental masterpiece. Instead, she left many small pieces and wrote out of a separate and predominantly female tradition, which coexisted with but remained in important ways largely independent of the masculine gospel of Great Works. Rose Terry Cooke's forte was the regional sketch, a form, as Marjorie Pryse has persuasively argued, not only pioneered by women but also developed and manipulated by them into what may very well be one of the few existing distinctly female genres.[2] The sketch does not seek to control its subject as do novels, epic poems, or traditional dramatic scripts. It does not aspire to omnipotence. It is, instead, admittedly marginal, as are women in patriarchally structured society.

The sketch concentrates on depicting a narrowly limited portion of life geographically and sociologically, and its intent, in addition to telling a story (if that function is present, which is not always the case), is to render the social and psychological life of the region as faithfully as possible. To be sure, the sketch—short, suggestive rather than definitive—may become, like sections of a quilt (also a women's art form), part of some larger design that does approach comprehensiveness, as in Sarah Orne Jewett's *The Country of the Pointed Firs* (1896), for example, or, likewise deriving from the work of nineteenth-century women, Sherwood Anderson's *Winesburg, Ohio* (1919). But even when that expansion happens, the aesthetic is one of accretion—aggregation—rather than of accelerating linear plot development.

Seen in this light, the tradition of the sketch, or as much twentieth-century literary criticism and history has belittlingly labeled it, the "local color tradition," has interesting connections with contemporary theories about the shape and nature of modern western female consciousness. As Nancy Chodorow explains in *The Reproduction of Mothering* and Carol Gilligan in *In a Different Voice*, women are reared in modern American culture (by modern I mean the Victorian era through the present) to value relationships over success-oriented individual goals and to place far more importance on process and context than do men in the culture, from whom end results and decontextualized abstract reasoning and judgments are expected. Perhaps this helps explain why the regional sketch developed as a literary form particularly hospitable to women, especially throughout the last century when a number of women writers were drawn to the form. It could be that the sketch had pragmatic advantages. We might theorize that nineteenth-century women, expected to run households and in many cases to raise children while they wrote, could fit the

2. Marjorie Pryse is presently writing a major study of nineteenth-century American regionalism as a women's form.

writing of short fictions into demanding domestic schedules with a little more ease than novel writing. However, the abundance of novels published by women in the last century suggests that this practical consideration may be more imaginary than real. A more likely explanation for women's affinity for and excellence with the sketch and short story, it seems to me, is the psychological one. The form permits women to offer ungrandiose, concrete art, shaped, more often than not, by the rhythms of domestic and feminine experience, which is cyclical, repetitive, and often inconclusive.

Individuals' relatedness to their specific environment rather than any abstract concept about universal human nature or experience lies at the heart of the regional sketch, which assumes it can know well only its own admittedly narrow field. Claims to vast masterful brilliance—the kind of overarching intellectual control aspired to by a Melville or Joyce, for example—are emphatically not part of the subtext of the sketch. To the contrary, it is the finiteness, the limitedness of the authorial project, brilliant in its detailed concrete accuracy perhaps, but lacking in any pretension to impressive scope, that makes the sketch appealing—as well perhaps as "feminine." A tiny piece of life is all, even if we are very lucky, that we can see clearly. True, in the pebble may be the boulder: that the author and reader can surmise. But what we are shown is the pebble.

Within this form, several thematic groupings emerge from Cooke's works, collected and uncollected.

Her love stories are for the most part more sentimental than we like today. An exception is "Amandar" (*Harper's*, 1880; reissued in *Somebody's Neighbors*), which looks at love between a father and son and dramatizes the feelings of a man who so loved his wife who died in childbirth that he named their son for her, to the boy's predictable embarrassment. Also successful because it avoids oversweetness is "Uncle Josh" (*Putnam's*, 1857; reissued in *Somebody's Neighbors*), a funny story about a sailor whose invete- rate cursing is cured not by his gentle first wife, whom he adores, but by his brusque second who refuses to police his language: she will not allow her self to be made his "pack mule to heaven." One of Cooke's best love stories, "Miss Lucinda" (reprinted here), is also one of her least conventional, showing the origins of love in a pigsty and treating with dignity the first love of an eccentric older woman.

Introduction

More distinctive than the love stories, however (or the pious religious sketches collected in *Root-Bound*, none of which is included here
because they are very formulaic and pat), are Cooke's biting—sometimes
grimly humorous, sometimes simply grim—tales about Calvinism, about
domestic violence in American society, and about life as a single woman
in rural, white, middle-class New England in the late eighteenth and early
nineteenth centuries.

Cooke had mixed feelings about Calvinism. In a few stories, such as
"Some Account of Thomas Tucker" (reprinted here), she expresses admiration for the strength of character fostered by the religion. Likewise, "The
Deacon's Week" (*Putnam's*, 1887; reissued in *The Sphinx's Children*), one of
Cooke's most popular stories in the nineteenth century, shows an uncompromising yet constructive Calvinism at work in a community; the parson
leads his flock through a series of reforms in which they focus their prayers
and willpower on a different topic each week, such as temperance, parent-
ing, and so forth. But in most cases Cooke brings a highly critical rather
than an admiring perspective to Calvinism. In "Aceldama Sparks; or, Old
and New" (*Harper's*, 1859; reissued in *The Sphinx's Children*) she considers
the conflict over religion between a father and son, the father professing a
hardline Calvinism while the son espouses a new, more tolerant and
compassionate Christianity. Nursed back to health by this gentle son, the
father finally concedes that the new faith may be an improvement. In
contrast to this reconciliation between parent and child, the communion
achieved by a mother and daughter in "Too Late" (reprinted here), also a
story about Calvinism's grip on the New England family, is bitter. Mother
and daughter come together, but, true to Cooke's title, it is otherwise too
late for the mother to find happiness or peace of mind in this life. The faith
of her father has blighted her life irremediably.

Yet to single out a category of fictions about Calvinism may be
misleading, for it could be argued that Calvinism so pervades the stories
and sketches, coloring the landscape and shaping the characters' lives, that
it does not really function as a discrete topic in Cooke. Rather, it reinforces
in negative ways the patriarchal authority that constricts the lives of almost
all of the women and children, and some of the men as well, in Cooke's
fictive New England. Not all men in Cooke's fiction are tyrants. Some are

kind, loving husbands, brothers, fathers, or friends. But many—and many of the most powerfully drawn—are neither kind nor loving. They are arrogant, cruel, despotic. Hardened by their constant struggle with an ungiving earth and fortified in that struggle by a religion forged out of fear and cast in an ironclad intellectuality, Cooke's men—fathers, deacons, husbands—brutalize their wives and daughters. Some of these women successfully rebel, as in "Grit" (*Harper's*, 1877; reissued in *Huckleberries*) or "Freedom Wheeler's Controversy with Providence" (reprinted here), but others are crushed, as Cooke also shows in "Freedom Wheeler's Controversy with Providence," as well as in "A Town Mouse and a Country Mouse" (*Atlantic*, 1891; reissued in *Huckleberries*) or "Mrs. Flint's Married Experience" (reprinted here).

Cooke's analysis of this patriarchal landscape receives blunt expression in her uncollected sketch "The West Shetucket Railway," published in the *Independent* in 1872, just about midway through her publishing career (and, interestingly, the year before her marriage). Surveying rural New England, she thinks about "life in lonely farms among its wild mountains, or on the bare, desolate hills that roll their sullen brown summits mile on mile through the lower tracts of this region" and states:

> There is nothing more painful than the prevalence of crime and disease in these isolated homes. Born to an inheritance of hard labor, labor necessary to mere life; fighting with that most valorous instinct of human nature, the instinct of self-preservation, against a climate not only rigorous but fatally changeful, a soil bitter and barren enough to need that gold should be sewn before more than copper can be harvested, without any excitement to stir the half torpid brain, without any pleasure, the New England farmer becomes in too many cases a mere creature of animal instincts akin to the beasts that perish—hard, cruel, sensual, vindictive. An habitual church-goer, perhaps; but none the less thoroughly irreligious. All the keener sensitiveness of his organization blunted by overwork and underfeeding till the finer emotions of his soul dwindle and perish for want of means of expression, he revenges himself on his condition in the natural way. And when you bring this same dreadful pressure to bear on women, whose more delicate nature is proportionately more

excitable, whose hearts bleed silently to the very last drop before their lips find utterance,—when you bring to bear on these poor weak souls, made for love and gentleness and bright outlooks from the daily dulness of work, the brutality, stupidness, small craft, and boorish tyranny of husbands to whom they are tied beyond escape, what wonder is it that a third of all the female lunatics in our asylums are farmers' wives, and that domestic tragedies, even beyond the scope of a sensitive novel, occur daily in these lonely houses, far beyond human help or hope?

The women who escape this tyranny are the occasional confrontive wife such as Melinda in "Freedom Wheeler's Controversy with Providence" or simply the lucky one, for example the heroine of "Dely's Cow" (reprinted here), or, as is most frequently the case, single women who have the good judgment to avoid marriage in the first place, such as Aunts Huldah and Hannah in "Freedom Wheeler." These two women prize their independence, and because they are financially self-sufficient they can, as Huldah illustrates, contradict masculine authority from a position of security (something a dependent wife or daughter cannot do).

But Huldah is the exception—as her timid sister Hannah freely owns. Most single women in Cooke's fictive world are either cowed by masculine authority or demoralized by the stigma against old maids, a bigotry that produces one of the most familiar patterns in Cooke, the story which traces the reckless decision of a spinster or widow, often someone with a comfortable home and respected social position in the community, to marry. "Odd Miss Todd" (*Harper's*, 1882; reissued in *Huckleberries*), "How Celia Changed Her Mind" (reprinted here), and "Mrs. Flint's Married Experience" all work variations on the theme of a misguided character's dissatisfaction with her life as a single woman, as does "Polly Mariner, Tailoress" (*Galaxy*, 1870; reissued in *Somebody's Neighbors*), although in that particular story Cooke finds the subject poignant rather than tragic. The parson's wife in "How Celia Changed Her Mind," a woman who knows from personal experience that "even married life had its own loneliness" and therefore is "inclined to agree with St. Paul, that the woman who did not marry 'doeth better,'" tries to influence Celia: "'Many, indeed, most of my best friends are maiden ladies, and I respect and love them just as much as if they were married women.'" But unfortunately it is not the respect and love of other women that the disgruntled spinster in Cooke's story wants. As Cooke ruefully observes in this story: "It may be said of men, as of elephants, that it is lucky they do not know their own power; for how many more women would become their worshipers and slaves than are so to-day if they knew the abject gratitude the average woman feels for the least attention, the smallest kindness, the faintest expression of affection or good will. We are all, like the Syrophenician woman, glad and ready to eat of the crumbs which fall from the children's table, so great is our faith—in men."

As this observation suggests, one disturbing theme in Cooke is the extent to which women are not merely victims, but complicit or willing victims in their oppression. To be sure, they comply because they have been shaped by the culture. Cooke does not suggest that women are naturally passive or abject, much less masochistic. The conditions of most women's lives—exhausting physical labor, repeated childbearing, endless indoctrination in the superiority of male intellect and spiritual authority—conspire to beat them down. Women reflect even in their most private moments, as a frightening tale like "Too Late" shows, attitudes they have been taught. But that is not the whole story. Cooke also believes that women at some level contribute to their own victimization when they unthinkingly participate in the type of psychological dependence on men which she criticizes in the statement quoted above and in the entire story "How Celia Changed Her Mind." Change would have to begin not simply in the attitudes of men, but of women as well.

The stories reprinted here are intended to represent Cooke's best work and to show some of her range and development over time. The first three are early stories, appearing, respectively, in the *Atlantic* in January 1858, *Harper's* in July of that same year, and the *Atlantic* in August 1859. Never anthologized by Cooke, they are far more Romantic—allegorical, even Gothic—than her better-known work. They also are three of her most interesting stories. Coming out of the same mid-century fascination with evil and darkness which produced Poe, Melville, Spofford, and Stowe, they are concerned, among other things, with death and the boundaries of human consciousness; with the invention of a creation myth that accounts anew not only for good and evil but also for the creation of earthly creators themselves, artists; and with the frightening power of human passion, including same-sex attachments as opposed to heterosexual bonds.

"Maya, the Princess" has no realistic level. It is a totally symbolic story: a parable about the woman artist which can also be read as a female creation myth. Cooke immerses us in an imaginary matriarchal realm (the father/king in this tale is a shadowy figure off at war at every crucial point in the development of his daughter, Maya: women, queens and fairies, exercise power in the mythic land of Maya's birthplace). The story of Maya's endowment with the Spark, symbol of wisdom, suffering, and creativity, deliberately echoes and rewrites Genesis (as well as Hawthorne). In place of Satan, the jealous spirit Anima stretches out "her wand, a snake of black diamonds, with a blood-red head," and touches the child Maya's eyes so that "from the serpent's rapid tongue a spark of fire darted into either eye," blessing/cursing the girl-child with vision not available to others in the realm.

As a parable of the Fall, "Maya, the Princess" tells the story of Everywoman, doomed to a life of suffering because she mistakenly places her faith in a man. As the woman artist's story, Maya's "Spark" becomes a curse segregating her from life—although still the Spark is a gift, though terrible. Unlike her innocent sisters, Maya comes to know suffering and pain and in the end experiences the lot of the beggar woman. She sees life from the bottom. Rich in symbols, this allegory about women and art can be read as creation myth or as veiled autobiography. In either case, it records the nineteenth-century woman artist's despair that she may never be able to use the magnificent yet frightening vision with which she has been endowed. It records her grief over being rendered "songless."

If "Maya" is a bitter parable, not unlike "The Valley of Childish Things" (1896) published by Edith Wharton almost half a century later, it is also witty and, oddly enough, darkly optimistic. In the imagined realm of female flesh and spirit from which Maya springs (again, the paternal presence is virtually nonexistent) there is a kind of empowering vision that anticipates Charlotte Perkins Gilman's *Herland* (1915). Cooke's creation of a powerful realm of mythic mothers, wicked as well as good (here she differs from Gilman), implies an alternative and potentially invigorating psychic heritage for women, one in which our imagined past, and therefore perhaps our future as well, might exist independent of the control of patriarchs.

In the tradition of Spofford's "The Amber Gods" (1860) as well as Gilman's "The Yellow Wallpaper" (1892), "My Visitation" is a tale told by a first-person disturbed narrator, who announces that she will not be able to give us a cool, neatly arranged narrative but, instead, the agonized, admittedly emotional outpourings of her heart. An avid reader of the Brontës, this woman offers us a love story as Gothic as any the Brontës wrote—a tale of wild, dangerous passion that defies the grave—with the difference here that the passion involved is, explicitly rather than implicitly, the love of a woman for another woman. The issue the narrator struggles with is her disinterest in, her relative lack of attraction to, heterosexuality. The narrator is never "without constant yearnings for Eleanor," whom she describes as "the one present and all-absorbing passion of my soul." She says: "I discovered in myself that I never could have loved any man as I did her," and realizes that "I had but the lesser part of a heart to give any man. I loved a woman too well to love or to marry." "My Visitation" charts the painful journey this woman is expected to make away from this passionate same-sex attachment to union with a man; and the fact that Cooke dramatizes that journey as a horror story—a kind of living nightmare that tips the narrator into madness—reveals both how dangerous the enforced journey into heterosexuality is and, in many cases, how damaging.

In part Cooke raises a sociological issue. Her narrator admits: "I shuddered at the possibility of loving a man so utterly, and then placing myself at his mercy for life." Given men's power over women in patriarchal culture, a power Cooke shows herself well aware of in story after story, love for a man can mean consigning oneself to a life of abuse and even torture from which escape, in an era before divorce, was impossible. The narrator's fear of heterosexuality is not prudish (as her feelings for Eleanor show, she is obviously able to own and express her passions) but realistic. Passionate dependence on a man, given the social structure, is dangerous.

Yet the struggle in "My Visitation" runs deeper than a critique of marriage in patriarchal society. In order to be "sane" and "normal" in her society, the narrator must rip herself away from the passionate attachment she feels for another woman. As Carroll Smith-Rosenberg explains in her study of middle-class white women's friendships in the nineteenth century, most women lived in a world sharply divided into separate masculine and feminine spheres—the former public, rational, and competitive in nature, the latter private, emotional, and relational. Therefore for many women emotional and even physical satisfaction came from relationships not with men but with other women: sisters, mothers, and especially friends. Defined as asexual creatures by their culture, respectable women could show their love for one another openly in speech, embraces, and letters, and, Smith-Rosenberg argues, they could continue their passionate attachments even after marriage, practicing obedience and conjugal compliance in their relations with their husbands, but reserving their intense affection and genuine love for other women. Cooke's story, while demonstrating the gulf between a nineteenth-century woman's feelings for men and her feelings for another woman, contradicts the principal argument of Smith-Rosenberg's essay: that the two kinds of feelings could coexist in adult female life. Cooke's heroine must renounce her feelings for Eleanor; she must come to see her beloved as a monster and her own passionate love for her as deranged. Anticipating Sarah Orne Jewett's "A White Heron" (1886), another story about enforced passage into heterosexuality, Cooke's horror story records the psychic pain—the descent into madness—that the injunction to love men has caused many women.

Stylistically, "The Ring Fetter" represents a bridge between Cooke's Romantic fiction and the more realistic stories and sketches that would typify her work throughout the rest of her career. Like "Maya, the Princess" and "My Visitation," its atmosphere is exotic, even Gothic: in this story a woman is literally the prisoner of a demonic villain, a murderer, who chains her to him in marriage. The settings are morbid; the characters, including an ancient black couple as hopelessly in the husband's thrall as the wife he abuses and tortures, are exaggerated. At the same time, this tale mounts the realistic criticism of marriage that Cooke would go on to offer repeatedly in her subsequent fiction: her horror at the unlimited power of husbands over wives within marriage. She says of her heroine married to a drunkard and criminal (the woman's own mother was so isolated as a wife that it maddened and finally killed her): "She could not leave him; she was utterly in his power; she was his,—like his boots, his gun, his dog; and till he should tire of her and fling her into some lonely chamber to waste and die, she was bound to serve him; he was safe." The sadistic conclusion of this fiction about the powerlessness of wives perfectly meshes the Romanticism and the realism that coexist throughout the narrative.

The next three stories, "Freedom Wheeler's Controversy with Providence," "Mrs. Flint's Married Experience," and "How Celia Changed Her Mind" are fully accomplished realistic pieces on the subjects of marriage and of Calvinist repression and rigidity.

"Freedom Wheeler's Controversy with Providence" brilliantly fuses several of Cooke's themes: the strength and grit of old women who remain single, the tyranny of Calvinist husbands, the drudgery and victimization of women in marriage, and the value of female rebellion. The piece is grimly funny, even macabre. Freedom Wheeler determines to have a son named after him, despite obvious providential signs to the contrary; and in the course of charting his battle against nature, God, the church, and— finally and most formidable—a woman not about to be intimidated by his masculine arrogance, Cooke converts her own rage into revenge. She brings Freedom Wheeler through a devastating series of losses to a confrontation with his own character which is profoundly humbling and life altering. The story, considered one of Cooke's best, represents an excellent introduction to its author's bedrock quarrel with patriarchal authority.

Equally typical is "Mrs. Flint's Married Experience," a story about mother-daughter loss, the abuse of women possible within patriarchal marriage, and the inability of men to judge women's lives. This sketch shows the terrible mistake a single woman makes when she decides to marry because she is lonely and feels unappreciated. When the Widow Gold marries Deacon Flint, thus becoming Mrs. Flint (the change in her name mirrors her fate), she signs her own death warrant. The deacon— model churchman and upstanding citizen—works his wife to exhaustion, starves her, refuses to let her see other people, deprives her of sufficient clothing in the winter, and then ignores her debilitation and deterioration. All of this he does in the name of Christian duty and economy; and as Cooke explains in the story, this man is not a figment of her imagination: "If this story were not absolutely true," she declares, "I should scarce dare to invent such a character as Deacon Flint." When his wife leaves this man, partly through the encouragement of a young woman who is horrified by his cruelty and determined that the old woman not submit to it any longer, the church deacons censure her for her disobedience, despite the protests, it is important to say, of a renegade parson who sides with the woman. This bitter story, especially in its closing fury—the young woman Mabel confronts Deacon Flint: "'Are you proper pleased now?' she said in a low voice of concentred contempt and rage. . . . 'You've killed her as good as if you took an axe to her'"—passionately illustrates Cooke's outrage at the victimization of women by tyrannical husbands.

Reiterating the central issue of "Mrs. Flint's Married Experience," "How Celia Changed Her Mind" records the fate of a spinster who marries late in life because she feels that "'a woman that's married is somebody; she's got a place in the world . . . but . . . you might as well be a dog as an old maid.'" The marriage she makes, like the wretched lovematch that inspires the tale's subplot, is typical ("It was no worse with Celia than with most of her sex in Bassett") and hellish:

> Admitted into the freemasonry of married women, she discovered how few among them were more than household drudges, the servants of their families, worked to the verge of exhaustion, and neither thanked nor rewarded for their pains. She saw here a woman whose children were careless of, and ungrateful to her, and her husband coldly indifferent; there was one on whom the man she had married wreaked all his fiendish temper in daily small injuries, little vexatious acts, petty tyrannies, a "street-angel, house-devil" of a man, of all sorts the most hateful. There were many whose lives had no other outlook than hard work until the end should come, who rose up to labor and lay down in sleepless exhaustion, and some whose days were a constant terror to them from the intemperate brutes to whom they had intrusted their happiness, and indeed their whole existence.

Celia, whose marriage is as bad as any of these, is very nearly broken by her husband's mean-spirited miserliness. Yet, mercifully, she is not. In contrast to "Mrs. Flint's Married Experience," in this story it is the husband who dies, and his widow meets the world with defiance. She refuses to wear mourning and replies to anyone who compliments her on her inheritance, "'I earned it.'" This sketch tells of tragedy but ends in triumph. Celia, surrounding herself with old maids, proudly presides over an all-female Thanksgiving dinner at which she vows: "'Every year, so long as I live, I'm going to keep an old maids' Thanksgivin' for a kind of a burnt-offering, sech as the Bible tells about, for I've changed my mind clear down to the bottom.'" And then, this widow, who was nearly starved to death by her husband, says to the hungry women surrounding her: "'let's go to work at the victuals.'"

Cooke did not always write gloomy or tragic fiction, as the next three stories—"Miss Lucinda," "Dely's Cow," and "Miss Beulah's Bonnet"—attest. She could be playful; she could be poignant; she could be raucously funny.

"Miss Lucinda" opens with a consciously literary declaration about realism. "Forgive me once more, patient reader," Cooke announces, "if I offer to you no tragedy in high life, no sentimental history of fashion and wealth, but only a little story about a woman who could not be a heroine." This nonheroine is a jolly, round-cheeked older woman who has her world well ordered. Her pets, flowers, lovely manners, and refined table give her great pleasure and fulfillment, persuading her that she needs nothing else. Then there appears a pig and on its heels a fastidious French dancing master to complicate her life. First her world turns slapstick and then into a kind of farce, with Miss Lucinda and the French dancing master pirouetting in the pigsty and the old maid appearing at dance class decked out in scarlet ribbons and "clouds of lace." The happy ending of this story, which plays with the Romantic fantasy of a wounded man's being tamed by the love of a woman (a familiar pattern in the Brontës, for example), shows the positive side of Cooke's vision. In this sweet, funny story, which incidentally reverses the Circe myth (here a man replaces a pig rather than the other way around), Cooke holds up two misfits, two "crazies"—an independent Eve in her unspoiled Garden and a down-at-the-heels Frenchman—as two of the healthiest, most likable characters in her fiction. Neither is a Calvinist; neither is central or "important" in New England society. Indeed, both are marginal, peculiar. Love between a man and a woman is possible in Cooke's world, this story suggests, but it thrives outside conventional patriarchal structures.

"Dely's Cow" is a delicate sketch. It shows us the loneliness and hardness of rural New England life for a young wife during wartime, yet it

Introduction

is not anger or social criticism but a gentle sympathy that Cooke seems to express here. Dely's husband, a good person, is a loyal patriot, and when he joins the army she is left on their farm miles away from any adult human contact. During her long months of isolation, with only her baby to keep her company, she finds consolation and friendship in the cow she daily grooms and milks. Dely's cow—sweet, sad, milky, given a name—represents a major presence, literal and symbolic, in this story about a young woman's isolation and deprivation. The two females, one human, the other bovine, form a nonverbal community that sees the young mother through her long period of killing solitude.

"Miss Beulah's Bonnet," a comical sketch, makes a serious point about cruelty to children and about the deep chasm between masculine and feminine culture in the white, rural, New England landscape surveyed by Cooke. When her prized (and ludicrously old-fashioned) Leghorn bonnet disappears, it does not occur to Beulah Larkin—a stereotypically "tall, gaunt, hard-featured, and good" old woman who has remained single and highly respected all her life—that it might be connected to her harsh treatment of one of her wards, a healthily high-spirited little boy whose sister the old maid pets but whose own antics and bids for attention she crushes. Similarly, when Miss Beulah fails to appear in church and the deacons, with dour ceremony and high self-importance, come to interrogate their backslid sister, they fail to see or properly appreciate the connection between the good woman's absence and her hatlessness. While unimportant to men, the possession of a proper church hat is a serious matter in female culture. It is not a question of fashion but of self-dignity. A seasonally inappropriate or hopelessly ragged bonnet makes a woman look as foolish in church as would a pair of knickers on a grown man; it is a matter of being able to present oneself as a serious, adult member of the community who understands that honoring God begins in self-respect and the observance of certain rules of decorum. None of this is understood by the jury of patriarchs who come to visit their judgment on—to their way of thinking—the unaccountably balky, even prideful, old maid. Much like Susan Glaspell's "A Jury of Her Peers" (1917) early in this century, Cooke's story criticizes the assumption of men that their rules and values are the only ones: the sketch affirms the integrity and dignity of women's culture and community in the face of male ignorance and even contempt. (Significantly, women band together to replace Miss Beulah's bonnet.) An amusing story about the differences between the male and female spheres, "Miss Beulah's Bonnet" forces both Miss Beulah and the church fathers to face the blindness that is produced by their radically segregated worlds.

The last two pieces in this volume return to tragedy, marriage, and the subject of Calvinism.

"Too Late"—quite possibly the best story Cook ever wrote—shows the tragic effect on a woman of the severe Calvinist upbringing that taught her to hate her own body and to scorn all pleasure and emotion in this life. Taking as her model her harsh Calvinist father, for whom existence "was a heavy and dreadful responsibility . . . a perpetual fleeing from the wrath to come," Hannah Blair impulsively and then methodically crushes her own spirit, taking out her pain on her own daughter, whose love she rejects and whose body, always with good Calvinist cause, she beats. As a mother-daughter story, this sketch in culturally produced self-mutilation, which spills over into child abuse, examines the suffering that women inflict on themselves and each other, including their daughters, when they buy into life-denying patriarchal values. Although the sketch finally offers a modicum of hope in its portrait of the last relationship we see in the story, it is uncompromising in its critique of Calvinism's destructive legacy for women.

"Some Account of Thomas Tucker," in contrast, ponders the inspiring side of Calvinism, its "ghastly honesty." The sketch traces the career of a repressed but relentlessly dutiful son of Puritanism whose father was cheerless and orthodox and whose mother was spiritless and drab. Parson Tucker constantly confronts his flock with their hypocrisy: he accosts the bride at the altar, commanding her to look into her heart and motives; he preaches the blessing of infant mortality at the annual baptismal service. This "aggressive honesty" isolates and exposes him. He cannot even hide from his own fear of death. Yet this honesty is strangely, bitterly, admirable. His refusal to compromise the truth as he sees it is both the blight on his life and the beauty of it in this highly critical and yet compassionate reflection on Calvinism.

Likewise the refusal of Rose Terry Cooke to compromise the truth as she saw it accounts for much of the energy—the force—of her best fiction. Cooke had a superb ear for dialect and dialogue. The speech of her characters in the realistic fiction rings true to life; we can believe that actual people are talking. She also had an eye for detail, as any regionalist must, and a keen fix on significant character types: the prophetic Native American, Moll Thunder, who appears in several of the sketches; the starchy Aunts Huldah and Hannah of "Freedom Wheeler's Controversy with Providence"; the series of cruel patriarchs who dominate Cooke's fictive New England landscape. In addition Cooke's dramatic sense is sharp. Often she opens a sketch with dialogue, drawing the reader in swiftly. In her best work she is skillful at looping exposition and history in after she has begun, and freqently her conclusions introduce the perfect last stroke that pulls the whole composition into brilliant focus. As a stylist, Cooke is impressive.

But finally it is for her honesty, I think, that Rose Terry Cooke stands out: her fierce commitment to telling the truth as she saw it. Harriet Prescott Spofford observed of her friend, "Possibly she would be as good a hater as lover should occasion rise, for indifference is impossible to her, and all her emotions are strong ones" (*Famous Women*, 191). Spofford's "possibly" here is decorative—a mere piece of tact. Clearly Rose Terry Cooke *was* as good a hater as she was a lover, and the strength of those emotions—Cooke's refusal to remain indifferent—is what gives her best work its aggressive honesty, even its "ghastly honesty," which speaks across the century that separates her life from ours.

SELECTED BIBLIOGRAPHY

WORKS BY ROSE TERRY COOKE

Happy Dodd. Boston: Ticknor, 1887.

"A Hard Lesson." *The Continent* 5 (June 1884): 682–88.

Huckleberries Gathered from New England Hills. Boston: Houghton Mifflin, 1891.

"A Letter to Mary Ann." *Sunday Afternoon* 3 (Jan. 1879): 79–83.

"Maya, the Princess." *Atlantic Monthly* 1 (Jan. 1858): 263–70.

"My Visitation." *Harper's* 17 (July 1858): 232–39.

"One More Letter to Mary Ann." *Sunday Afternoon* 3 (Aug. 1879): 752–55.

Poems. Boston: Ticknor and Fields, 1861.

Poems. New York: Gottsberger, 1888.

"The Ring Fetter." *Atlantic Monthly* 4 (Aug. 1859): 154–70.

Root-Bound and Other Sketches. Boston: Congregational Sunday School and Publishing Society, 1885.

Somebody's Neighbors. Boston: Osgood, 1881.

The Sphinx's Children and Other People's. Boston: Ticknor, 1886.

Steadfast, the Story of A Saint and A Sinner. Boston: Ticknor, 1889.

Selected Bibliography

SOURCES AND FURTHER READINGS

Chodorow, Nancy. *The Reproduction of Mothering: Psychoanalysis and the Sociology of Gender.* Berkeley: U of California P, 1978.

Donovan, Josephine. *New England Local Color Literature: A Women's Tradition.* New York: Frederick Ungar, 1983. 68–81.

Downey, Jean. "*Atlantic* Friends: Howells and Cooke." *American Notes and Queries* 1 (May 1963): 132–33.

———. "A Biographical and Critical Study of Rose Terry Cooke." Diss. U of Ottawa, 1956.

———. "Rose Terry Cooke: A Bibliography." *Bulletin of Bibliography* 21 (May-Aug. 1955): 159–63; (Sept.-Dec. 1955): 191–92.

Gilligan, Carol. *In a Different Voice: Psychological Theory and Women's Development.* Cambridge, MA: Harvard UP, 1982.

Herron, Ima Honaker. *The Small Town in American Literature.* New York: Pageant Books, 1959.

Howells, William Dean. *W. D. Howells as Critic.* Ed. Edwin H. Cady. London: Routledge & Kegan Paul, 1973.

Kleitz, Katherine. "Essence of New England: The Portraits of Rose Terry Cooke." *American Transcendental Quarterly* 47–48 (Summer-Fall 1980): 127–39.

Martin, Jay. *Harvests of Change: American Literature, 1865–1914.* Princeton: Princeton UP, 1967. 139–42.

Newlyn, Evelyn. "Rose Terry Cooke and the Children of the Sphinx." *Regionalism and the Female Imagination* 4 (Winter 1979): 49–57.

Smith-Rosenberg, Carroll. "The Female World of Love and Ritual: Relations Between Women in Nineteenth-Century America." *Signs* 1 (Autumn 1975): 1–28.

Spofford, Harriet Prescott. *A Little Book of Friends.* Boston: Little, Brown, 1916. 143–56.

———. "Rose Terry Cooke." *Our Famous Women, An Authorized Record of the Lives and Deeds of Distinguished American Women of Our Times.* By Elizabeth Stuart Phelps et al. Hartford: A. D. Worthington, 1884. 174–206.

Selected Bibliography

Toth, Susan Allen. "Character Studies in Rose Terry Cooke: New Faces for the Short Story." *Kate Chopin Newsletter* 2 (1976): 19–26.

Westbrook, Perry D. *Acres of Flint: Sarah Orne Jewett and Her Contemporaries.* Metuchen, NJ: Scarecrow Press, 1951; rev. ed. 1981. 78–85.

A NOTE ON THE TEXT

The overall arrangement of the fictions in this anthology is not chronological. Date of publication is not always a reliable reflection of composition for Cooke, and she herself mixed early and later stories when she compiled her anthologies. Therefore an arrangement that illustrates stylistic and thematic developments has been followed, although chronology does obtain in two respects: the first stories in this volume represent work Cooke published early in her career, and within each grouping of pieces (see the Introduction) the fictions appear chronologically.

The publication history of the pieces is as follows: "Maya, the Princess," *Atlantic* 1 (Jan. 1858), 263–70, not reprinted by Cooke; "My Visitation," *Harper's* 17 (July 1858), 232–39, not reprinted by Cooke; "The Ring Fetter," *Atlantic* 4 (Aug. 1859), 154–70, not reprinted by Cooke; "Freedom Wheeler's Controversy with Providence," *Atlantic* 40 (July 1877), 65–84, reprinted in *Somebody's Neighbors* (1881); "Mrs. Flint's Married Experience," *Harper's* 62 (Dec. 1880), 79–101, reprinted in *Somebody's Neighbors*; "How Celia Changed Her Mind," printed in *Huckleberries* (1892), no journal publication found; "Miss Lucinda," *Atlantic* 8 (Aug. 1861), 141–59, reprinted in *Somebody's Neighbors*; "Dely's Cow," *Atlantic* 15 (June 1865), 665–72, reprinted in *Somebody's Neighbors*; "Miss Beulah's Bonnet," *Harper's* 60 (Mar. 1880), 570–79, reprinted in *Somebody's Neighbors*; "Too Late," *Galaxy* 19 (Jan. 1875), 32–43, reprinted in *The Sphinx's Children* (1886); "Some Account of Thomas Tucker," *Atlantic* 50 (Aug. 1882), 177–93, reprinted in *The Sphinx's Children*. Stories anthologized by Cooke have been reprinted from the anthology in which they appeared. Changes in punctuation and spelling have not been made.

"HOW CELIA CHANGED HER MIND"

CHANGED HER MIND"

and Selected Stories

MAYA, THE PRINCESS

THE SEA floated its foam-caps upon the gray shore, and murmured its inarticulate love-stories all day to the dumb rocks above; the blue sky was bordered with saffron sunrises, pink sunsets, silver moon-fringes, or spangled with careless stars; the air was full of south-winds that had fluttered the hearts of a thousand roses and a million violets with long, deep kisses, and then flung the delicate odors abroad to tell their exploits, and set the butterflies mad with jealousy, and the bees crazy with avarice. And all this bloom was upon the country of Larrièrepensée, when Queen Lura's little daughter came to life in the Topaz Palace that stood on Sunrise Hills, and was King Joconde's summer pavilion.

Now there was no searching far and wide for godfathers, god-mothers, and a name, as there is when the princesses of this world are born: for, in the first place, Larrièrepensée was a country of pious heathen, and full of fairies; the people worshipped an Idea, and invited the fairy folk to all their parties, as we who are proper here invite the clergy; only the fairy folk did not get behind the door, or leave the room, when dancing commenced.

And the reason why this princess was born to a name, as well as to a kingdom, was, that, long ago, the people who kept records in Larrièrepensée were much troubled by the ladies of that land never growing old: they staid at thirty for ten years; at forty, for twenty; and all died before fifty, which made much confusion in dates,—especially when some women were called upon to tell traditions, the only sort of history endured in that kingdom; because it was against the law to write either lies or romances, though you might hear and tell them, if you would, and some people would; although to call a man a historian there was the same thing as to say, "You lie!" here.

But as I was saying, this evergreen way into which the women fell caused much trouble, and the Twelve Sages made a law that for six hundred years every female child born in any month of the seventy-two hundred following should be named by the name ordained for that month; and then they made a long list, containing seventy-two hundred names of women, and locked it up in the box of Great Designs, which stood always under the king's throne; and thenceforward, at the beginning of every month, the Twelve Sages unlocked the box, consulted the paper, and sent a herald through the town to proclaim the girl-name for that month. So this saved a world of trouble; for if some wrinkled old maid should say, "And that happened long ago, some time before I was born," all her gossips laughed, and cried out, "Ho! ho! there's a historian! do we not all know you were a born Allia, ten years before that date?"—and then the old maid was put to shame.

Now it happened well for Queen Lura's lovely daughter, that on her birthmonth was written the gracious name of Maya, for it seemed well to fit her grace and delicacy, while but few in that country knew its sad Oriental depth, or that it had any meaning at all.[1]

It was all one flush of dawn upon Sunrise Hills, when the maids-of-honor, in curls and white frocks, began to strew the great Hall of Amethyst with geranium leaves, and arrange light tripods of gold for the fairies, who were that day gathered from all Larrièrepensée to see and gift the new princess. The Queen had written notes to them on spicy magnolia-petals, and now the head-nurse and the grand-equerry wheeled her couch of state into the Hall of Amethyst, that she might receive the tender wishes of the good fairies, while yet the sweet languor of her motherhood kept her from the fresh wind and bright dew out of doors.

The couch of state was fashioned like a great rose of crimson velvet; only where there should have been the gold anthers of the flower lay the lovely Queen, wrapped in a mantle of canary-birds' down, and nested on one arm slept the Child of the Kingdom, Maya. Presently a cloud of honey-bees swept through the wide windows, and settling upon the ceiling began a murmurous song, when, one by one, the flower-fairies entered, and flitting to their tripods, each garlanded with her own blossom, awaited the coming of their Head,—the Fairy Cordis.

As the Queen perceived their delay, a sudden pang crossed her pale and tranquil brow.

"Ah!" said she, to the nurse-in-chief, Mrs. Lita, "my poor baby, Maya! What have I done? I have neglected to ask the Fairy Anima, and now she will come in anger, and give my child an evil gift, unless Cordis hastens!"

"Do not fear, Madam!" said Mrs. Lita, "your nerves are weak,—take a little cordial."

So she gave the Queen a red glass full of honeybell whiskey; but she called it a fine name, like Rose-dew, or Tears-of-Flax, and then Queen Lura drank it down nicely;—so much depends on names, even in Larrièrepensée!

But as Mrs. Lita set away the glass, the bees upon the ceiling began to buzz in a most angry manner, and rally about the queen-bee; the south-wind cried round the palace corner; and a strange light, like the sun shining when it rains, threw a lurid glow over the graceful fairy forms. Then the door of the hall flung open, and a beautiful, wrathful shape crossed the threshold;—it was the Fairy Anima. Where she gathered the gauzes that made her rainbow vest, or the water-diamonds that gemmed her night-black hair, or the sun-fringed cloud of purple that was her robe, no fay or mortal knew; but they knew well the power of her presence, and grew pale at her anger.

With swift feet she neared the couch of state, but her steps lingered as she saw within those crimson leaves the delicate, fear-pale face of the Queen, and her sleeping child.

"Always rose-folded!" she murmured, "and I tread the winds abroad! A fair bud, and I am but a stately stem! You were foolish and frail, Queen Lura, that you sent me no word of your harvest-time; now I come angry. Show me the child!"

Mrs. Lita, with awed steps, drew near, and lifted the baby in her arms, and the child's soft hazel eyes looked with grave innocence at Anima. Truly, the Princess was a lovely piece of nature: her hair, like fine silk, fell in dark, yet gilded tresses from her snow-white brow; her eyes were thoughtless, tender, serene; her lips red as the heart of a peach; her skin so fair that it seemed stained with violets where the blue veins crept livingly beneath; and her dimpled cheeks were flushed with sleep like the sunset sky.

Anima looked at the baby.—"Ah! too much, too much!" said she. "Queen Lura, a butterfly can eat honey only; let us have a higher life for the Princess of Larrièrepensée. Maya, I give thee for a birth-gift another crown. Receive the Spark!"

Queen Lura shrieked; but Anima stretching out her wand, a snake of black diamonds, with a blood-red head, touched the child's eyes, and from the serpent's rapid tongue a spark of fire darted into either eye, and sunk deeper and deeper,—for two tears flowed above, and hung on Maya's silky lashes, as she looked with a preternatural expression of reproach at the Fairy.

Now all was confusion. Queen Lura tried to faint,—she knew it was proper,—and the grand-equerry rang all the palace bells in a row. Anima gave no glance at the little Princess, who still sat upright in Mrs. Lita's petrified arms, but went proudly from the hall alone.

The flower-fairies dropped their wands with one sonorous clang upon the floor, and with bitter sighs and wringing hands flitted one after another to the portal, bewailing, as they went, their wasted gifts and powers.

"Why should I give her beauty?" cried the Fairy Rose; "all eyes will be dazzled with the Spark; who will know on what form it shines?"

So the red rose dropped and died.

"Why should I bring her innocence?" said the Fairy Lily; "the Spark will burn all evil from her, thought and deed!"

Then the white lily dropped and died.

"Is there any use to her in grace?" wept the Fairy Eglantine; "the Spark will melt away all mortal grossness, till she is light and graceful as the clouds above."

And the eglantine wreaths dropped and died.

"She will never want humility," said the Fairy Violet; "for she will find too soon that the Spark is a curse as well as a crown!"

So the violet dropped and died.

Then the Sun-dew denied her pity; the blue Forget-me-not, constancy; the Iris, pride; the Butter-cup, gold; the Passion-flower, love; the

Amaranth, hope: all because the Spark should gift her with every one of these, and burn the gift in deeply. So they all dropped and died; and she could never know the flowers of life,—only its fires.

But in the end of all this flight came a ray of consolation, like the star that heralds dawn, springing upward on the skirt of night's blackest hour. The raging bees that had swarmed upon the golden chandelier returned to the ceiling and their song; the scattered flowers revived and scented the air: for the Fairy Cordis came,—too late, but welcome; her face bright with flushes of vivid, but uncertain rose,—her deep gray eyes brimming with motherhood, a sister's fondness, and the ardor of a child. The tenderest garden-spider-webs made her a robe, full of little common blue-eyed flowers, and in her gold-brown hair rested a light circle of such blooms as beguile the winter days of the poor and the desolate, and put forth their sweetest buds by the garret window, or the bedside of a sick man.

Mrs. Lita nearly dropped the baby, in her great relief of mind; but Cordis caught it, and looked at its brilliant face with tears.

"Ah, Head of the Fairies, help me!" murmured Queen Lura, extending her arms toward Cordis; for she had kept one eye open wide enough to see what would happen while she fainted away.

"All I can, I will," said the kindly fairy, speaking in the same key that a lark sings in. So she sat down upon a white velvet mushroom and fell to thinking, while Maya, the Princess, looked at her from the rose where she lay, and the Queen, having pushed her down robe safely out of the way, leaned her head on her hand, and very properly cried as much as six tears.

Soon, like a sunbeam, Cordis looked up. "I can give the Princess a countercharm, Queen Lura," said she,—"but it is not sure. Look you! she will have a lonely life,—for the Spark burns, as well as shines, and the only way to mend that matter is to give the fire better fuel than herself. For some long years yet, she must keep herself in peace and the shade; but when she is a woman, and the Spark can no more be hidden,—since to be a woman is to have power and pain,—then let her veil herself, and with a staff and scrip[2] go abroad into the world, for her time is come. Now in this kingdom of Larrièrepensée there stand many houses, all empty, but swept and garnished, and a fire laid ready on the hearth for the hand of the Coming to kindle. But sometimes, nay, often, this fire is a cheat: for there be men who carve the semblance of it in stone, and are so content to have the chill for the blaze all their lives; and on some hearths the logs are green wood, set up before their time; and on some they are but ashes, for the fire has burned and died, and left the ghostly shape of boughs behind; and sometimes, again, they are but icicles clothed in bark, to save the shame of the possessor. But there are some hearths laid with dry and goodly timber; and if the Princess Maya does not fail, but chooses a real and honest heap of wood, and kindles it from the Spark within her, then will she have a most perfect life; for the fire that consumes her shall leave its evil work, and make the light and warmth of a household, and rescue her forever from the accursed crown of the Spark. But—I grieve to tell you, yet one of my name cannot lie—if the Princess mistake the false for the true, if she flashes her fire upon stone, or ice, or embers, either the Spark will recoil and burn her to ashes, or it will die where she placed it and turn her to stone, or—worst fate of all, yet likeliest to befall the tenderest and best—it will reënter her at her lips, and turn her whole nature to the bitterness of gall, so that neither food shall refresh her, sleep rest her, water quench her thirst, nor fire warm her body. Is it worth the trial? or shall she live and burn slowly to her death, with the unquenchable fire of the Spark?"

"Ah! let her, at the least, try for that perfect life," said Queen Lura.

Then the Fairy Cordis drew from her delicate finger a ring of twisted gold, in which was set an opal wrought into the shape of a heart, and in it palpitated, like throbbing blood, one scarlet flash of flame.

"Let her keep this always on her hand," said Cordis. "It will serve to test the truth of the fire she strives to kindle; for if it be not true wood, this heart will grow cold, the throb cease, the glow become dim. The talisman may, will, save her, unless in the madness of joy she forget to ask its aid, or the Spark flashing upon its surface seems to create anew the fire within, and thus deceives her."

So the Fairy put the ring upon Queen Lura's hand, and kissed Maya's fair brow, already shaded with sleep. The bees upon the ceiling followed her, dropping honey as they went; the maids-of-honor wheeled away the couch of state; the castle-maids swept up the fading leaves and blossoms, drew the tulip-tree curtains down, fastened the great door with a sandal-wood bar, sprinkled the corridors with rosewater; and by moon-rise, when the nightingales sung loud from the laurel thickets, all the country slept,—even Maya; but the Spark burned bright, and she dreamed.

So the night came on, and many another night, and many a new day,—till Maya, grown a girl, looked onward to the life before her with strange foreboding, for still the Spark burned.

Hitherto it had been but a glad light on all things, except men and women; for into their souls the Spark looked too far, and Maya's open brow was shadowed deeply and often with sorrows not her own, and her heart ached many a day for pains she could not or dared not relieve; but if she were left alone, the illumination of the Spark filled everything about her with glory. The sky's rapturous blue, the vivid tints of grass and leaves, the dismaying splendor of blood-red roses, the milky strawberry-flower, the brilliant whiteness of the lily, the turquoise eyes of water-plants,—all these gave her a pleasure intense as pain; and the songs of the winds, the love-whispers of June midnights, the gathering roar of autumn tempests, the rattle of thunder, the breathless and lurid pause before a tropic storm,—all these the Spark enhanced and vivified; till, seeing how blest in herself and the company of Nature the Child of the Kingdom grew, Queen Lura deliberated silently and long whether she should return the gift of the Fairy Cordis, and let Maya live so tranquil and ignorant forever, or whether she should awaken her from her dreams, and set her on her way through the world.

But now the Princess Maya began to grow pale and listless. Her eyes shone brighter than ever, but she was consumed with a feverish longing to see new and strange things. On her knees, and weeping, she implored her mother to release her from the court routine, and let her wander in the woods and watch the village children play.

So Queen Lura, having now another little daughter, named Maddala, who was just like all other children, and a great comfort to her mother, was the more inclined to grant Maya's prayer. She therefore told Maya all that was before her, and having put upon her tiny finger the fairy-ring, bade the tiring-woman take off her velvet robe, and the gold circlet in her hair, and clothe her in a russet suit of serge, with a gray kirtle and hood. King Joconde was gone to the wars, Queen Lura cried a little, the Princess Maddala laughed, and Maya went out alone,—not lonely, for the Spark burned high and clear, and showed all the legends written on the world everywhere, and Maya read them as she went.

Out on the wide plain she passed many little houses; but through all their low casements the red gleam of a fire shone, and on the door-steps clustered happy children, or a peasant bride with warm blushes on her cheek sat spinning, or a young mother with pensive eyes lulled her baby to its twilight sleep and sheltered it with still prayers.

One of these kindly cottages harbored Maya for the night; and then her way at dawn lay through a vast forest, where the dim tree-trunks stretched far away till they grew undefined as a gray cloud, and only here and there the sunshine strewed its elf-gold on ferns and mosses, feathery and soft as strange plumage and costly velvet. Sometimes a little brook with bubbling laughter crept across her path and slid over the black rocks, gurgling and dimpling in the shadow or sparkling in the sun, while fish, red and gold-speckled, swam noiseless as dreams, and darting water-spiders, poised a moment on the surface, cast a glittering diamond reflection on the yellow sand beneath.

The way grew long, and Maya weary. The new leaves of opalescent tint shed odors of faint and passionate sweetness; the birds sang love-songs that smote the sense like a caress; a warm wind yearned and complained in the pine boughs far above her; yet her heart grew heavy, and her eyes dim; she was sick for home;—not for the palace and the court; not for her mother and Maddala; but for home;—she knew her exile, and wept to return.

That night, and for many nights, she slept in the forest; and when at length she came out upon the plain beyond, she was pale and wan, her dark eyes drooped, her slender figure was bowed and languid, and only the mark upon her brow, where the coronet had fretted its whiteness, betrayed that Maya was a princess born.

And now dwellings began to dot the country: brown cottages, with clinging vines; villas, aërial and cloud-tinted, with pointed roofs and capricious windows; huts, in which some poor wretch from his bed of straw looked out upon the wasteful luxury of his neighbor, and, loathing his bitter crust and turbid water, saw feasts spread in the open air, where tropic fruits and beaded wine mocked his feverish thirst; and palaces of stainless marble, rising tower upon tower, and turret over turret, like the pearly heaps of cloud before a storm, while the wind swept from their gilded lattices bursts of festal music, the chorus that receives a bride, or the triumphal notes of a warrior's return.

All these Maya passed by, for no door was open, and no fireless hearth revealed; but before night dropped her starry veil, she had travelled to a mansion whose door was set wide, and, within, a cold hearth was piled with boughs of oak and beech. The opal upon Maya's finger grew dim, but she moved toward the unlit wood, and at her approach the false pretence betrayed itself; the ice glared before her, and chilled her to the soul, as its shroud of bark fell off. She fled over the threshold, and the house-spirit laughed with bitter mirth; but the Spark was safe.

Now came thronging streets, and many an open portal wooed Maya, but wooed in vain. Once, upon the steps of a quaint and picturesque cottage stood an artist, with eyes that flashed heaven's own azure, and lit his waving curls with a gleam of gold. His pleading look tempted the Child of the Kingdom with potent affinities of land and likeness; his fair cottage called her from wall and casement, with the spiritual eyes of ideal faces looking down upon her, forever changeless and forever pure; but when, from purest pity, kindness, and beauty-love, she would have drawn near the hearth, a sigh like the passing of a soul shivered by her, and before its breath the shapely embers fell to dust, the hearth beneath was heaped with ashes, and with tearful lids Maya turned away, and the house-spirit, weeping, closed the door behind her.

Long days and nights passed ere she essayed again; and then, weary and faint with home-woe, she lingered on the steps of a lofty house whose carved door was swung open, whose jasper hearthstone was heaped with goodly logs, and beside it, on the soft flower-strewn skin of a panther, slept a youth beautiful as Adonis, and in his sleep ever murmuring, "Mother!" Maya's heart yearned with a kindred pang. She, too, was orphaned in her soul, and she would gladly have the fire upon this lonely hearth, and companioned the solitude of the sleeper; but, alas! the boughs still wore their summer garland, and from each severed end slow tears of dryad-life distilled honeyedly upon the stone beneath. Of such withes and saplings comes no living fire! Maya, smiling, set a kiss upon the boy-sleeper's brow, but the Spark lay quiet, and the house-spirit flung a blooming cherry-bough after its departing guest.

Maya, the Princess

The year was now wellnigh run. The Princess Maya despaired of home. The earth seemed a harsh stepmother, and its children rather stones than clay. A vague sense of some fearful barrier between herself and her kind haunted the woman's soul within her, and the unquenchable flames of the Spark seemed to girdle her with a defence that drove away even friendly ingress. Night and day she wept, oppressed with loneliness. She knew not how to speak the tongues of men, though well she understood their significance. Only little children mated rightly with her divine infancy; only the mute glories of nature satisfied for a moment her brooding soul. The celestial impulses within her beat their wings in futile longing for freedom, and with inexpressible anguish she uttered her griefs aloud, or sung them to such plaintive strains that all who heard wept in sympathy. Yet she had no home.

After many days she came upon a broad, champaign, fertile land, where, on a gentle knoll, among budding orchards, and fields green with winter grains, stood a low, wide-eaved house, with gay parterres and clipped hedges around it, all ordered with artistic harmony, while over chimney and cornice crept wreaths of glossy ivy, every deep green leaf veined with streaks of light, and its graceful sprays clasping and clinging wherever they touched the chiselled stone beneath. Upon the lawn opened a broad, low door, and the southern sun streamed inward, showing the carved panels of the fireplace and its red hearth, where heavy boughs of wood and splinters from the heart of the pine lay ready for the hand of the Coming to kindle. Upon the threshold, plucking out the dead leaves of the ivy, stood one from whose face strength, and beauty, and guile that the guileless knew not, shone sunlike upon Maya; and as she faltered and paused, he spoke a welcome to her in her own language, and held toward her the clasping hand of help. A thrill of mad joy cleft the heart of the Princess, a glow of incarnate summer dyed with rose her cheek and lip, the Spark blazed through her brimming eyes, weariness vanished. "Home! home!" sung her rapt lips; and in the delirious ecstasy of the hour she pressed toward the hearth, laid down her scrip and staff upon the heaped wood, flung herself on the red stone, and, heedless of the opal talisman, flashed outward from her joyful eyes the Spark,—the Crown, the Curse! So a forked tongue of lightning speeds from its rain-fringed cloud, and cleaves the oak to its centre; so the blaze of a meteor rushes through midheaven, and—is gone! The Spark lit, quivered, sunk, and flashed again; but the wood lay unlighted beneath it. Maya gasped for breath, and with the long respiration the Spark returned, lit upon her lips, seared them like a hot iron, and entered into her heart,—the blighting canker of her fate, a bitterness in flesh and spirit forevermore.

Writhing with anguish and contempt, she turned away from the wrought stone whose semblance had beguiled her to her mortal loss; and as she passed from the step, another hand lit a consuming blaze beneath her staff and scrip, sending a sword of flame after her to the threshold, and the house-spirit shrieked aloud, "Only stones together strike fire, Maya!"—while from the casement above looked forth two faces, false and fair, with eyes of azure ice, and disdainful smiles, and bound together by a curling serpent, that ringed itself in portentous symbol about their waists.

With star-like eyes, proud lips, and erect head, Maya went out. Her laugh rang loud; her song soared in wild and mocking cadence to the stars; her rigid brow wore scorn like a coronal of flame; and with a scathed nature she trod the streets of the city, mixed with its wondering crowds, made the Spark a blaze and a marvel in all lands,—but hid the opal in her bosom; for its scarlet spot of life-blood had dropped away, and the jewel was broken across.

So the wide world heard of Maya, the Child of the Kingdom, and from land to land men carried the stinging arrows of her wit, or signalled the beacon-fires of her scorn, while seas and shores unknown echoed her mad and rapt music, or answered the veiled agony that derided itself with choruses of laughter, from every mystic whisper of the wave, or roar of falling headlands.

And then she fled away, lest, in the turbulent whirl of life, the Curse should craze, and not slay her. For sleep had vanished with wordless moans and frighted aspect from her pillow,—or if it dared, standing afar off, to cast its pallid shadow there, still there was neither rest nor refreshing in the troubled spell. Nor could the thirst that consumed her quench itself with red wine or crystal water, translucent grapes or the crimson fruits that summer kisses into sweetness with her heats; forever longing, and forever unsated, it parched her lips and burnt her gasping mouth, but there was no draught to allay it. And even so food failed of its office. Kindly hands brought to her, whose queenliness asserted itself to their souls with an innocent loftiness, careless of pomp or insignia, all delicate cates and exquisite viands; but neither the keen and stimulating odors of savory meat, the crisp whiteness of freshest bread, nor the slow-dropping gold of honeycomb could tempt her to eat. The simplest peasant's fare, in measure too scanty for a linnet, sustained her life; but the Curse lit even upon her food, and those lips of fire burned all things in their touch to tasteless ashes.

So she fled away; for the forest was cool and lonely, and even as she learned the lies and treacheries of men, so she longed to leave them behind her and die in bitterness less bitter for its solitude. But Maya fled not from herself: the winds wailed like the crying of despair in her harp-voiced pines; the shining oak-leaves rustled hisses upon her unstrung ear; the timid forest-creatures, who own no rule but patient love and caresses, hid from her defiant step and dazzling eye; and when she knew herself in no wise healed by the ministries of Nature, in the very apathy of desperation she flung herself by the clear fountain that had already fallen upon her lips and cooled them with bitter water, and hiding her head under the broad, fresh leaves of a calla that bent its marble cups above her knitted brow and loosened hair, she lay in deathlike trance, till the Fairy Anima swept her feet with fringed garments, and cast the serpent wand writhing and glittering upon her breast.

"Wake, Maya!" said the organ-tones of the Spark-Bringer; and Maya awoke.

"So! the Spark galls thee?" resumed those deep, bitter-sweet tones; and for answer the Princess Maya held toward her, with accusing eyes, the broken, bloodless opal.

"Cordis's folly!" retorted Anima. "Thou hadst done best without it, Maya; the Spark abides no other fate but shining. Yet there is a little hope for thee. Wilt thou die of the bitter fire, or wilt thou turn beggar-maid? The sleep that charity lends to its couch shall rest thee; the draught a child brings shall slake thy thirst; the food pity offers shall strengthen and renew. But these are not the gifts a Princess receives; she who gathers them must veil the Crown, shroud the Spark, conceal the Curse, and in torn robes, with bare and bleeding feet, beg the crumbs of life from door to door. Wilt thou take up this trade?"

Maya, the Princess

Maya rose up from the leaves of the cool lily, and put aside the veiling masses of her hair.

"I will go!" she whispered, flutelike, for hope beat a living pulse in her brain.

So with scrip and hood she went out of the forest and begged of the world's bounty such life as a beggar-maid may endure.

Long ago the King and Queen died in Larrièrepensée, and there the Princess Maddala reigns with a goodly Prince beside her, nor cares for her lost sister; but songless, discrowned, desolate, Maya walks the earth.

All ye whose fires burn bright on the hearth, whose dwellings ring with child-laughter, or are hushed with love-whispers and the peace of home, pity the Princess Maya! Give her food and shelter; charm away the bitter flames that consume her life and soul; drop tears and alms together into the little wasted hand that pleads with dumb eloquence for its possessor; and even while ye pity and protect, revere that fretted mark of the Crown that still consecrates to the awful solitude of sorrow Maya, the Child of the Kingdom!

MY VISITATION

"Is not this she of whom,
When first she came, all flushed you said to me,

. . . .

Now could you share your thought; now should men see
Two women faster welded in one love
Than pairs of wedlock?"
            —*The Princess*[1]

IF THIS STORY is incoherent—arranged rather for the writer's thought than for the reader's eye—it is because the brain which dictated it reeled with the sharp assaults of memory, that living anguish that abides while earth passes away into silence; and because the hand that wrote it trembled with electric thrills from a past that can not die, forever fresh in the soul it tested and tortured—powerful after the flight of years as in its first agony, to fill the dim eye with tears, and throb the languid pulses with fresh fever and passion.

Take, then, the record as it stands, and ask not from a cry of mortal pain the liquid cadence and accurate noting of an operatic bravura.

The first time *It* came was in broad day. I was ill, unable to rise; the day was cold; autumnal sunshine, pure and still, streamed through the house and came in at both the south windows of my room, the curtains drawn side to receive it, for the ague of sickness is worse to me than its pain, and not yet had my preparations for winter enabled me to have a fire. Every thing was clear and chill; Aunt Mary, down stairs in the parlor, sat and knitted, as it was her custom to do of an afternoon; Uncle Seth was not at home; the servant had gone to mass, for it was some feast-day of her Church—no sound or echo disturbed the solitude.

There is something peculiar in a silent day of autumn; melancholy pierces its fine sting through the rays of sunshine; sadness cries in the cricket's monotonous voice; separation and death symbolize in the slow leaves that quit the bough reluctantly, and lie down in dust to be over-

14

trodden—to rot. I can endure any silence better than this hush of decay; it fills me with preternatural horror; it is as if a tomb opened and breathed out its dank, morbid breath across the murmur of life, to paralyze and to chill.

But that day I had taken refuge from the awe and foreboding, the ticking of the clock, the dust-motes floating on light, the startling crack that now and then a springing board or an ill-hung window made. I had taken a book. I was deep in *Shirley*; it excited, it affected me; it is always to me like a brief and voluntary brain-fever to read that book. *Jane Eyre* is insanity for the time. *Villette* is like the scarlet fever; it possesses, it chokes, flushes, racks you; it leaves you weak and in vague pain, apprehensive of some bad result; but it was *Shirley* I read, so forgetting every thing.[2] I am not lonely usually, yet I know when I am alone; there is an indescribable freedom in the sense of solitude, no alien sphere crosses and disturbs mine, no intrusive influence distorts the orbit; I am myself—or I was, then. Presently, as I lay there, the clock struck three. I was to take some potion at that hour. I must rise and get it. I set one foot on the floor, and was putting a shoe upon the other cautiously, when it occurred to me, why was I so careful? and I remembered that it had seemed to me something was on the bed when I moved—my kitten perhaps. I looked, there was nothing there; but I was not alone in the room—there was something else I could not see. I did not hear, but I knew it.

A horror of flesh and sense crept over me; but I was ashamed; I treated it with contempt. Shivering, I walked to the shelf, reached the cup, swallowed my nauseous dose—now tasteless—and went back to bed. It is not worth denying that I trembled. I am a coward. I am always afraid, even when I face the fear; so, shaking, I lay down. My throat was parched, my lips beaded with a sweat of terror, but the consciousness of solitude returned in time to save me from faintness. *It* had gone. And that was the first time.

Here, perhaps, it is best to interpolate my own story, as much of it as is needful to the understanding of this visitation.

I was an orphan, living in the family of my guardian and uncle by marriage, Mr. Van Alstyne. I was not an orphan till fifteen years of happy life at home had fitted me to feel the whole force of such a bereavement. My parents had died within a year of each other, and at the time my story begins I had been ten years under my uncle's roof. He was kind, gentle, generous, and good; all that he could be, not being my father.

It is not necessary to say that I grieved long and deeply over my loss; my nature is intense as well as excitable, and I had no mother. What that brief sentence expresses many will feel; many, more blessed, can not imagine. It is to all meaning enough to define my longing for what I had not, my solitude in all that I had, my eager effort to escape from both longing and solitude.

After I had been a year under my guardian's care, Eleanor Wyse, a far-off cousin of Mr. Van Alstyne, came to board at the house and go to school with me. She was fifteen, I sixteen, but she was far the oldest. In the same family as we were, in the same classes, there were but two ways for us to take, either rivalry or friendship; between two girls of so much individuality there was no neutral ground, and within a month I had decided the matter by falling passionately in love with Eleanor Wyse.

I speak advisedly in the use of that term; no other phrase expresses the blind, irrational, all-enduring devotion I gave to her; no less vivid word belongs to that madness. If I had not been in love with her I should have seen her as I can now—as what she really was; for I believe in physiognomy. I believe that God writes the inner man upon the outer as a restraint upon society; what the moulding of feature lacks, expression, subtle traitor, supplies; and it is only years of repression, of training, of diplomacy, that put the flesh totally in the power of the spirit, and enable man or woman to seem what they are not, what they would be thought.

Eleanor's face was very beautiful; its Greek outline, straight and clear, cut to a perfect contour; the white brow; the long, melancholy eye, with curved, inky lashes; the statuesque head, its undulant, glittering hair bound in a knot of classic severity; the proud, serene mouth, full of carved beauty, opening its scarlet lips to reveal tiny pearl-grains of teeth of that rare delicacy and brilliance that carry a fatal warning; the soft, oval cheek, colorless but not pale, opaque and smooth, betraying Southern blood; the delicate throat, shown whiter under the sweeping shadow and coil of her black-brown tresses; the erect, stately, perfect figure, slight as became her years, but full of strength and promise; all these captivated my intense adoration of beauty. I did not see the label of the sculptor; I did not perceive in that cold, strict chiseling the assertion that its material was marble. I believed the interpretation of its hieroglyphic legend would have run thus: "This is the head of young Pallas; power, intellect, purity are her ægis; the daughter of Jove has not yet tasted passion; virgin, stainless, strong for sacrifice and victory, let the ardent and restless hearts of women seek her to be calmed and taught. *Evoe Athena!*"[3] Nor did I like to see the goddess moved; expression did not become her; the soul that pierced those deep eyes was eager, unquiet, despotic; nothing divine, indeed, yet, in my eyes, it was the unresting, hasting meteor that flashed and faded through mists of earth toward its rest—where I knew not, but its flickering seemed to me atmospheric, not intrinsic.

I looked up to Eleanor with respect as well as fervor. She was full of noble theories. To hear her speak you would have been inwardly shamed by the great and pure thoughts she expressed, the high standard by which she measured all. Truth, disinterestedness, honor, purity, humility, found in her a priestess garmented in candor. If I thought an evil thought, I was thereafter ashamed to see her; if I was indolent or selfish, her presence reproached me; her will, irresistible and mighty, awoke me; if she was kind in speech or act—if she spoke to me caressingly—if she put her warm lips upon my cheek—I was thrilled with joy; her presence affected me, as sunshine does, with a sense of warm life and delight; when we rode, walked, or talked together, I wished the hour eternal; and when she fell into some passion, and burned me with bitter words, stinging me into retort by their injustice, their hard cruelty, it was I who repented—I who humiliated myself—I who, with abundant tears, asked her pardon, worked, plead, prayed to obtain it; and if some spasmodic conscientiousness roused her to excuse herself—to say she had been wrong—my hand closed her lips: I could not hear that: the fault was mine, mine only. I was glad to be clay as long as she was queen and deity.

I do not think this passion of mine moved Eleanor much. She liked to talk with me; our minds mated, our tastes were alike. I had no need to explain my phrases to her, or to do more than indicate my thoughts; she was receptive and appreciative of thought, not of emotion. Me she never knew. I had no reserve in my nature—none of what is commonly called pride; what I felt I said, to the startling of good usual persons; and because I said it, Eleanor did not think I felt it. To her organization utterance and simplicity were denied; she could not speak her emotions if she would; she would not if she could; and she had no faith in words from others. My demonstrations annoyed her; she could not return them; they could not be ignored; there was a certain spice of life and passion in them that asserted itself poignantly and disturbed her. My services she liked better; yet there was in her the masculine contempt for spaniels; she despised a creature that would endure a blow, mental or physical, without revenging itself; and from her I endured almost any repulse, and forgot it.

She was with us in the house three years, and in that time she learned to love me after a fashion of her own, and I, still blind, adored her more. She found in me a receptivity that suited her, and a useful power of patient endurance. Her will made me a potent instrument. What she wanted she must have, and her want was my law. No time, no pains, no patience were wanting in me to fulfill her ends. I served her truly, and I look back upon it with no regret; futile or fertile, such devotion widens and ripens the soul that it inhabits. No aftershock of anguish can contract the space or undo the maturity; and even in my deepest humiliation before her sublime theories and superhuman ideals I unconsciously grew better myself. A capacity for worship implies much, and results in much.

Yet I think I loved her without much selfishness. I desired nothing better than to see her appreciated and admired. It was inexplicable to me when she was not; and I charged the coolness with which she was spoken of, and the want of enthusiasm for her person and character in general society, to her own starry height above common people, and their infinite distance from her nature.

So these years passed by. We went to school; we finished our school-days; we came out into the world; for, in the mean time, her mother had died, and her father removed to Bangor. She liked the place as a residence, and it had become home to her of late. I hoped it was pleasanter for her to be near me. When Eleanor was about twenty a nephew of Uncle Van Alstyne's came to make us a visit; he was no new acquaintance; he had come often in his boyhood, but since we grew up he had been in college, at the seminary, last in Germany for two years' study, and we did not know him well in his maturer character until this time. Herman Van Alstyne was quiet and plain, but of great capacity; I saw him much, and liked him. Love did not look at us. I was absorbed in Eleanor; so was he; but to her he was of no interest. I think she respected him, but her manner was careless and cold, even neglectful. Herman perceived the repulsion. At first he had taken pains to interest her—to mould her traits—to develop some inner nature in which he had faith; but the stone was intractable; neither ductile nor docile was Pallas; her soul yielded no more to him than the strong sea yields place or submission to the winged wind that smites it in passing.

He was with us three months waiting for a call he said, but stricter chains held him till he broke them with one blow and went to a Western parish.

He had not offered himself to Eleanor and been refused. Wisely he refrained from bringing the matter to a foreknown crisis: he spared himself the pain and Eleanor the regret of a refusal that he regarded truly as certain. I was sorry for the whole affair, for I believed she would scarcely know a better man, but it passed away; I promised to write him when his mother found the correspondence wearying, and we interchanged a few letters at irregular intervals till we met again, letters into which Eleanor's name found no entrance.

Three years after he left I went, early in July, to spend some weeks at the sea-side, for I was not strong; in the last few years my health had failed slowly, but progressively, till I was alarmingly weak and ordered to breathe salt air and use sea-bathing as the best hope of restoration. I do not know why I should reserve the cause of this long languor and sinking: it was nothing wrong in me that I owed it to the breaking of a brief engagement. A young girl, totally inexperienced, I had loved a man and been taught by himself to despise him—a tragedy both trite and sharp; one that is daily reacted, noted, and forgotten by observers, to find a cold record in marble or the catalogues of insane asylums, another perhaps in the eternal calendar of the heavens above. I was too strong in nature to grace either of these mortal lists, and I loved Eleanor too well. I had always loved her more than that man; and when the episode was over, I discovered in myself that I never could have loved any man as I did her, and I went out into the world in this conviction, finding that life had not lost all its charms—that so long as she lived for me I should neither die nor craze. But the shock and excitement of the affair shattered my nervous system and undermined my health, and the listless, aimless life of a young lady offered no reactive agency to help me: so I went from home to new scenes and fresh atmosphere.

My Visitation

The air of Gloucester Beach strengthened me day by day. The exquisite scenery was a pleasure endless and pure. I asked nothing better than to sit upon some tide-washed rock and watch the creeping waves slide back in half-articulate murmur from the repelling shore, or, eager with the strength of flood, fling themselves, in mock anger, against cliff and crag, only to break in wreaths of silver spray and foam-bells—to glitter and fall in a leap of futile mirth, then rustling in the shingle and sea-weed with vague whispers, that

"Song half asleep or speech half awake,"[4]

which has lulled so many restless hearts to a momentary quiet, singing them the long lullaby that preludes a longer slumber.

It was excitement enough to walk alone upon the beach when a hot cloudy night drooped over land and sea; when the soft trance and enchantment of summer lulled cloud and wave into stillness absolute and cherishing, when the sole guide I had in that warm gloom was the white edge of surf, and the only sound that smote the quiet, the still-recurring, apprehensive dash, as wave after wave raced, leaped, panted, and hissed after its forerunner.

The Beach House was almost empty at that early season, and I enjoyed all this alone, not without constant yearnings for Eleanor; wanting her, even this scenery lost a charm, and I gave it but faint admiration since I could not see it with her eyes. It must be a very pure love of nature that can exist alone, and without flaw, in the absence of association. The austere soul of the great mother offers no sympathy to the petulant passion or irrational grief of her children. It is only to the heart that has proved itself strong and lofty that her potent and life-giving traits reveal themselves. In this love, as in all others, save only the love of God, the return that is yielded is measured by the power of the adorer, not his want. Truly,

"Nature never did betray
The heart that loved her;"[5]

but she has many and many a time betrayed the partial love—scoffed at the divided worship.

After I had been a fortnight at the Beach, I was joined by Herman Van Alstyne. He had come on from the West to recruit his own health, suffering from a long intermittent fever, by sea-air; and hearing I was at Gloucester, had come there, and asked my leave to remain, gladly accorded to him. We had always been good friends, and my unspoken sympathy with his liking for, and loss of, Eleanor had established a permanent bond between us. In the constant association into which we were now thrown I learned daily to like him better. He was very weak indeed, quite unable to walk or drive far, and the connection of our families was a sufficient excuse to others for our intimacy. I delighted to offer him any kindness or service in my power, and he repaid me well by the charm of his society.

We spent our mornings always together in some niche of the lofty cliff that towered from the tide below in bare grandeur, reflecting the sun from its abrupt brown crags till every fibre of grass rooted in their crevices grew blanched, and the solitary streamer of bramble or wild creeper became crisp long ere autumn. But this heat was my element; the slow blood quickened in my veins under its vital glow; I felt life stealing back to its deserted and chilly conduits; I basked like a cactus or a lizard into brighter tints and a gayer existence.

There we often sat till noon, talking or silent as we would; for though there was a peculiar charm in the appreciative, thoughtful conversation of Herman Van Alstyne, a better and a rarer trait he possessed in full measure—the power of "a thousand silences."

Or, perhaps, under the old cedars that shed aromatic scents upon the sun-thrilled air, and strewed bits of dry, sturdy leaves upon the short grass that carpeted the summit of the cliff, we preferred shadow to sunshine; and while I rested against some ragged bole, and inhaled all odor and health, he read to me some quaint German story, some incredibly exquisite bit of Tennyson, some sensitively musical passage of Kingsley, or, better and more apt, a song or a poem of Shelley's—vivid, spiritual, supernatural; the ideal of poetry; the leaping flame-tongue of lonely genius hanging in mid-air, self-poised, self-containing, glorious, and unattainable.

I have never known so delicate an apprehension as Mr. Van Alstyne possessed; his nobler traits I was afterward to know—to feel; but now it suited me thoroughly to be so well understood—to feel that I might utter the wildest imagination, or the most unexpected peculiarity of opinion, and never once be asked to explain what I meant—to reduce into social formulas that which was not social but my own. If there is one rest above

another to a weary mind it is this freedom from shackles, this consciousness of true response. Never did I perceive a charm in the landscape that he
had not noticed before or simultaneously with me; the same felicity of
diction or of thought in what we read struck us as with one stroke; we
liked the same people, read the same books, agreed in opinion so far as to
disagree on and discuss many points without a shadow of impatience or an
uncandid expression. We talked together as few men talk—perhaps no
women—

> "Talked at large of worldly fate,
> And drew truly every trait"

—but we never spoke of Eleanor.

And so the summer wore on. I perceived a gradual change creep over
Herman's manner in its process; he watched me continually. I felt his eyes
fixed on me whenever I sat sewing or reading; I never looked up without
meeting them. He grew absent and fitful. I did not know what had
happened. I accused myself of having pained him. I feared he was ill.
I never once thought of the true trouble; and one day it came—he asked
me to marry him.

Never was any woman more surprised. I had not thought of the
thing. I could not speak at first. I drew from him the hand he attempted to
grasp. I did not collect my stricken and ashamed thoughts till, looking up, I
saw him perfectly pale, his eyes dark with emotion, waiting, in rigid self-
control, for my answer.

I could not, in justice to him or to myself, be less than utterly candid.
I told him how much I liked him; how grieved I was that I could have
mistaken his feeling for me so entirely; and then I said what I then
believed—that I could not marry him—for I had but the lesser part of a
heart to give any man. I loved a woman too well to love or to marry. A deep
flush of relief crossed his brow.

"Is that the only objection you offer to me?" asked he, calmly.

"It is enough," said I. "If you think that past misery of mine interferes
against you, you are in the wrong. I know now that I never loved that man
as a woman should love the man she marries, and had I done so, the utter
want of respect or trust I feel for him now would have silenced the love
forever."

"I did not think of that," said he. "I needed but one assurance—that, except for Miss Wyse, you might have loved me; is it so?"

I could not tell him—I did not know. The one present and all-absorbing passion of my soul was Eleanor; beside her, no rival could enter. I shuddered at the possibility of loving a man so utterly, and then placing myself at his mercy for life. I felt that my safety lay in my freedom from any such tie to Eleanor. She made me miserable often enough as it was; what might she not do were I in her power always? Yet this face of the subject I did not suggest to Mr. Van Alstyne; it was painful enough to be kept to myself. I told him plainly that I could not love another as I did her; that I would not if I could.

He looked at me, not all unmoved, though silently; a gentle shading of something like pity stole across his regard, fixed and keen at first. He neither implored nor deprecated, but lifted my hand reverently to his lips, and said, in a tone of supreme calmness, "I can wait."

I should have combated the hope implied in those words. I was afterward angry with myself for enduring them; but at the moment uncertainty, shaped out of instinct and apprehension, closed my lips; I could not speak, and he left me. I went to my room more moved than I liked to acknowledge; and when he went away the next morning, though I felt the natural relief from embarrassment—knowing that I should not meet him as before—I still missed him, as a part of my daily life.

A month longer at the Beach protracted my stay into autumn; and then, with refreshed health and new strength, I returned home—home! whose chief charm lay in the prospect of seeing Eleanor.

It is true that this hope was not unalloyed. I am possessed of a nature singularly instinctive, and for some weeks past a certain shadow had crept into her letters that pained me. No word or phrase denoted change; but I perceived the uncertain aura, and was irrationally harassed by a trouble too vague for expression.

When I reached Bangor it lay waiting for me sufficiently tangible and legible in the shape of a note from Eleanor.

AND HERE must I leave a blank. The forgiveness which stirs me to this record refuses to define for alien eyes what that trouble was. All that I can say to justify the extreme and piteous result which followed is, that Eleanor

Wyse had utterly, cruelly, and deliberately deceived me; and when it was no longer possible to do so, had been obliged by circumstances to show me what she had done.

Of that day it is best to say but little: the world cracked and reeled under me; I returned from a brief stupor into one bitter, blind tempest of contempt; and in its strength I answered her note concisely and coldly. An hour's time brought me a rejoinder not worth answering, simply perfidious—a regret, "deep and true," that she had been compelled to grieve me, to "reserve" from me any thing.

True! I had believed in truth, in goodness, in disinterested love, in principle; where now were such faiths swept? Verily, over the cliff into the sea! I was morally destroyed; I made shipwreck of myself and my life; my whole soul was a salt raging wave, tideless and foaming, without rest, without intent, without faith or hope in God—for he who loses faith in man loses faith in man's Maker—and this had Eleanor Wyse done for me.

Doubtless, to many, this emotion of mine will seem exaggerated. Let them remember that it was the loss of all that bound to life a lonely, morbid, intense, and excitable woman. Need I say more? If, after many years, with the kind help of nobler men and women, and the great patience of God, I have worn my way, inch by inch, back to some foothold of belief, I feel even yet—in some recoils of memory, some recurring habit of my soul—the reflex influence of those wretched days, months, years, when I suspected every one—"hateful, and hating," of a truth.

Death is hard to bear when its angel breathes upon the face we love, and extinguishes therein the fiery spark of life; but what is death compared to such dissolution as treachery brings? If Eleanor Wyse had died when I loved her and trusted her, I should have gone mourning softly all my days, but not in pain; to find her untrue admitted no remedy, no palliation. Truth was the ruling passion of my mind; that, and nothing else, contented me. Its absence or its loss were the loss and absence of all in those whom I loved; and it was only within a brief time, as years go, that I had grown into the discovery that men are liars in spite of education or policy; what was it, then, to know this of my ideal—Eleanor?

But let those helpless, miserable weeks go by. If I detail so much as I have, it is to show the reason of my righteous indignation—of my tenacious memory. After a time I supposed that I forgave Eleanor. I thought myself good, most Pharisaically good, to have forgiven such an injury. I made some little comedy of friendship for visible use; I visited her, though not as often as I had done before. I saw her try to supply, with the love of others, the lavish devotion and service I had given her; I saw her fail and suffer in the consciousness of want and dissatisfaction, and, self-righteously, I forgave again! Senseless that I was!—as if forgiveness rankled and grew bitter in one's heart—as if pardon, full and pure, rejoiced in the retributions of this life—fed itself with salt recollections of the past, and evil foreshadowings of the future; as if it could exist without love, without forgetfulness; as if good deeds were its pledge, or good words its seal!

No! I never forgave her. I never forgot one pang she inflicted on me, one untruth she uttered; I never trusted her word or her smile again. I gathered up every circumstance of the past, and hunted it to its source; I discovered that she had not simply deceived but deluded me, and laughed at me in the process.

How my blood boiled over these revelations! how my flesh failed with my heart! Slow, persistent fever gnawed me; my nights were without sleep or rest; my days laggard and delirious. Why I did not go crazy is yet unexplained to myself. I think I did, only that there was a method in my madness that won for it the milder name of nervousness. I was ill—I tottered on the very tempting brink of death, without awe or regret; I made no effort to live, nor any to die, except to pray that I might—the only prayer that ever passed my seared lips. I was sent away from home again; and while I was gone Eleanor married a certain Mr. Mason, of Bangor, and they removed to Illinois—in time, still further West. I was no better for this absence; and, impatient of strangers and intrusive acquaintance, I came home, and, strange as it may seem, I missed Eleanor! Habit is the anchor of half the love in this world, and my habit of loving her survived the love—or held it, perhaps—for I missed her sorrowfully.

I found Herman Van Alstyne at my uncle's when I came, and I was glad—glad of any thing to break the desperate monotony of sorrow. He knew nothing more than every one knew of this affair, except that he knew me, and from that gathered intuitively a part of the truth; and, by long patience, unwearied and delicate care—watching, waiting, forbearing, and enduring—he brought me nearer a certain degree of calm than I had believed possible, when a sudden summons called him away from Bangor;

and it was during his absence that *It* began to come; as I said in the beginning, more than two years after I had lost Eleanor.

I lay still in my bed on that day of which I had spoken; the long stress of misery that I had undergone in the past years resulted in so much physical exhaustion as to have brought on the exquisite tortures of neuralgia, and it was a sudden access of this chronic rack that to-day held me prisoner. The draught I had taken was an anodyne, and under its influence I fell asleep. I must have slept an hour, when I woke abruptly with a renewed sense of something in the dusk beside me, at my pillow. I screamed as I woke into this terror, and instantly Aunt Mary came in. A cold sigh crossed my cheek; I shivered with a horror strange and unearthly. Aunt Mary asked if I had been asleep? I said yes. If I had been dreaming painfully? I did not answer that. I asked for some water, and getting it she forgot her question; but I could not bear to be alone. I begged her to sit beside me and to sleep with me, for I could not endure solitude; perpetual apprehension made me cringe in every nerve and fibre. I started at the slightest stir of leaf or insect upon the pane, and the repining autumn wind seemed to come over mile on mile of graves, bringing thence no mealy scent of white daisies—no infant-breathing violet odors—no frutescent perfume of sweet-briar, nor funereal smells of cypress, and plaintive whispers of fir and pine; but wave after wave of cries from half-free souls; sobbing with dull pain, and moans of deprecating anguish; a cry that neither heaven nor earth answered, but which crept—a live desolation—into the ear attent, and the brain morbidly excited.

Yet gradually this left me. I kept by some kindly human presence all day, and feared night no more till—

Let me say that all this time I was imperceptibly growing better than I had been. Hope, the very ministrant of Heaven, was by tiny crevice and unguarded postern stealing into my heart, though I knew it not, and softening all my hard thoughts of Eleanor, for I am moved to the outer world rather by my own moods than theirs; sorrow and pain make me selfish and unkind; peace, joy, even unconscious hope, expand my love for all mankind. I am better, more tender, more benevolent to others, when I receive some light and life within.

One night I was all alone; the low, unearthly glimmer of a waning moon lit the naked earth, a few leaves rustled on the fitful wind that lulled, and rose, and lulled again, with almost articulate meaning. I lay listening; a long pause came, of most significant quiet—a faint sigh crossed my brow. *It* was there beside me!—unseen, unheard, but felt in the secretest recesses of life and consciousness; a spirit, whereat my marrow curdled, my heart was constricted, my blood refused to run, my breath failed—fluttered—was it death? I sprung from my pillow; the presence drew farther away. I could see nothing, but I felt that something yearning, restless, pained, and sad regarded me. I began to gather courage. I began to pity a soul that had cast off life yet could not die to life; and now it drew nearer, as if some magnetism, born of my kindlier sympathies, melted the barrier between us, close—closer—till something rustled like a light touch the cover of my bed, stirred at my ear! Good Heaven! could I bear that? I could not shriek or cry, I fell forward upon my face. It went, and the wind began its wail; now reproachful sobs filled it: the moon sank, rain gathered overhead, and dripped with sullen persistence all night upon the roof, for all night I heard it.

It is tedious to recount each instance of this visitation. For weeks it staid beside me. I felt it on my bed at night; I felt it by my chair in the day; it swept past me in the garden paths, a cold waft of air; it watched me through the window-blinds; it hung over me sleeping; yet never was I wonted to the presence; every day thrilled me with fresh surprise, and daily it grew, for daily it became more perceivable.

At first I felt only a sense of alien life in a room otherwise solitary; then a breath of air, air from some other sphere than this, penetrative, dark, chilling; then a sound, not of voice, or pulse, but of motion in some inanimate thing, the motion of contact; then came a touch, the gentlest, faintest approach of lips or fingers, I knew not which, to my brow; and last, a growing, gathering, flickering into sight. I saw nothing at first, directly; from the oblique glance that fear impelled I drew an impression of quivering air beside me; then of a shadow, frail and variant; then a shapeless shape of mist, a cloud, dark and portentous and significant; and next those sidelong glances revealed to me an expression; no face, no feature, but, believe it who can, an expression, earnest, melancholy, beseeching; a look that pierced me, that pleaded with my soul's depth, that entreated shelter, succor, consolation, which even in my terror I longed to give.

I might perhaps have suffered physically more than I did from this visiting, but the winged hope of which I spoke before upheld me still, daily, with stronger hands.

Herman had returned to Bangor after a brief absence, and was there still. I could not see him so constantly as I did and refuse my admiration to those traits that ever rule and satisfy me. Mr. Van Alstyne passed with some people for a philosopher, with some for a reformer: there were those who called him singular and self-opinionated; there were others who revered him for his devout nature and stainless life. He was more than any of these, he was a true man: and even in his plain exterior the eye that knew him found a charm peculiar and salient; the deep-sunken, clear, earnest eyes, kindled with a spark of profound depth and meaning; the thin, sharply cut, aquiline outline; the flexible, pure, refined mouth; the bronzed coloring; the overhanging brow—all these wore beauty indefinable, fired by the sweet and vivid smile of the irradiate soul within. In his presence, calm, restful, and strengthening, no subterfuge or evasion could live. He was just, direct, and tenderly strong; it was to him, to him it is, that I owed and owe a new and higher life than I had known before; he saw my sinking and lonely soul, but he saw its self-recuperative power, and with the most delicate and careful tenderness beguiled that motive force into action. He did far more than that; he recalled to me the higher motives that anguish had well-nigh scourged out from my horizon; he taught me as a father teaches his little child a newer trust in the Father of us all. I returned to those divine consolations that he laid before me with a pierced and penitent heart; and in knowing that I was prayed and cared for on earth, I learned anew that God is more tender and more patient than his creatures, and the logic of strong emotion made the truth living and potent. In all this was I drawn toward Herman by the strongest tie that can bind one heart to another—a tie that overarches and outlasts all the fleeting passions of time, for it is the adamantine link of eternity; and had I lost him then, I should have felt for all my life that there was a relation between us, undying and sure, to be renewed and acknowledged at length where such relations respire their native air, where there is neither marrying nor giving in marriage.

But it pleased God that I should live to receive my heart's desire; what began in gratitude ended in love. I might have shrunk from admitting so potent a guest again into my soul, had any other soul sent the messenger thither; but I trusted him when I disbelieved every other creature, and with this trust had crept back to me my faith in God, in good, in life and its ends. Truly, so far as man can do it, he saved my soul alive!

Now it was the early part of December. It was still haunting me. I could see more—eyes, deep and pleading, the outline of a head, pure lineaments, seemed hovering beside me, but if I turned for a direct look they were gone. I did not fear it; my happy faith and Herman shielded me.

The year drew on. The day before Christmas came, still, crisp, but yet warm for its season; no snow shrouded the earth; the far-off sun beamed out benign and pale; the few dry leaves lay quiet as they fell; the firs upon the lawn with curved boughs waited for their ermine, stately and dark. Herman asked me to walk with him. I cloaked and hooded myself, and we went away, away into the deep woods. What we said in that sweet silence of a leafless, sunny forest is known to us two: it is not for you, reader, friendly though you be; it is enough to tell you that I had promised to be his wife, that I was homesick no more.

It was well for me that this happened that day—should I not rather say God ordered it?—for as ever in this life sorrow tramples upon the foregoing footsteps of joy, so I found upon my return a household in tears. Mr. Mason, Eleanor's husband, had written, at last, two months after it happened, and another month had the letter been in coming—ah! how ever shall I say it? Eleanor was dead! her latest breath had gasped out a cry for me!

If Death is the Spoiler, so is he the Restorer; who shall dare to soil the shroud with any thing but tears? I could do no more but weep; but I mourned for Eleanor again as I had never thought to do; evil, treachery, anguish, and distrust vanished—I remembered only love.

For hours I could not see or speak with Herman, the flood of misery overpowered me; and he too sorrowed, deeply, but serenely. It was late in the evening before I recovered any sort of composure. He sent to my chamber a brief penciled request, and I went down; worn out with weeping, I obeyed like a child. I ate the food he brought me; I drank the restorative draught; quiet, but languid, I laid my head upon his breast, and, held by the firm grasp of his arm, I rested, and he consoled me; a deep and vital draught of peace slaked my soul's feverish thirst. Such peace had I never known, for it was the daughter of experience and trust.

My Visitation

You who, full of youth and its intact passion, give a careless hour to these pages, wonder not that I could find it just to give so noble a man a heart once given and wasted! Know that it is not the flower of any tropic palm that is fit to feed and sustain man, but the ripened clusters of its fruitage—the result of time, and sun, and storm. The first blush, the earliest kiss, the tender and timid glance are sweet indeed; but the true household fire, deep and abiding, is oftenest kindled in the heart matured by passion and by pain, tested in the stress of life, deepened and strengthened by manifold experience; and such a heart receives no unworthy guest, lights its altar-fire for no idol of wood or clay. I felt that I rendered Herman Van Alstyne far nobler and higher homage, that I did him purer justice in loving him now than it had ever been in my power to do before.

First love is a honeyed and dewy romance, fit for novels and school-girls; but of the myriad women who have lived to curse their marriage-day nine-tenths have been those who married in their ignorant girlhood, and married boys.

I have digressed to honor Herman, to vindicate myself. That Christmas-eve I lay sheltered and at rest on his arm, till the toll of midnight rang clear upon my ear. I could forever sing the angels' song now, that for years had been a blank repetition to my wretched and ungodly soul.

"Peace on earth!" was no more a chimera; I knew it at heart. "Good will to men!" that was spontaneous; I loved all in and for one. "Glory to God in the highest!" What did that ask to utter it but a full thankfulness that bore me upward like the flood-tide of a summer sea?

Blessed as I was, my common sense reminded me that it was far into the night, that I ought to sleep; so I said good-night to Herman, and crept with weak steps to my room. I fell asleep to dream of him, of Eleanor, of peace, and I woke into the deep silence that always preceded—*It*.

I woke knowing what stood beside me. Keen starlight pierced the pane, and shed a dim, obscure perception of place and outline over my room. A long, restful, sobbing sigh parted my lips; I perceived *It* was at hand; fear fled; terror died out; I turned my eyes—oh God! it was Eleanor!

Wan—frail—a flowing outline of shadow, but the face in every faultless line and vivid expression; now an expression of intense longing, of wistful prayer, of pleading that would never be denied.

I lifted my heavy arms toward the vision; it swayed and bent above me: the white lips parted; no murmur nor sound clave them, yet they spoke—"Forgive! forgive!"

"Eleanor! Yes love, darling! yes, forever, as I hope to be forgiven!" I cried out aloud. A gleam of rapture and rest relaxed the brow, the sad eyes; love ineffable glowed along each lineament, and transfused to splendor the frigid moulding of snow.

I closed my eyes to crush inward the painful tears, and a touch of lips sealed them with sacred and unearthly repose. I looked again; *It* had gone forever. The Christmas bells pealed loud and clear for dawn, and my thoughts rung their own joy bells beside the steeple chimes. Herman and Eleanor both loved me—I had forgiven; I was forgiven.

Yet must day and space echo that word once more. Hear me, Eleanor! hear me, from that mystic country where thou hast fled before!

I repeat that forgiveness again. So may Heaven pardon me in the hour of need; so may God look upon me with strong affection in the parting of soul and body, even as I pardon and love thee, Eleanor, with a truth and faith eternal! Thee, forever loved, but, ah! not now forever lost?

THE RING FETTER

A New England Tragedy

THERE ARE long stretches in the course of the Connecticut River, where its tranquil current assumes the aspect of a lake, its sudden bends cut off the lovely reach of water, and its heavily wooded banks lie silent and green, undisturbed, except by the shriek of the passing steamer, casting golden-green reflections into the stream at twilight, and shadows of deepest blackness, star-pierced, at remoter depths of night. Here, now and then, a stray gull from the sea sends a flying throb of white light across the mirror below, or the sweeping wings of a hawk paint their moth-like image on the blue surface, or a little flaw of wind shudders across the water in a black ripple; but except for these casual stirs of Nature, all is still, oppressive, and beautiful, as earth seems to the trance-sleeper on the brink of his grave.

In one of these reaches, though on either side the heavy woods sweep down to the shore and hang over it as if deliberating whether to plunge in, on the eastern bank there is a tiny meadow just behind the tree-fringe of the river, completely hedged in by the deep woods, and altogether hidden from any inland road; nor would the traveller on the river discover it, except for the chimney of a house that peers above the yellow willows and seems in that desolate seclusion as startling as a daylight ghost. But this dwelling was built and deserted and weather-beaten long before the date of our story. It had been erected and inhabited during the Revolution, by an old Tory, who, foreseeing the result of the war better than some of his contemporaries, and being unwilling to expose his person to the chances of battle or his effects to confiscation, maintained a strict neutrality, and a

secret trade with both parties; thereby welcoming peace and independence, fully stocked with the dislike and suspicion of his neighbors, and a
large quantity of Continental "fairy-money." So, when Abner Dimock
died, all he had to leave to his only son was the red house on "Dimock's
Meadow," and a ten-acre lot of woodland behind and around the green
plateau where the house stood. These possessions he strictly entailed on
his heirs forever, and nobody being sufficiently interested in its alienation
to inquire into the State laws concerning the validity of such an entail, the
house remained in the possession of the direct line, and in the year 18——
belonged to another Abner Dimock, who kept tavern in Greenfield, a town
of Western Massachusetts, and, like his father and grandfather before him,
had one only son. In the mean time, the old house in Haddam township
had fallen into a ruinous condition, and, as the farm was very small, and
unprofitable chestnut-woodland at that, the whole was leased to an old
negro and his wife, who lived there in the most utter solitude, scratching
the soil for a few beans and potatoes, and in the autumn gathering nuts, or
in the spring roots for beer, with which Old Jake paddled up to
Middletown, to bring home a return freight of salt pork and rum.

The town of Greenfield, small though it was, and at the very top of a
high hill, was yet the county town, subject to annual incursions of lawyers,
and such "thrilling incidents" as arise from the location of a jail and a
court-room within the limits of any village. The scenery had a certain
summer charm of utter quiet that did it good service with some healthy
people of well-regulated and insensitive tastes. From Greenfield Hill one
looked away over a wide stretch of rolling country; low hills, in long,
desolate waves of pasturage and grain, relieved here and there by a mass of
black woodland, or a red farm-house and barns clustered against a hill-
side, just over a wooden spire in the shallow valley, about which were
gathered a few white houses, giving signs of life thrice a day in tiny threads
of smoke rising from their prim chimneys; and over all, the pallid skies of
New England, where the sun wheeled his shorn beams from east to west as
coldly as if no tropic seas mirrored his more fervid glow thousands of miles
away, and the chilly moon beamed with irreproachable whiteness across
the round gray hills and the straggling pond, beloved of frogs and mud-
turtles, that Greenfield held in honor under the name of Squam Lake.

Perhaps it was the scenery, perhaps the air, possibly the cheapness of the place as far as all the necessaries of life went, that tempted Judge Hyde to pitch his tent there, in the house his fathers had built long ago, instead of wearing his judicial honors publicly, in the city where he attained them; but, whatever the motive might be, certain it is that at the age of forty he married a delicate beauty from Baltimore, and came to live on Greenfield Hill, in the great white house with a gambrel roof and dormer windows, standing behind certain huge maples, where Major Hyde and Parson Hyde and Deacon Hyde had all lived before him.

A brief Northern summer bloomed gayly enough for Adelaide Howard Hyde when she made her bridal tour to her new home; and cold as she found the aspect of that house, with its formal mahogany chairs, high-backed, and carved in grim festoons and ovals of incessant repetition,—its penitential couch of a sofa, where only the iron spine of a Revolutionary heroine could have found rest,—its pinched, starved, and double-starched portraits of defunct Hydes, Puritanic to the very ends of toupet and periwig,—little Mrs. Hyde was deep enough in love with her tall and handsome husband to overlook the upholstery of a home he glorified, and to care little for comfort elsewhere, so long as she could nestle on his knee and rest her curly head against his shoulder. Besides, flowers grew, even in Greenfield; there were damask roses and old-fashioned lilies enough in the square garden to have furnished a whole century of poets with similes; and in the posy-bed under the front windows were tulips of Chinese awkwardness and splendor, beds of pinks spicy as all Arabia, blue hyacinths heavy with sweetness as well as bells, "pi'nies" rubicund and rank, hearts-ease clustered against the house, and sticky rose-acacias, pretty and impracticable, not to mention the grenadier files of hollyhocks that contended with fennel-bushes and scarlet-flowered beans for the precedence, and the hosts of wild flowers that bloomed by wood-edges and pond-shores wherever corn or potatoes spared a foot of soil for the lovely weeds. So in Judge Hyde's frequent absences, at court or conclave, hither and yon, (for the Judge was a political man,) it was his pretty wife's chief amusement, when her delicate fingers ached with embroidery, or her head spun with efforts to learn housekeeping from old Keery, the time-out-of-mind authority in the Hyde family, a bad-humored, good-tempered old maid,—it was, indeed, the little Southerner's only amusement,—to make the polish and mustiness of those dreary front-parlors gay and fragrant with flowers; and though Judge Hyde's sense of the ridiculous was not remarkably keen, it was too much to expect of him that he should do otherwise than laugh long and loud, when, suddenly returning from Taunton one summer day, he tracked his wife by snatches of song into the "company rooms," and found her on the floor, her hair about her ears, tying a thick garland of red peonies, intended to decorate the picture of the original Hyde, a dreary old fellow, in bands, and grasping a Bible in one wooden hand, while a distant view of Plymouth Bay and the Mayflower tried to convince the spectator that he was transported, among other antedeluvians, by that Noah's ark, to the New World. On either hand hung the little Flora's great-grandmother-in-law, and her great-grandfather accordingly, Mrs. Mehitable and Parson Job Hyde, peering out, one from a bushy ornament of pink laurel-blossoms, and the other from an airy and delicate garland of the wanton sweet-pea, each stony pair of eyes seeming to glare with Medusan intent at this profaning of their state and dignity. "Isn't it charming, dear?" said the innocent little beauty, with a satisfaction half doubtful, as her husband's laugh went on.

But for every butterfly there comes an end to summer. The flowers dropped from the frames and died in the garden; a pitiless winter set in; and day after day the mittened and mufflered schoolboy, dragging his sled through drifts of heavy snow to school, eyed curiously the wan, wistful face of Judge Hyde's wife pressed up to the pane of the south window, its great restless eyes and shadowy hair bringing to mind some captive bird that pines and beats against the cage. Her husband absent from home long and often, full of affairs of "court and state,"—her delicate organization, that lost its flickering vitality by every exposure to cold,—her lonely days and nights,—the interminable sewing, that now, for her own reasons, she would trust to no hands but her own,—conscious incapacity to be what all the women about her were, stirring, active, hardy housekeepers,—a vague sense of shame, and a great dread of the future,—her comfortless and motherless condition,—slowly, but surely, like frost, and wind, and rain, and snow, beat on this frail blossom, and it went with the rest. June roses were laid against her dark hair and in her fair hands, when she was carried to the lonely graveyard of Greenfield, where mulleins and asters, golden-rod, blackberry-vines, and stunted yellow-pines adorned the last sleep of the weary wife and mother; for she left behind her a week-old baby,—a girl,—wailing prophetically in the square bedroom where its mother died.

Judge Hyde did not marry again, and he named his baby Mehitable. She grew up as a half-orphaned child with an elderly and undemonstrative father would naturally grow,—shy, sensitive, timid, and extremely grave. Her dress, thanks to Aunt Keery and the minister's wife, (who looked after her for her mother's sake,) was always well provided and neat, but no way calculated to cultivate her taste or to gratify the beholder. A district school provided her with such education as it could give; and the library, that was her resort at all hours of the day, furthered her knowledge in a singular and varied way, since its lightest contents were histories of all kinds and sorts, unless one may call the English Classics lighter reading than Hume or Gibbon.

But at length the district-schoolma'am could teach Mehitable Hyde no more, and the Judge suddenly discovered that he had a pretty daughter of fourteen, ignorant enough to shock his sense of propriety, and delicate enough to make it useless to think of sending her away from home to be buffeted in a boarding-school. Nothing was left for him but to undertake her education himself; and having a theory that a thorough course of classics, both Greek and Latin, was the foundation of all knowledge, half a score of dusty grammars were brought from the garret, and for two hours every morning and afternoon little Miss Hitty worried her innocent soul over conjugations and declensions and particles, as perseveringly as any professor could have desired. But the dreadful part of the lessons to Hitty was the recitation after tea; no matter how well she knew every inflection of a verb, every termination of a noun, her father's cold, gray eye, fixed on her for an answer, dispelled all kinds of knowledge, and, for at least a week, every lesson ended in tears. However, there are alleviations to everything in life; and when the child was sent to the garret after her school-books, she discovered another set, more effectual teachers to her than Sallust or the "Græca Minora," even the twelve volumes of "Sir Charles Grandison," and the fewer but no less absorbing tomes of "Clarissa Harlowe"; and every hour she could contrive not to be missed by Keery or her father was spent in that old garret, fragrant as it was with sheaves of all the herbs that grow in field or forest, poring over those old novels, that were her society, her friends, her world.

So two years passed by. Mehitable grew tall and learned, but knew little more of the outside world than ever; her father had learned to love her, and taught her to adore him; still shy and timid, the village offered no temptation to her, so far as society went; and Judge Hyde was beginning to feel that for his child's mental health some freer atmosphere was fast becoming necessary, when a relentless writ was served upon the Judge himself, and one that no man could evade; paralysis smote him, and the strong man lay prostrate,—became bedridden.

Now the question of life seemed settled for Hitty; her father admitted no nursing but hers. Month after month rolled away, and the numb grasp gradually loosed its hold on flesh and sense, but still Judge Hyde was bedridden. Year after year passed by, and no change for better or worse ensued. Hitty's life was spent between the two parlors and the kitchen; for the room her dead mother had so decorated was now furnished as a bedroom for her father's use; and her own possessions had been removed into the sitting-room next it, that, sleeping or waking, she might be within call. All the family portraits held a conclave in the other front-parlor, and its north and east windows were shut all the year, save on some sultry summer day when Keery flung them open to dispel damp and must, and the school-children stared in reverentially, and wondered why old Madam Hyde's eyes followed them as far as they could see. Visitors came now and then to the kitchen-door, and usurped Keery's flag-bottomed chair, while they gossiped with her about village affairs; now and then a friendly spinster with a budget of good advice called Hitty away from her post, and, after an hour's vain effort to get any news worth retailing about the Judge from those pale lips, retired full of disappointed curiosity to tell how stiff that Mehitable Hyde was, and how hard it was to make her speak a word to one! Friends were what Hitty read of in the "Spectator,"[1] and longed to have; but she knew none of the Greenfield girls since she left school, and the only companion she had was Keery, rough as the east wind, but genuine and kind-hearted,—better at counsel than consolation, and no way adapted to fill the vacant place in Hitty's heart.

So the years wore away, and Miss Hyde's early beauty went with them. She had been a blooming, delicate girl,—the slight grace of a daisy in her figure, wild-rose tints on her fair cheek, and golden reflections in her light brown hair, that shone in its waves and curls like lost sunshine; but ten years of such service told their story plainly. When Hitty Hyde was twenty-six, her blue eyes were full of sorrow and patience, when the shy lids let their legend be read; the little mouth had become pale, and the corners drooped; her cheek, too, was tintless, though yet round; nothing but the beautiful hair lasted; even grace was gone, so long had she stooped over her father. Sometimes the unwakened heart within her dreamed, as a girl's heart will. Stately visions of Sir Charles Grandison bowing before her,—shuddering fascinations over the image of that dreadful Lovelace,—nothing more real haunted Hitty's imagination. She knew what she had to do in life,—that it was not to be a happy wife or mother, but to waste by a bedridden old man, the only creature on earth she loved as she could love. Light and air were denied the plant, but it grew in darkness,— blanched and unblooming, it is true, but still a growth upward, toward light.

Ten years more of monotonous patience, and Miss Hyde was thirty-six. Her hair had thinned, and was full of silver threads; a wrinkle invaded either cheek, and she was angular and bony; but something painfully sweet lingered in her face, and a certain childlike innocence of expression gave her the air of a nun; the world had never touched nor taught her.

But now Judge Hyde was dead; nineteen years of petulant, helpless, hopeless wretchedness were at last over, and all that his daughter cared to live for was gone; she was an orphan, without near relatives, without friends, old, and tired out. Do not despise me that I say "old," you plump and rosy ladies whose life is in its prime of joy and use at thirty-six. Age is not counted by years, nor calculated from one's birth; it is a fact of wear and work, altogether unconnected with the calendar. I have seen a girl of sixteen older than you are at forty. I have known others disgrace themselves at sixty-five by liking to play with children and eat sugar-plums!

One kind of youth still remained to Hitty Hyde,—the freshness of inexperience. Her soul was as guileless and as ignorant as a child's; and she was stranded on life, with a large fortune, like a helmless ship, heavily loaded, that breaks from its anchor, and drives headlong upon a reef.

Now it happened, that, within a year after Judge Hyde's death, Abner Dimock, the tavern-keeper's son, returned to Greenfield, after years of absence, a bold-faced, handsome man, well-dressed and "free-handed," as the Greenfield vernacular hath it. Nobody knew where Abner Dimock had spent the last fifteen years; neither did anybody know anything against him; yet he had no good reputation in Greenfield. Everybody looked wise and grave when his name was spoken, and no Greenfield girl cared to own him for an acquaintance. His father welcomed him home with more surprise than pleasure; and the whole household of the Greenfield Hotel, as Dimock's Inn was new-named, learned to get out of Abner Dimock's way, and obey his eye, as if he were more their master than his father.

Left quite alone, without occupation or amusement, Miss Hyde naturally grasped at anything that came in her way to do or to see to; the lawyer who had been executor of her father's will had settled the estate and gone back to his home, and Miss Hyde went with him, the first journey of her life, that she might select a monument for her father's grave. It was now near a year since Judge Hyde's death, and the monument was on its way from Boston; the elder Dimock monopolized the cartage of freight as well as passengers to the next town, and to him Miss Hyde intrusted the care of the great granite pillar she had purchased; and it was for his father that Abner Dimock called on the young lady for directions as to the disposal of the tombstone just arrived. Hitty was in the garden; her white morning-dress shone among the roses, and the morning air had flushed her pale cheek; she looked fair and delicate and gracious; but her helpless ignorance of the world's ways and usages attracted the world-hardened man more than her face. He had not spent a *roué*[2] life in a great city for nothing; he had lived enough with gentlemen, broken-down and lost, it is true, but well-bred, to be able to ape their manners; and the devil's instinct that such people possess warned him of Hitty Hyde's weakest points. So, too, he contrived to make that first errand lead to another, and still another,—to make the solitary woman depend on his help, and expect his coming; fifty thousand dollars, with no more incumbrance than such a woman, was worth scheming for, and the prey was easily snared.

It is not to be expected that any country village of two streets, much less Greenfield, could long remain ignorant of such a new and amazing phase as the devotion of any man to any woman therein; but, as nobody liked to interfere too soon in what might only be, after all, a mere business arrangement, Greenfield contented itself with using its eyes, its ears, and its tongues, with one exception to the latter organ's clatter, in favor of Hitty Hyde; *to* her no one dared as yet approach with gossip or advice.

In the mean time Hitty went on her way, all regardless of the seraphs at the gate. Abner Dimock was handsome, agreeable, gentlemanly to a certain lackered extent;—who had cared for Hitty, in all her life, enough to aid and counsel her as he had already done? At first she was half afraid of him; then she liked him; then he was "so good to me!" and then—she pitied him! for he told her, sitting on that hard old sofa, in the June twilight, how he had no mother, how he had been cast upon the charities of a cruel and evil world from his infancy; reminded her of the old red school-house where they had been to school together, and the tyranny of the big boys over him,—a little curly, motherless boy. So he enlarged upon his life; talked a mildly bitter misanthropy; informed Miss Hyde by gradual insinuations that she was an angel sent on earth to console and reform a poor sinner like him; and before the last September rose had dropped, so far had Abner Dimock succeeded in his engineering, that his angel was astounded one night by the undeniably terrestrial visitation of an embrace and a respectfully fervid kiss.

Perhaps it would have been funny, perhaps pathetic, to analyze the mixed consternation and delight of Mehitable Hyde at such *bonâ-fide* evidence of a lover. Poor woman's heart!—altogether solitary and deso-late,—starved of its youth and its joy,—given over to the chilly reign of patience and resignation,—afraid of life,—without strength, or hope, or pleasure,—and all at once Paradise dawns!—her cold, innocent life bursts into fiery and odorous bloom; she has found her fate, and its face is keen with splendor, like a young angel's. Poor, deluded, blessed, rapture-smitten woman!

Blame her as you will, indignant maidens of Greenfield, Miss Flint, and Miss Sharp, and Miss Skinner! You may have had ten lovers and twenty flirtations apiece, and refused half-a-dozen good matches for the best of reasons; you, no doubt, would have known better than to marry a man who was a villain from his very physiognomy; but my heart must needs grow tender toward Miss Hyde; a great joy is as pathetic as a sorrow. Did you never cry over a doting old man?

But when Mrs. Smith's son John, a youth of ten, saw, by the light of an incautious lamp that illuminated a part of the south parlor, a good-night kiss bestowed upon the departing Abner by Miss Hitty Hyde and abso-lutely returned by said Abner, and when John told his mother, and his mother revealed it to Miss Flint, Miss Flint to Miss Skinner, and so forth, and so on, till it reached the minister's wife, great was the uproar in Greenfield; and the Reverend Mrs. Perkins put on her gray bonnet and went over to remonstrate with Hitty on the spot.

Whether people will ever learn the uselessness of such efforts is yet a matter for prophecy. Miss Hyde heard all that was said, and replied very quietly, "I don't believe it." And as Mrs. Perkins had no tangible proofs of Abner Dimock's unfitness to marry Judge Hyde's daughter, the lady in question got the better of her adviser, so far as any argument was concerned, and effectually put an end to remonstrance by declaring with extreme quiet and unblushing front,—

"I am going to marry him next week. Will you be so good as to notify Mr. Perkins?"

Mrs. Perkins held up both hands and cried. Words might have hardened Hitty; but what woman that was not half tigress ever withstood another woman's tears?

Hitty's heart melted directly; she sat down by Mrs. Perkins, and cried, too.

"Please, don't be vexed with me," sobbed she. "I love him, Mrs. Perkins, and I haven't got anybody else to love,—and—and—I never shall have. He's very good to love me,—I am so old and homely."

"Very good!" exclaimed Mrs. Perkins, in great wrath, "*good!* to marry Judge Hyde's daughter, and—fifty thousand dollars," Mrs. Perkins bit off. She would not put such thoughts into Hitty's head, since her marriage was inevitable.

"At any rate," sighed Hitty, on the breath of a long-drawn sob, "nobody else ever loved me, if I am Judge Hyde's daughter."

So Mrs. Perkins went away, and declared that things had gone too far to be prevented; and Abner Dimock came on her retreating steps, and Hitty forgot everything but that he loved her; and the next week they were married.

Here, by every law of custom, ought my weary pen to fall flat and refuse its office; for it is here that the fate of every heroine culminates. For what are women born but to be married? Old maids are excrescences in the social system,—disagreeable utilities,—persons who have failed to fulfil their destiny,—and of whom it should have been said, rather than of ghosts, that they are always in the wrong. But life, with pertinacious facts, is too apt to transcend custom and the usage of novel-writers; and though the one brings a woman's legal existence to an end when she merges her independence in that of a man, and the other curtails her historic existence at the same point, because the novelist's catechism hath for its preface this creed,—"The chief end of woman is to get married"; still, neither law nor novelists altogether displace this same persistent fact, and a woman lives, in all capacities of suffering and happiness, not only her wonted, but a double life, when legally and religiously she binds herself with bond and vow to another soul.

Happy would it have been for Hitty Hyde, if with the legal fiction had chimed the actual existent fact!—happy indeed for Abner Dimock's wife to have laid her new joy down at the altar, and been carried to sleep by her mother under the mulleins and golden-rods on Greenfield Hill! Scarce was the allotted period of rapture past half its term, scarce had she learned to phrase the tender words aloud that her heart beat and choked with, before Abner Dimock began to tire of his incumbrance, and to invent plans and excuses for absences; for he dared not openly declare as yet that he left his patient, innocent wife for such scenes of vice and reckless dissipation as she had not even dreamed could exist.

Yet for week after week he lingered away from Greenfield; even months rolled by, and, except for rare and brief visits home, Hitty saw no more of her husband than if he were not hers. She lapsed into her old solitude, varied only by the mutterings and grumblings of old Keery, who had lifted up her voice against Hitty's marriage with more noise and less effect than Mrs. Perkins, and, though she still staid by her old home and haunts, revenged herself on fate in general and her mistress in particular by a continual course of sulking, all the time hiding under this general quarrel with life a heart that ached with the purest tenderness and pity. So some people are made, like chestnuts; one gets so scratched and wounded in the mere attempt to get at the kernel within, that it becomes matter of question whether one does not suffer less from wanting their affection than from trying to obtain it. Yet Hitty Dimock had too little love given her to throw away even Keery's habit of kindness to her, and bore with her snaps and snarls as meekly as a saint,—sustained, it is true, by a hope that now began to solace and to occupy her, and to raise in her oppressed soul some glimmer of a bright possibility, a faint expectation that she might yet regain her husband's love, a passion which she began in her secret heart to fear had found its limit and died out. Still, Hitty, out of her meek, self-distrusting spirit, never blamed Abner Dimock for his absences; rather, with the divine unselfishness that such women manifest, did she blame herself for having linked his handsome and athletic prime with her faded age, and struggle daily with the morbid conscience that accused her of having forgotten his best good in the indulgence of her own selfish ends of happiness. She still thought, "He is so good to me!" still idealized the villain to a hero, and, like her kind, predestined to be the prey and the accusing angel of such men, prayed for and adored her husband as if he had been the best and tenderest of gentlemen. Providence has its mysteries; but if there be one that taxes faith and staggers patience more than another, it is the long misery that makes a good woman cringe and writhe and agonize in silence under the utter rule and life-long sovereignty of a bad man. Perhaps such women do not suffer as we fancy; for after much trial every woman learns that it is possible to love where neither respect nor admiration can find foothold,—that it even becomes necessary to love some men, as the angels love us all, from an untroubled height of pity and tenderness, that, while it sees and condemns the sin and folly and uncleanness of its object, yet broods over it with an all-shielding devotion, laboring and beseeching and waiting for its regeneration, upheld above the depths of suffering and regret by the immortal power of a love so fervent, so pure, so self-forgetting, that it will be a millstone about the necks that disregard its tender clasping now, to sink them into a bottomless abyss in the day of the Lord.

Now had one long and not unhappy autumn, a lingering winter, a desolate spring, a weary summer, passed away, and from an all-unconscious and protracted wrestling with death Hitty Dimock awoke to find her hope fulfilled,—a fair baby nestled on her arm, and her husband, not all-insensible, smiling beside her.

It is true, that, had she died then, Abner Dimock would have regretted her death; for, by certain provisions of her father's will, in case of her death, the real estate, otherwise at her own disposal, became a trust for her child or children, and such a contingency ill suited Mr. Dimock's plans. So long as Hitty held a rood of land or a coin of silver at her own disposal, it was also at his; but trustees are not women, happily for the world at large, and the contemplation of that fact brought Hitty Hyde's husband into a state of mind well fitted to give him real joy at her recovery.

So, for a little while, the sun shone on this bare New England hill-side, into this grim old house. Care and kindness were lavished on the delicate woman, who would scarce have needed either in her present delight; every luxury that could add to her slowly increasing strength, every attention that could quiet her fluttering and unstrung nerves, was showered on her, and for a time her brightest hopes seemed all to have found fruition.

As she recovered and was restored to strength, of course these cares ceased. But now the new instincts of motherhood absorbed her, and, brooding over the rosy child that was her own, caressing its waking, or hanging above its sleep, she scarce noted that her husband's absences from home grew more and more frequent, that strange visitors asked for him, that he came home at midnight oftener than at dusk. Nor was it till her child was near a year old that Hitty discovered her husband's old and rewakened propensity,—that Abner Dimock came home drunk,—not drunk as many men are, foolish and helpless, mere beasts of the field, who know nothing and care for nothing but the filling of their insatiable appetite;—this man's nature was too hard, too iron in its moulding, to give way to temporary imbecility; liquor made him savage, fierce, brutal, excited his fiendish temper to its height, nerved his muscular system, inflamed his brain, and gave him the aspect of a devil; and in such guise he entered his wife's peaceful Eden, where she brooded and cooed over her child's slumbers, with one gripe of his hard hand lifted her from her chair, kicked the cradle before him, and, with an awful though muttered oath, thrust mother and child into the entry, locked the door upon them, and fell upon the bed to sleep away his carouse.

Here was an undeniable fact before Hitty Dimock, one she could no way evade or gloss over; no gradual lesson, no shadow of foreboding, preluded the revelation; her husband was unmistakably, savagely drunk. She did not sit down and cry;—drearily she gathered her baby in her arms, hushed it to sleep with kisses, passed down into the kitchen, woke up the brands of the ash-hidden fire to a flame, laid on more wood, and, dragging old Keery's rush-bottomed chair in front of the blaze, held her baby in her arms till morning broke, careless of anything without or within but her child's sleep and her husband's drunkenness. Long and sadly in that desolate night did she revolve this new misery in her mind; the fact was face to face, and must be provided for,—but how to do it? What could she do, poor weak woman, even to conceal this disgrace, much more to check it? Long since she had discovered that between her and her husband there was no community of tastes or interests; he never talked to her, he never read to her, she did not know that he read at all; the garden he disliked as a useless trouble; he would not drive, except such a gay horse that Hitty dared not risk her neck behind it, and felt a shudder of fear assail her whenever his gig left the door; neither did he care for his child. Nothing at home could keep him from his pursuits; that she well knew; and, hopeful as she tried to be, the future spread out far away in misty horror and dread. What might not become of her boy, with such a father's influence? was her first thought;—nay, who could tell but in some fury of drink he might kill or maim him? A chill of horror crept over Hitty at the thought,—and then, what had not she to dread? Oh, for some loophole of escape, some way to fly, some refuge for her baby's innocent life! No,—no,—no! She was his wife; she had married him; she had vowed to love and honor and obey,—vow of fearful import now, though uttered in all pureness and truth, as to a man who owned her whole heart! Love him!—that was not the dread; love was as much her life as her breath was; she knew no interval of loving for the brute fiend who mocked her with the name of husband; no change or chance could alienate her divine tenderness,—even as the pitiful blue sky above hangs stainless over reeking battle-fields and pest-smitten cities, piercing with its sad and holy star-eyes down into the hellish orgies of men, untouched and unchanged by just or unjust, forever shining and forever pure. But honor him! could that be done? What respect or trust was it possible to keep for a self-degraded man like that? And where honor goes down, obedience is sucked into the vortex, and the wreck flies far over the lonely sea, historic and prophetic to ship and shore.

No! there was nothing to do! her vow was taken, past the power of man to break; nothing now remained but endurance. Perhaps another woman, with a strong will and vivid intellect, might have set herself to work, backed by that very vow that defied poor Hitty, and, by sheer resolution, have dragged her husband up from the gulf and saved him, though as by fire; or a more buoyant and younger wife might have passed it by as a first offence, hopeful of its being also the only one. But an instinctive knowledge of the man bereft Hitty of any such hope; she knew it was not the first time; from his own revelations and penitent confessions while she was yet free, she knew he had sinned as well as suffered, and the past augured the future. Nothing was left her, she could not escape, she must shut her eyes and her mouth, and only keep out of his way as far as she could. So she clasped her child more tightly, and, closing her heavy eyes, rocked back and forth till the half-waked boy slept again; and there old Keery found her mistress, in the morning, white as the cold drifts without, and a depth of settled agony in her quiet eyes that dimmed the old woman's only to look at.

Neither spoke; nor when her husband strode into the breakfast-room and took his usual place, sober enough, but scarcely regretful of the over-night development, did any word of reproach or allusion pass the wife's white lips. A stranger would have thought her careless and cold. Abner Dimock knew that she was heart-broken; but what was that to him? Women live for years without that organ; and while she lived, so long as a cent remained of the Hyde estate, what was it to him if she pined away? She could not leave him; she was utterly in his power; she was his,—like his boots, his gun, his dog; and till he should tire of her and fling her into some lonely chamber to waste and die, she was bound to serve him; he was safe.

And she offered no sort of barrier to his full indulgence of his will to drink. Had she lifted one of her slender fingers in warning, or given him a look of reproachful meaning, or uttered one cry of entreaty, at least the conscience within him might have visited him with a temporary shame, and restrained the raging propensity for a longer interval; but seeing her apparent apathy, knowing how timid and unresisting was her nature,— that nothing on earth will lie still and be trodden on but a woman,— Abner Dimock rioted and revelled to his full pleasure, while all his pale and speechless wife could do was to watch with fearful eyes and straining ears for his coming, and slink out of the way with her child, lest both should be beaten as well as cursed; for faithful old Keery, once daring to face him with a volley of reproaches from her shrill tongue, was levelled to the floor by a blow from his rapid hand, and bore bruises for weeks that warned her from interference. Not long, however, was there danger of her meddling.

The Ring Fetter

When the baby was a year and a half old, Keery, in her out-doors labors,—now grown burdensome enough, since Mr. Dimock neither worked himself nor allowed a man on the premises,—Keery took a heavy cold, and, worn out with a life of hard work, sank into rest quickly, her last act of life being to draw Hitty's face down to her own, wrinkled and wan as it was, scarce so old in expression as her mistress's, and with one long kiss and sob speak the foreboding and anxious farewell she could not utter.

"Only you now!" whispered Hitty to her child, as Keery's peaceful, shrouded face was hidden under the coffin-lid and carried away to Greenfield Hill. Pitiful whisper! happily all-unmeaning to the child, but full of desolation to the mother, floating with but one tiny plank amid the wild wrecks of a midnight ocean, and clinging as only the desperate can cling to this vague chance of life.

A rough, half-crazed girl, brought from the alms-house, now did the drudgery of the family. Abner Dimock had grown penurious, and not one cent of money was given for comfort in that house, scarce for need. The girl was stupid and rude, but she worked for her board,—recommendation enough in Mr. Dimock's eyes; and so hard work was added to the other burdens loaded upon his silent wife. And soon came another, all-mysterious, but from its very mystery a deeper fear. Abner Dimock began to stay at home, to be visited at late hours by one or two men whose faces were full of evil and daring; and when, in the dead of the long nights, Hitty woke from her broken and feverish sleep, it was to hear muffled sounds from the cellar below, never heard there before; and once, wrapping a shawl about her, she stole down the stairways with bare feet, and saw streams of red light through the chinks of the cellar-door, and heard the ring of metal, and muttered oaths, all carefully dulled by such devices as kept the sounds from chance passers in the street, though vain as far as the inhabitants of the house itself were concerned. Trembling and cold, she stole back to her bed, full of doubts and fears, neither of which she dared whisper to any one, or would have dared, had she possessed a single friend to whom she could speak. Troubles thickened fast over Hitty; her husband was always at home now, and rarely sober; the relief his absences had been was denied her entirely; and in some sunny corner of the uninhabited rooms up-stairs she spent her days, toiling at such sewing as was needful, and silent as the dead, save as her life appealed to God from the ground, and called down the curse of Cain upon a head she would have shielded from evil with her own life.

Keen human legislation! sightless justice of men!—one drunken wretch smites another in a midnight brawl, and sends a soul to its account with one sharp shudder of passion and despair, and the maddened creature that remains on earth suffers the penalty of the law. Every sense sobered from its reeling fury, weeks of terrible expectation heaped upon the cringing soul, and, in full consciousness, that murderer is strangled before men and angels, because he was drunk!—necessary enough, one perceives, to the good of society, which thereby loses two worse than useless members; but what, in the name of God's justice, should His vicegerent, law, visit upon the man who wrings another life away by slow tortures, and torments heart and soul and flesh for lingering years, where the victim is passive and tenacious, and dies only after long-drawn anguish that might fill the cup of a hundred sudden deaths? Yet what escapes the vicegerent shall the King himself visit and judge. "For He cometh! He cometh to judge the earth; with righteousness shall He judge the world, and the people with equity."

Six months passed after Keery's death, and now from the heights of Greenfield and her sunny window Hitty Dimock's white face looked out upon a landscape of sudden glory; for October, the gold-bringer, had come, pouring splendor over the earth, and far and wide the forests blazed; scarlet and green maples, with erect heads, sentinelled the street, gay lifeguards of autumn; through dark green cedars the crimson creeper threaded its sprays of blood-red; birches, gilded to their tops, swayed to every wind, and drooped their graceful boughs earthward to shower the mossy sward with glittering leaves; heavy oaks turned purple-crimson through their wide-spread boughs; and the stately chestnuts, with foliage of tawny yellow, opened wide their stinging husks to let the nuts fall for squirrel and blue-jay. Splendid sadness clothed all the world, opal-hued mists wandered up and down the valleys or lingered about the undefined horizon, and the leaf-scented south wind sighed in the still noon with foreboding gentleness.

One day, Abner Dimock was gone, and Hitty stole down to the garden-door with her little child, now just trying to walk, that he might have a little play on the green turf, and she cool her hot eyes and lips in the air. As she sat there watching the pretty clumsiness of her boy, and springing forward to intercept his falls, the influence of the sun and air, the playful joy of the child, the soothing stillness of all Nature, stole into her heart till it dreamed a dream of hope. Perhaps the budding blossom of promise might become floral and fruitful; perhaps her child might yet atone for the agony of the past;—a time might come when she should sit in that door, white-haired and trembling with age, but as peaceful as the autumn day, watching the sports of his children, while his strong arm sustained her into the valley of shadow, and his tender eyes lit the way.

As she sat dreaming, suddenly a figure intercepted the sunshine, and, looking up, she saw Abner Dimock's father, the elder Abner, entering the little wicket-gate of the garden. A strange, tottering old figure, his nose and chin grimacing at each other, his bleared eyes telling unmistakable truths of cider-brandy and New England rum, his scant locks of white lying in confusion over his wrinkled forehead and cheeks, his whole air squalid, hopeless, and degraded,—not so much by the poverty of vice as by its demoralizing stamp penetrating from the inner to the outer man, and levelling it even below the plane of brutes that perish.

"Good-day! good-day!" said he to his son's wife, in a squeaking, tremulous tone, that drove the child to his mother's arms,—"Abner to home?"

"No, Sir," said Hitty, with an involuntary shudder, that did not escape the bleared blue eye that fixed its watery gaze upon her.

"Cold, a'n't ye? Better go in, better go in! Come, come along! How d'e do, little feller? don't know yer grandper, hey?"

The child met his advances with an ominous scream, and Hitty hurried into the house to give him to the servant's charge, while she returned to the sitting-room, where the old man had seated himself in the rocking-chair, and was taking a mental inventory of the goods and chattels with a momentary keenness in his look that no way reassured Hitty's apprehensive heart.

"So, Abner a'n't to home?"

"No, Sir."

"Don't know where he's gone, do ye?"

"No, Sir."

"Don't never know where he goes, I expect?"

"No, Sir."

"Well, when he comes home,—know when he's a-comin' home?"

"No, Sir."

"Well, when he doos, you tell him 't some folks come to the tavern last night, 'n' talked pretty loud, 'n' I heerd—Guess 'ta'n't best, though, to tell what I heerd. Only you tell Abner 't I come here, and I said he'd better be a-joggin'. He'll know, he'll know,—h'm, yes," said the old man, passing his hand across his thin blue lips, as if to drive away other words better left unsaid,—and then rising from his seat, by the aid of either arm, gained his balance, and went on, while he fumbled for his stick:—

"I'd ha' writ, but black and white's a hangin' matter sometimes, 'n' words a'n't; 'n' I hadn't nobody to send, so I crawled along. Don't ye forget now! don't ye! It's a pretty consider'ble piece o' business; 'n' you'll be dreffully on't, ef you do forget. Now *don't* ye forget!"

"No, I won't," said Hitty, trembling as she spoke; for the old man's words had showed her a depth of dreadful possibility, and an old acquaintance with crime and its manœuvres, that chilled the blood in her veins. She watched him out of the gate with a sickening sense of terror at her heart, and turned slowly into the house, revolving all kinds of plans in her head for her husband's escape, should her fears prove true. Of herself she did not think; no law could harm her child; but, even after years of brutality and neglect, her faithful affection turned with all its provident thoughtfulness and care at once to her husband; all her wrongs were forgotten, all her sorrows obliterated by this one fear! Well did St. Augustine say, "God is patient because He is eternal"; but better and truer would the saying have been, had it run, "God is patient because He is love": a gospel that He publishes in the lives of saints on earth, in their daily and hourly "anguish of patience," preaching to the fearful souls that dare not trust His long-suffering by the tenacious love of those who bear His image, saying, in resistless human tones, "Shall one creature endure and love and continually forgive another, and shall I, who am not loving, but Love, be weary of thy transgressions, O sinner?" And so does the silent and despairing life of many a woman weave unconsciously its golden garland of reward in the heavens above, and do the Lord's work in a strange land where it cannot sing His songs.

The Ring Fetter

The day crept toward sunset, and Hitty sat with her wan face pressed to the window-pane, hushing her child in his cradle with one of those low, monotoned murmurs that mothers know; but still her husband did not come. The level sun-rays pierced the woods into more vivid splendor, burnished gold fringed the heavy purple clouds in the west, and warm crimson lights turned the purple into more triumphant glory; the sun set, unstained with mist or tempest, behind those blue and lonely hills that guard old Berkshire with their rolling summits, and night came fast, steel-blue and thick with stars; but yet he did not come, the untouched meal on the table was untouched still. Hour after hour of starry darkness crept by, and she sat watching at the window-pane; overhead, constellations marched across the heavens in relentless splendor, careless of man or sorrow; Orion glittered in the east, and climbed toward the zenith; the Pleiades clustered and sparkled as if they missed their lost sister no more; the Hyades marked the celestial pastures of Taurus, and Lyra strung her chords with fire. Hitty rested her weary head against the window-frame and sent her wearier thoughts upward to the stars; there were the points of light that the Chaldeans watched upon their plains by night, and named with mystic syllables of their weird Oriental tongue,—names that in her girlhood she had delighted to learn, charmed by that nameless spell that language holds, wherewith it plants itself ineradicably in the human mind, and binds it with fetters of vague association that time and chance are all-powerless to break,—Zubeneschamali and Zubenelgunebi, Bellatrix and Betelguese, sonorous of Rome and Asia both, full of old echoes and the dry resonant air of Eastern plains,—names wherein sounded the clash of Bellona's armor, and the harsh stir of palm-boughs rustled by a hot wind of the desert, and vibrant with the dying clangor of gongs, and shouts of worshipping crowds reverberating through horrid temples of grinning and ghastly idols, wet with children's blood.

Far, far away, the heavenly procession and their well-remembered names had led poor Hitty's thoughts; worn out with anxiety, and faint for want of the food she had forgotten to take, sleep crept upon her, and her first consciousness of its presence was the awakening grasp of a rough hand and the hoarse whisper of her husband.

"Get up!" said he. "Pick up your brat, get your shawl, and come!"

Hitty rose quickly to her feet. One faculty wretchedness gives, the power of sudden self-possession,—and Hitty was broad awake in the very instant she was called. Her husband stood beside her, holding a lantern; her boy slept in the cradle at her feet.

"Have you seen your father?" said she, with quick instinct.

"Yes, d——n you, be quick! do you want to hang me?"

Quick as a spirit Hitty snatched her child, and wrapped him in the blanket where he lay; her shawl was on the chair she had slept in, her hood upon a nail by the door, and flinging both on, with the child in her arms, she followed her husband down-stairs, across the back-yard, hitting her feet against stones and logs in the darkness, stumbling often, but never falling, till the shadow of the trees was past, and the starlight showed her that they were traversing the open fields, now crisp with frost, but even to the tread,—over two or three of these, through a pine-wood that was a landmark to Hitty, for she well knew that it lay between the turnpike-road and another, less frequented, that by various windings went toward the Connecticut line,—then over a tiny brook on its unsteady bridge of logs, and out into a lane, where a rough-spoken man was waiting for them, at the head of a strong horse harnessed to one of those wagons without springs that New-Englanders like to make themselves uncomfortable in. Her husband turned to her abruptly.

"Get in," said he; "get in behind; there's hay enough; and don't breathe loud, or I'll murder you!"

She clambered into the wagon and seated herself on the hay, hushing her child, who nestled and moaned in her arms, though she had carried him with all possible care. A sharp cut of the whip sent the powerful horse off at full speed, and soon this ill-matched party were fast traversing the narrow road that wound about the country for the use of every farm within a mile of its necessary course, a course tending toward the Connecticut.

Hour after hour crept by. Worn out with fatigue, poor Hitty dozed and fell back on the soft hay; her child slept, too, and all her troubles faded away in heavy unconsciousness, till she was again awakened by her husband's grasp, to find that dawn was gathering its light roseate fleeces in the east, and that their flight was for the present stayed at the door of a tavern, lonely and rude enough, but welcome to Hitty as a place of rest, if only for a moment. The sullen mistress of the house asked no questions and offered no courtesy, but, after her guests had eaten their breakfast, rapidly prepared, she led the way to a bedroom in the loft, where Abner Dimock flung himself down upon the straw bed and fell sound asleep, leaving Hitty to the undisturbed care of her child. And occupation enough that proved; for the little fellow was fretful and excited, so that no hour for thought was left to his anxious and timid mother till the dinner-bell awoke her husband and took him down-stairs. She could not eat, but, begging some milk for her boy, tended, and fed, and sung to him, till he slept; and then all the horrors of the present and future thronged upon her, till her heart seemed to die in her breast, and her limbs failed to support her when she would have dragged herself out of doors for one breath of fresh air, one refreshing look at a world untroubled and serene.

So the afternoon crept away, and as soon as night drew on the journey was resumed. But this night was chill with the breath of a sobbing east wind, and the dim stars forboded rain. Hitty shivered with bitter cold, and the boy began to cry. With a fierce curse Abner bade her stop his disturbance, and again the poor mother had hands and heart full to silence the still recurring sobs of the child. At last, after the midnight cocks had ceased to send their challenges from farm to farm, after some remote church-clocks had clanged one stroke on the damp wind, they began to pass through a large village; no lights burned in the windows, but white fences gleamed through the darkness, and sharp gable ends loomed up against the dull sky, one after another, and the horse's hoofs flashed sparks from the paved street before the church, that showed its white spire, spectre-like, directly in their path. Here, by some evil chance, the child awoke, and, between cold and hunger and fear, began one of those long and loud shrieks that no power can stop this side of strangulation. In vain Hitty kissed, and coaxed, and half-choked her boy, in hope to stop the uproar; still he screamed more and more loudly. Abner turned round on his seat with an oath, snatched the child from its mother's arms, and rolled it closely in the blanket.

"Hold on a minute, Ben!" said he to his companion; "this yelp must be stopped"; and stepping over to the back of the wagon, he grasped his wife tightly with one arm, and with the other dropped his child into the street. "Now drive, Ben," said he, in the same hoarse whisper,—"drive like the Devil!"—for, as her child fell, Hitty shrieked with such a cry as only the heart of a mother could send out over a newly-murdered infant. Shriek on shriek, fast and loud and long, broke the slumbers of the village; nothing Abner could do, neither threat nor force, short of absolute murder, would avail,—and there was too much real estate remaining of the Hyde property for Abner Dimock to spare his wife yet. Ben drove fiend-fashion; but before they passed the last house in the village, lights were glancing and windows grating as they were opened. Years after, I heard the story of such a midnight cry borne past sleeping houses with the quick rattle of wheels; but no one who heard it could give the right clue to its explanation, and it dried into a legend.

Now Hitty Dimock became careless of good or evil, except one absorbing desire to get away from her husband,—to search for her child, to know if it had lived or died. For four nights more that journey was pursued at the height of their horse's speed; every day they stopped to rest, and every day Hitty's half-delirious brain laid plans of escape, only to be balked by Abner Dimock's vigilance; for if he slept, it was with both arms round her, and the slightest stir awoke him,—and while he woke, not one propitious moment freed her from his watch. Her brain began to reel with disappointment and anguish; she began to hate her husband; a band of iron seemed strained about her forehead, and a ringing sound filled her ears; her lips grew parched, and her eye glittered; the last night of their journey Abner Dimock lifted her into the wagon, and she fainted on the hay.

"What in hell did you bring her for, Dimock?" growled his companion; "women are d——d plagues always."

"She'll get up in a minute," coolly returned the husband; "can't afford to leave a goose that lays golden eggs behind; hold on till I lift her up. Here, Hitty! drink, I tell you! drink!"

A swallow of raw spirit certainly drove away the faintness, but it brought fresh fire to the fever that burned in her veins, and she was muttering in delirium before the end of that night's journey brought them to a small village just above the old house on the river that figured in the beginning of this history, and which we trust the patient reader has not forgotten. Abner Dimock left his wife in charge of the old woman who kept the hovel of a tavern where they stopped, and, giving Ben the horse to dispose of to some safe purchaser, after he had driven him down to the old house, returned at night in the boat that belonged to his negro tenant, and, taking his unconscious wife from her bed, rowed down the river and landed her safely, to be carried from the skiff into an upper chamber of the old house, where Jake's wife, Aunt Judy, as Mr. Dimock styled her, nursed the wretched woman through three weeks of fever, and "doctored" her with herbs and roots.

The tenacious Hyde constitution, that was a proverb in Greenfield, conquered at last, and Hitty became conscious, to find herself in a chamber whose plastered walls were crumbling away with dampness and festooned with cobwebs, while the uncarpeted floor was checkered with green stains of mildew, and the very old four-post bedstead on which she lay was fringed around the rickety tester with rags of green moreen, mould-rotted.

Hitty sank back on her pillow with a sigh; she did not even question the old negress who sat crooning over the fire, as to where she was, or what had befallen her; but accepted this new place as only another misty delirium, and in her secret heart prayed, for the hundredth time, to die.

Slowly she recovered; for prayers to die are the last prayers ever answered; we live against our will, and tempt living deaths year after year, when soul and body cry out for the grave's repose, and beat themselves against the inscrutable will of God only to fall down before it in bruised and bleeding acquiescence. So she lived to find herself immured in this damp and crumbling house, with no society but a drinking and crime-haunted husband, and the ignorant negroes who served him,—society varied now and then by one or two men revolting enough in speech and aspect to drive Hitty to her own room, where, in a creaking chair, she rocked monotonously back and forth, watching the snapping fire, and dreaming dreams of a past that seemed now but a visionary paradise.

For now it was winter, and the heavy drifts of snow that lay on Dimock's meadow forbade any explorations which the one idea of finding her child might have driven her to make; and the frozen surface of the river no white-sailed ship could traverse now, nor the hissing paddle-wheels of a steamer break the silence with intimations of life, active and salient, far beyond the lonely precinct of Abner Dimock's home.

So the winter passed by. The noises and lights that had awoke Hitty at midnight in the house at Greenfield had become so far an institution in this lonely dwelling that now they disturbed her sleep no more; for it was a received custom, that, whenever Abner Dimock's two visitors should appear, the cellar should resound all night with heavy blows and clinking of metal, and red light as from a forge streamed up through the doorway; but it disturbed Hitty no more; apathy settled down in black mist on her soul, and she seemed to think, to care, for nothing.

But spring awoke the dead earth, and sleeping roots aroused with fresh forces from their torpor, and sent up green signals to the birds above. A spark of light awoke in Hitty's eye; she planned to get away, to steal the boat from its hidden cove in the bushes and push off down the friendly current of the river,—anywhere away from him! anywhere! though it should be to wreck on the great ocean, but still away from him! Night after night she rose from her bed to hazard the attempt, but her heart failed, and her trembling limbs refused their aid. At length moonlight came to her aid, and when all the house slept she stole down-stairs with bare, noiseless feet, and sped like a ghost across the meadow to the river-bank. Poor weak hands! vainly they fumbled with the knotted rope that bound the skiff to a crooked elm overhanging the water,—all in vain for many lingering minutes; but presently the obdurate knot gave way, and, turning to gather up her shawl, there, close behind her, so close that his hot breath seemed to sear her cheek, stood her husband, clear in the moonlight, with a sneer on his face, and the lurid glow of drunkenness, that made a savage brute of a bad man, gleaming in his deep-set eyes. Hitty neither shrieked nor ran; despair nerved her,—despair turned her rigid before his face.

"Well," said he, "where are you going?"

"I am going away,—away from you,—anywhere in the world away from you!" answered she, with the boldness of desperation.

"Ha, ha! going away from me!—that's a d——d good joke, a'n't it? Away from your husband! You fool! you can't get away from me! you're mine, soul and body,—this world and the next! Don't you know that? Where's your promise, eh?—'for better, for worse!'—and a'n't I worse, you cursed fool, you? You didn't put on the handcuffs for nothing; heaven and hell can't get you away from me as long as you've got on that little shiny fetter on your finger,—don't you know that?"

The maddened woman made a quick wrench to pull away from him her left hand, which he held in his, taunting her with the ring that symbolized their eternal bonds; but he was too quick for her.

"Hollo!" laughed he; "want to get rid of it, don't you? No, no! that won't do,—that won't do! I'll make it safe!"

And lifting her like a child in his arms, he carried her across the meadow, back to the house, and down a flight of crazy steps into the cellar, where a little forge was all ablaze with white-hot coal, and the two ill-visaged men she well knew by sight were busy with sets of odd tools and fragments of metal, while on a bench near by, and in the seat of an old chair, lay piles of fresh coin. They were a gang of counterfeiters.

Abner Dimock thrust his wife into the chair, sweeping the gilt eagles to the floor as one of the men angrily started up, demanding, with an oath, what he brought that woman there for to hang them all.

"Be quiet, Bill, can't you?" interposed the other man. "Don't you see he's drunk? you'll have the Devil to pay, if you cross a drunk Dimock!"

But Abner had not heard the first speaker; he was too much occupied with tying his wife's arms to the chair,—a proceeding she could nowise interfere with, since his heavy foot was set upon her dress so as to hold her own feet in helpless fixedness. He proceeded to take the ring from her finger, and, searching through a box of various contents that stood in one corner, extracted from it a delicate steel chain, finely wrought, but strong as steel can be; then, at the forge, with sundry tools, carefully chosen and skilfully used, he soldered one end of the chain to the ring, and, returning to his wife, placed it again upon her finger.

"Here, Bill," growled he, "where's that padlock off the tool-chest, eh? give it here! This woman's a fool,—ha, ha, ha!—she wanted to get away from me, and she's my wife!"

Another peal of dissonant laughter interrupted the words.

"What a d——d good joke! I swear I haven't laughed before, this dog's age! And then she was goin' to rid herself of the ring! as if that would help it! Why, there's the promise in black and white,—'love, honor, and obey.'—'I take thee, Abner,'—ha, ha! that's good! But fast bind, fast find; she a'n't going to get rid of the ring. I'll make it as tight as the promise; both of 'em 'll last to doomsday. Give me the padlock, you scoundrel!"

Bill, the man he addressed, knew too much to hesitate after the savage look that sent home the last words,—and, drawing from a bag of tools and dies a tiny padlock and key, he handed them to Dimock, who passed the chain about Hitty's thin white wrist, and, fastening it with the padlock, turned the key, and, withdrawing it from the lock, dropped it into the silvery heat of the forge, and burst into a fit of laughter, so savage and so inhuman that the bearded lips of his two comrades grew white with horror to hear the devil within so exult in his possession of a man.

Hitty sat, statue-like, in her chair; stooping, the man unbound her, and she rose slowly and steadily to her feet, looking him in the face.

"Look!" said she, raising her shackled arm high in air,—"I shall carry it to God!"—and so fled, up the broken stairway, out into the moonlight, across the meadow,—the three men following fast,—over the fallen boughs that winter had strewn along the shore, out under the crooked elm, swift as light, poising on the stern of the boat, that had swung out toward the channel,—and once more lifting her hand high into the white light, with one spring she dropped into the river, and its black waters rolled down to the sea.

FREEDOM WHEELER'S
CONTROVERSY WITH PROVIDENCE

A Story of Old New England

I

AUNT HULDY and Aunt Hannah sat in the kitchen,—Aunt Huldah bolt upright in a straight-backed wooden chair, big silver-bowed spectacles astride her high nose, sewing carpet-rags with such energy that her eyes snapped, and her brown, wrinkled fingers flew back and forth like the spokes of a rapid wheel; Aunt Hannah in a low, creaky old rocker, knitting diligently but placidly, and rocking gently. You could almost hear her purr, and you wanted to stroke her; but Aunt Huldah!—an electric machine could not be less desirable to handle than she, or a chestnut-burr pricklier.

The back-log simmered and sputtered; the hickory-sticks in front shot up bright, soft flames; and through the two low, green-paned windows the pallid sun of February sent in a pleasant shining on to the clean kitchen-floor. Cooking-stoves were not made then, nor Merrimac calicoes. The two old women had stuff petticoats and homespun short-gowns, clean mob-caps over their decent gray hair, and big blue-check aprons: hair-dye, wigs, flowered chintz, and other fineries had not reached the lonely farms of Dorset in those days. "Spinsters" was not a mere name. The big wool wheel stood in one corner of the kitchen, and a little flax-wheel by the window. In summer both would be moved to the great garret, where it was cool and out of the way.

"Curus, ain't it?" said Aunt Huldah. "Freedom never come home before, later'n nine-o'clock bell, and he was mortal mighty then; kep' his tongue between his teeth same way he did to breakfast this mornin'. There's suthin' a-goin' on, Hanner, you may depend on't."

"Mabbe he needs some wormwood-tea," said Aunt Hannah, who, like Miss Hannah More, thought the only two evils in the world were sin and bile, and charitably preferred to lay things first to the physical disorder.

"I du b'lieve, Hanner, you think 'riginal sin is nothin' but a bad stomick."

"Ef 'tain't 'riginal sin, it's actual transgression pretty often, Huldy," returned the placid old lady with a gentle cackle. The Assembly's Catechism[1] had been ground into them both, as any old-fashioned New-Englander will observe, and they quoted its forms of speech, as Boston people do Emerson's Essays, by "an automatic action of the unconscious nervous centres."

The door opened, and Freedom walked in, scraping his boots upon the husk-mat, as a man will who has lived all his days with two old maids, but nevertheless spreading abroad in that clean kitchen an odor of the barn that spoke of "chores," yet did not disturb the accustomed nostrils of his aunts. He was a middle-sized, rather "stocky" man, with a round head well covered with tight-curling short hair, that revenged itself for being cut too short to curl by standing on end toward every point of the compass. You could not call him a common-looking man: something in his keen blue eye, abrupt nose, steady mouth, and square chin, always made a stranger look at him twice. Rugged sense, but more rugged obstinacy, shrewdness, keen perception, tempered somewhat by a certain kindliness that he himself felt to be his weak spot,—all these were to be read in Freedom Wheeler's well-bronzed face, sturdy figure, positive speech, and blunt manner.

He strode up to the fireplace, sat down in an arm-chair rudely shaped out of wood by his own hands, and plunged, after his fashion, at once into the middle of things.

"Aunt Huldy and Aunt Hanner, I'm a-goin' to git married." The domestic bombshell burst in silence. Aunt Hannah dropped a stitch, and couldn't see to pick it up for at least a minute. Aunt Huldah's scissors snipped at the rags with a vicious snap, as if they were responsible agents, and she would end their proceedings then and there; presently she said,

"Well, I *am* beat!" To which rather doubtful utterance Freedom made no reply, and the scissors snipped harder yet.

Aunt Hannah recovered herself first. "Well, I'm real glad on't," purred she. It was her part to do the few amenities of the family.

"I dono whether I be or not, till I hear who 'tis," dryly answered Aunt Huldah, who was obviously near akin to Freedom.

"It's Lowly Mallory," said the short-spoken nephew, who by this time was whittling busily at a peg for his ox-yoke.

"Du tell!" said Aunt Hannah in her lingering, deliberate tones, the words running into each other as she spoke. "She's jest's clever's the day is long. You've done a good thing, Freedom, 's sure's you live."

"He might ha' done wuss: that's a fact." And with this approval Freedom seemed satisfied; for he brushed his chips into the fire, ran his fingers through his already upright hair, eyed his peg with the keen aspect of a critic in pegs, and went off to the barn. He knew instinctively that his aunts must have a chance to talk the matter over.

"This is the beateree!" exclaimed Aunt Huldah as the door shut after him. "Lowly Mallory, of all creturs! Freedom's as masterful as though he was the Lord above, by natur; and ef he gets a leetle softly cretur like that, without no more grit'n a November chicken, he'll ride right over every thing, and she won't darst to peep nor mutter a mite. Good land!"

"Well, well," murmured Aunt Hannah, "she is a kind o' feeble piece, but she's real clever; an' I dono but what it's as good as he could do. Ef she was like to him, hard-headed, 'n' sot in her way, I tell ye, Huldy, the fur'd fly mightily; and it's putty bad to have fight to home when there's a fam'ly to fetch up."

"Well, you be forecastin', I must say, Hanner; but mabbe you're abaout right. Besides, I've obsarved that folks will marry to suit themselves, not other people. An' mabbe it's the best way, seein' it's their own loss or likin' more'n anybody else's."

"But, Huldy, 'pears as if you'd forgot one thing: I expect we'd better be a-movin' out into the old house, ef there's goin' to be more folks here."

"Well, I declare! I never thought on't. 'Tis best, I guess. I wonder ef Freedom's got the idee."

"I dono. But that hadn't oughter make no difference. There never was a house big enough for two families; an', ef we go before we're obleeged to, it's a sight better'n stayin' till we be."

"That's so, Hanner: you allers was a master-hand for takin' things right end foremost. I'll sort out our linen right off, 'nd set by our furnitoor into the back-chamber. I guess the old house'll want a leetle paintin' an' scrapin'. It's dreadful lucky Amasy Flint's folks moved to Noppit last week: seems as though there was a Providence about it."

"I shouldn't wonder ef Freedom had give 'em a sort o' hint to go, Huldy."

"Well, you do beat all! I presume likely he did."

And Aunt Huldah picked up the rags at her feet, piled them into a splint basket, hung the shears on a steel chain by her side, and lifting her tall, gaunt figure from the chair, betook herself up stairs. But Aunt Hannah kept on knitting. She was the thinker, and Huldah the doer, of the family. Now her thoughts ran before her to the coming change, and she sighed; for she knew her nephew thoroughly, and she pitied the gentle, sweet nature that was to come in contact with his.

Dear Aunt Hannah! She had never had any romance in her own life: she did not know anything about love, except as the placid and quite clear-eyed affection she felt for Freedom, who was her only near relation, and she saw little Lowly Mallory's future on its hardest side. But she could not help it; and her nature was one that never frets against a difficulty, any more than the green turf beats against the rock to whose edge it clings.

So the slow, sad New-England spring, with storm and tempest, drifting snows and beating rains, worked its reluctant way into May. And when the lilacs were full of purple and white plumes, delicate as cut coral sprays, and luscious with satiating odor, and the heavy-headed daffodils thrust golden locks upward from the sward, Aunt Huldah and Aunt Hannah moved their wool-wheel and their flax-wheel, the four stiff-backed chairs, the settle and big red chest, the high four-post bedstead, and the two rush-bottomed rockers that had been Grandsir Wheeler's, back into the small red house, for which these furnishing had been purchased sixty years before, laid the rag-carpet, that Aunt Huldah had sewed and dyed and woven, on the "settin'-room" floor, and, with a barrel of potatoes and a keg of salt pork, went to housekeeping.

There was some home-made linen belonging to them, and a few cups and dishes, also a feather-bed, and a pair of blankets. Freedom kept them supplied with what necessaries they wanted, and, though he was called "dreadful near" in the town, he was not an unjust man. His two aunts had taken him in charge, an orphan at six, and been faithful and kind to him all his days, and he could do no less than care for them now. Beside, they owned half the farm, and though one was fifty-six, and the other fifty-eight, there was much hard work left in them yet. Aunt Huldah was a skilful tailoress, in demand for miles about; and Aunt Hannah was the best sick-nurse in the county. They would not suffer: and, truth to tell, they rather enjoyed the independence of their own house; for Freedom and Aunt Huldah were chips of the same block, and only Aunt Hannah's constant, quiet restraint and peace-making kept the family tolerably harmonious. And in the farmhouse a new reign began,—the reign of Queen Log.[2]

Lowly Mallory was a fragile, slender, delicate girl, with sweet gray eyes and plenty of brown hair; pale as a spring anemone, with just such faint pinkness in her lips and on her high cheek-bones as tints that pensile, egg-shaped bud, when its

> "Small flower layeth
> Its fairy gem beneath some giant tree"

on the first warm days of May. She had already the line of care that marks New-England women across the forehead, like a mark of Cain,—the signal of a life in which work has murdered health and joy and freedom; for Lowly was the oldest of ten children, and her mother was bed-ridden. Lovina was eighteen now, and could take her place; and Lowly loved Freedom with the reticent, undemonstrative affection of her race and land: moreover, she was glad of change, of rest. Rest!—much of that awaited her! Freedom's first step after the decorous wedding and home-coming was to buy ten cows—he had two already—and two dozen new milk-pans.

"I calkerlate we can sell a good lot of butter 'n' cheese down to Dartford, Lowly," he said, on introducing her to the new dairy he had fitted up at one end of the woodshed; and, if the gentle creature's heart sank within her at the prospect, she did not say so, and Freedom never asked how she liked it. He was "masterful" indeed; and having picked out Lowly from all the other Dorset girls, because she was a still and hard-working maiden, and would neither rebel against nor criticise his edicts, he took it for granted things would go on as he wished.

Poor little Lowly! Her simple, tender heart went out to her husband like a vine feeling after a trellis; and, even when she found it was only a bowlder that chilled and repelled her slight ardors and timid caresses, she did still what the vine does,—flung herself across and along the granite faces of the rock, and turned her trembling blossoms sunward, where life and light were free and sure.

Aunt Huldah and Aunt Hannah soon grew to be her ministering angels; and if they differed from the gold-haired, pink-enamelled, straight-nosed creations of Fra Angelico, and would have figured ill,—in their shortgowns and mob-caps,—bowing before an ideal Madonna, Lowly wanted no better tendance and providing than they gave her, when in due season there appeared in the farmhouse a red and roaring baby, evidently patterned after his father, morally as well as physically; the white down on his raw pink head twisting into tight kinks, and his stubby fists set in as firm a grasp as ever Freedom's big brown paws were. Lowly was a happy little woman: she had loved children always, and here was one all her own. Two weeks were dreamed away in rest and rapture; then Freedom began to bustle and fret, and growl about the neglected dairy, and the rusty pork, and the hens that wanted care.

"Don't ye s'pose she'll git 'raound next week, Aunt Huldy? Things is gittin' dredful behind-hand!" Freedom had left the bedroom-door open on purpose. Aunt Huldah got up, and shut it with a slam, while he went on: "Them hens had oughter be set, 'n' I never git time to be a half a day prowlin' araound after 'em: they've stole their nests, I expect, the hull tribe; 'nd Hepsy don't make butter to compare along-side o' Lowly's; then there's that 'ere pork a-gittin' rusty, 'n' Aunt Hanner, she's over to Mallory's, nussin' Loviny, so's't I can't call on you; 'n' it doos seem's though two weeks was a plenty for well folks to lie in bed."

Here Aunt Huldah exploded: "Freedom Wheeler, you hain't got a mite o' compassion into ye! Lowly ain't over 'n' above powerful, anyway: she'll break clear down ef she ain't real keerful; mabbe I ain't"—

The shutting of the back-door stopped her tirade. While she hunted in a table-drawer for her thimble, Freedom had coolly walked off: he did not choose to argue the subject. But next day Lowly got up, and was dressed. There were two lines across the sad, low forehead now, but she went about her work in silence. There is a type of feminine character that can endure to the edge of death, and endure silently, and that character was eminently hers.

"Good little feller, so he was, as ever was; there, there, there! should be cuddled up good 'n' warm, so he should," Aunt Hannah purred to the small boy a month after, seeing him for the first time, as she had been taking care of Lovina Mallory through a low fever, when he was born.

"What be ye a-goin' to call him, Freedom?"

"I calkerlate he'll be baptized Shearjashub. There's allus ben a Shearjashub 'nd a Freedom amongst our folks. I've heered Grandsir Wheeler tell on't more'n forty times, how the' was them two names away back as fur as there's gravestones to tell on't down to Litchfield meetin'-house, 'nd back o' that in the old graveyard to Har'ford. I expect this here feller'll be called Shearjashub, 'nd the next one Freedom: that's the way they've allus run."

"For the land's sakes!" sputtered Aunt Huldah. "I was in hopes you hadn't got that notion inter your head. Why can't ye call the child some kind o' pootty Scripter name, like David, or Samwell, or Eber, 'nd not set him a-goin' with a kite's tail like that tied on to him?"

"I guess what's ben good 'nough for our folks time out o' mind'll be good 'nough for him," stiffly answered Freedom. And Aunt Huldah, with inward rage, accepted the situation, and went out to the barn to help Lowly set some refractory hens, where she found the poor little woman, with suspiciously red eyes, counting eggs on a corner of the hay-mow.

"Hanner's come, Lowly," said she, "so she's got baby, 'nd I come out to give ye a lift about them hens. I've ben a-dealin' with Freedom about that there child's name; but you might jest as well talk to White Rock: I will say for't he's the sottest man I ever see. I b'lieve he'd set to fight his own way out with the Lord above, if he hed to."

Lowly gave a little plaintive smile, but, after the manner of her sex, took her husband's part. "Well, you see, Aunt Huldy, it's kind o' nateral he should want to foller his folks's ways. I don't say but what I did want to call baby Eddard, for my little brother that died. I set great store by Eddy,"— here Lowly's checked apron wiped a certain mist from her patient eyes,— "and 'twould ha' been my mind to call him for Eddy; but Freedom don't feel to, and you know Scripter says wives must be subject to husbands."

"Hm!" sniffed Aunt Huldah, who was lost to the strong-minded party of her sex by being born before its creation,—"Scripter has a good deal to answer for!" with which enigmatical and shocking remark, she turned, and pounced upon the nearest hen. Poor old hen! She evidently represented a suffering and abject sex to Aunt Huldah, and exasperated her accordingly. Do I not know? Have not I, weakly and meekly protesting against their ways and works, also been hustled and bustled by the Rights Women?[3]—even as this squawking, crawking, yellow biddy was fluffed and cuffed and shaken up by Aunt Huldah, and plunged at last, in spite of nips and pecks and screaks, into the depths of a barrel, the head wedged on above her, and the unwilling matron condemned to solitary confinement, with hard labor, on thirteen eggs!

So Freedom had his way, of course; and Lowly went on, with the addition of a big naughty baby to take care of, waking before light to get her "chores" out of the way, prepare breakfast, skim cream, strain new milk and set it, scald pans, churn, work and put down butter, feed pigs and hens, bake, wash, iron, scrub, mend, make, nurse baby, fetch wood from the shed, and water from the well,—a delicate, bending, youthful figure, with hands already knotted, and shoulders bowed by hard work; her sole variety of a week-day being when one kind of pie gave place to another, or when the long winter evenings, with dim light of tallow candles, made her spinning shorter, and her sewing longer.

For Sundays were scarce a rest: breakfast was as early, milk as abundant, on that day as on any other and then there was a five-mile ride to meeting, for which ample lunch must be prepared, since they staid at noon; there was baby to dress, and her own Sunday clothes to put on, in which stiff and unaccustomed finery she sat four mortal hours, with but the brief interval of nooning, on a hard and comfortless seat, and then home again to get the real dinner of the day, to feed her pigs and hens, to get the clamorous baby quiet: this was hardly rest. And summer—that brings to overstrained nerves and exhausted muscles the healing of sun, sweet winds, fresh air, and the literal "balm of a thousand flowers"—only heralded to her the advent of six strong hungry men at haying, shearing, and reaping time, with extra meals, increased washing, and, of course, double fatigue. Yet this is the life that was once the doom of all New-

England farmers' wives; the life that sent them to early graves, to mad-houses, to suicide; the life that is so beautiful in the poet's numbers, so terrible in its stony, bloomless, oppressive reality. It would have been hard to tell if Lowly was glad or sorry, when, on a soft day in June, Aunt Hannah, this time at home, was hurriedly called from the red house to officiate as doctor and nurse both at the arrival of another baby. This time, Freedom growled and scowled by himself in the kitchen, instead of condescending to look at and approve the child; for it was a girl.

Aunt Hannah chuckled in her sleeve. Freedom had intimated quite frankly that this child was to be called after himself, nothing doubting but that another boy was at hand; and great was his silent rage at the disappointment.

"Imperdent, ain't it?" queried Aunt Huldah, who sat by the kitchen-fire stirring a mess of Indian-meal porridge, "To think it darst to be a girl when ye was so sot on its turnin' out a boy! Seems as though Providence got the upper hand on ye, Freedom, arter all!"

But Freedom never gave retort to Aunt Huldah. He had been brought up in certain superstitions, quite obsolete now, about respecting his elders; and, though the spirit was wanting sometimes, the letter of the law had observance. He could rage at Aunt Huldah privately, but before her he held his tongue. It was his wife who suffered as the sinner should for disturbing his plans in this manner. He snubbed her, he despised the baby, and forthwith bought two more cows, with the grim remark, "Ef I've got to fetch up a pack o' girls, I guess I'd better scratch around 'n' make a leetle more money."

But, if the new baby was an eyesore to Freedom, she was a delight to Lowly. All the more because her father ignored and seemed to dislike her, the affluent mother-heart flowed out upon her. She was a cooing, clinging, lovely little creature; and when, worn out with her day's work, Lowly had at last coaxed her cross, teething boy to sleep, and she sat down in the old creaky rocker to nurse and tend her baby, the purest joy that earth knows stole over her like the tranquil breath of heaven. The touch of tiny fingers on her breast; the warm shining head against her heart; the vague baby-smile and wandering eyes that neither the wistfulness of doubt, the darkness of grief, nor the fire of passion, clouded as yet; the inarticulate murmurs of satisfaction; the pressure of the little helpless form upon her lap; the silent, ardent tenderness that awoke and burned in her own heart for this precious creature,—all made for the weary woman a daily oasis of peace and beauty that perhaps saved her brain from that common insanity we call nervousness, and her body from utter exhaustion; for happiness is a medicine of God's own sending: no quack has ever pretended to dispense its potent and beneficent cordial; and the true, honest physician, he whose very profession is the nearest approach to that of the Saviour and Healer of men, knows well that one drop of the only elixir he cannot bring out-weighs all he can. Shearjashub grew up to the height of three years, and the baby toddled about, and chattered like a merry chipping-bird, when, one Fast Day morning, Lowly staid at home from meeting with a sinking heart, and Aunt Hannah was sent for again. Freedom went off to hear the usual sermon, on a pretence of taking Shearjashub out of the way; he being irrepressible except by his father, whom alone he feared. Mother and aunts the youngster manfully defied and scorned; but the very sound of his father's steps reduced him to silence. Shingles were not out of fashion then as a means of discipline; and the hot tingle of the application dwelt vividly in the boy's mind ever since he had been "tuned mightily," as his father phrased it, for disobedience and obstinacy; Aunt Huldah's comment at the first punishment being, "Hemlock all three on 'em,—man an' boy an' shingle: it's tough to tell which'll beat."

Little Love staid at home with old Hepsy, and prattled all day long in the kitchen. Lowly could not spare the sweet voice from her hearing, and she had need of all its comfort: for, when Freedom came home from Dorset Centre, a great girl-baby lay by Lowly in the bed; and if its welcome from the mother had been bitter tears, whose traces still shone on her wan face, from her father came far bitterer words,—curses in all but the wording; for Freedom was a "professor," and profanity was a sin. Mint and anise and cumin he tithed scrupulously; but mercy and judgment fled from him, and hid their shamefaced heads. Aunt Huldah and Aunt Hannah made their tansy-pudding that day, after the custom of their forefathers, and ate it with unflinching countenances; but Lowly fasted in her secret soul; and since her husband grimly remarked, "Tain't nothin' to me what ye call her: gals ain't worth namin' anyhow!" the new baby was baptized Marah, and behaved herself neither with the uproarious misconduct of Shearjashub, nor the gentle sweetness of Love, but, quite in defiance of her name, was the merriest, maddest little grig that could be, afraid of nothing and nobody, but as submissive to Lovey as a lamb could be, and full of fight when Shearjashub intruded himself on her domains. For this baby was a sturdy, rosy girl of three, before the fourth appeared. Lowly by this time had fallen into a listless carelessness toward her husband, that was simply the want of all spring in a long down-trodden heart. Lovey alone could stir her to tears or smiles. Marah tired and tormented her with her restless and overflowing vitality, though she loved her dearly; and her boy was big enough now to cling a little to "mother," and reward her for her faithful patience and care: but Lovey was the darling of her secret heart; and, being now five years old, the little maid waited on mother like a cherub on a saint, ran of errands, wound yarn, and did many a slight task in the kitchen that saved Lowly's bent and weary fingers.

It was with an impotent rage beyond speech that Freedom took the birth of another daughter,—a frail, tiny creature, trembling and weak as a new-born lamb in a snow-drift, but for that very reason rousing afresh in Lowly's breast the eternal floods of mother-love, the only love that never fails among all earthly passions, the only patience that is never weary, the sole true and abiding trust for the helpless creatures who come into life as waifs from the great misty ocean to find a shelter or a grave. Lowly was not only a mother according to the flesh,—for there are those whose maternity goes no further, and there are childless women who have the mother-liness that could suffice for a countless brood,—but she had, too, the real heart: she clung to her weakling with a fervor and assertion that disgusted Freedom, and astounded Aunt Huldah, who, like the old Scotch woman, sniffed at the idea of children in heaven: "No, no! a hantle o' weans there! an' me that could never abide bairns anywhere! I'll no believe it."

"It doos beat all, Hanner, to see her take to that skinny, miser'ble little crittur! The others was kind o' likely, all on 'em; but this is the dreadfulest weakly, peeked thing I ever see. I should think she'd be sick on't."

"I expect mothers—anyway them that's real motherly, Huldy— thinks the most of them that needs it the most. I've seen women with children quite a spell now, bein' out nussin' 'round, an' I allers notice that the sickly ones gets the most lovin' an' cuddlin'. I s'pose it's the same kind o' feelin' the Lord hez for sinners: they want him a sight more'n the righteous do."

"Why, Hanner Wheeler, what be you a-thinkin' of! Where's your Catechis'? Ain't all men by nater under the wrath an' cuss o' God 'cause they be fallen sinners? And here you be a-makin' out he likes 'em better'n good folks."

"Well, Huldy, I warn't a-thinkin' of Catechism: I was a-thinkin' about what it sez in the Bible."

Here the new baby cried; and Aunt Huldah, confounded but unconvinced, gave a loud sniff, and carried off Shearjashub and Marah to the red house, where their fights and roars and general insubordination soon restored her faith in the Catechism.

Lowly got up very slowly from little Phœbe's birth; and Freedom grumbled loud and long over the expense of keeping Hepsy a month in the kitchen. But his wife did not care now: a dumb and sudden endurance possessed her. She prayed night and morning, with a certain monomaniac persistence, that she and Lovey and the baby might die; but she did her work just as faithfully and silently as ever, and stole away at night to lie down on the little cot-bed in the back-chamber by Lovey and Marah, her hot cheek against the cool, soft face of her darling, and the little hand hid deep in her bosom, for an hour of rest and sad peace.

Freedom, meanwhile, worked all day on the farm, and carried Shearjashub, whose oppressive name had lapsed into Bub, into wood and field with him; taught him to drive the oxen, to hunt hens' nests in the barn on the highest mow, to climb trees, in short to risk his neck however he could "to make a man of him"; and the boy learned, among other manly ways, a sublime contempt for "gals," and a use of all the forcible words permitted to masculine tongues. But Shearjashub's spectre was about to tremble. Little Phœbe had lingered in the world through a year of fluttering life, when another baby was announced; but this time it was a boy!—small even to Phœbe's first size, pallid, lifeless almost, but still a boy.

"By Jinks!" exclaimed Freedom, his hard face glowing with pleasure. "I told ye so, Aunt Huldy! There's bound to be a Freedom Wheeler in this house, whether or no."

"Hm!" said Aunt Huldah. "You call to mind old Hepsy Tinker, don't ye?—she that was a-goin' to Har'ford a Tuesday, Providence permittin', an' Wednesday whether or no. Mabbe ye'll live to wish ye hadn't fit with the Lord's will the way ye hev."

"I've got a boy, anyhow," was the grim exultant answer. "And he'll be Freedom Wheeler afore night; for I'm a-goin' to fetch the parson right off."

Strenuously did Parson Pitcher object to private baptism: but he was an old man now; and Freedom threatened that he would go to Hartford and fetch the Episcopal minister, if Parson Pitcher refused, and the old doctor knew he was quite sure to keep his word: so, with a groan at the stiff-necked brother, he got out his cloak and hat, and rode home with victorious Freedom to the farmhouse. Here the punch-bowl was made ready on a stand in the parlor, and a fire kindled on the hearth, for it was a chilly April day; and from the open door into Lowly's bedroom the wailing day-old baby was brought, and given into its father's arms, a mere scrid and atom of humanity, but a boy.

The rite was over, the long prayer said, and Freedom strode into the chamber to lay his namesake beside its mother; but, as he stooped, the child quivered suddenly all over, gasped, opened its half-shut eyes glazed with a fatal film, and then closed the pallid, violet-shadowed lids forever.

The next entry in the family Bible was,—

"Freedom. Born April 11; died same day."

"Well, he hain't got nobody but the Lord to querrel with this bout!" snapped Aunt Huldah. "He's had his way, 'nd now see what come on't!"

Lowly got up again, after the fashion of her kind, without a murmur. She felt her baby's death, she mourned her loss, she was sorry for Freedom. She had loved him once dearly; and, if she had known it, Freedom loved her as much as he could any thing but himself: but it was not his way to show affection, even to his boy; as much of it as ever came to the surface was a rough caress offered now and then to Lowly,—a usage that had died out, and died with no mourning on either side. But as there is a brief sweet season often-times in our bitter climate, that comes upon the sour and angry November weather like a respite of execution, a few soft, misty, pensively sweet days, when the sun is red and warm in the heavens, the dead leaves give out their tender and melancholy odor, and the lingering birds twitter in the pine-boughs as if they remembered spring, so there came to Lowly a late and last gleam of tranquil pleasure.

Aunt Huldah brought it about, for her tongue never failed her for fear. She caught Freedom by himself one day, looking like an ill-used bull-dog, all alone in the barn, setting some new rake-teeth.

"I've hed it on my mind quite a spell, Freedom," began the valorous old woman, "to tell ye, that, ef ye expect Lowly is ever a-goin' to hev a rousin' hearty child agin, you'll hev to cosset her up some. She ain't like our folks."

"That's pretty trew, Aunt Huldy," was the bitter interruption.

"She ain't a nether millstone, thet's a fact," answered Aunt Huldah with vigor; "nor she ain't band leather, by a good sight: she's one o' the weakly, meekly sort; 'nd you can't make a whistle out o' a pig's tail, I've heerd fathers say, 'nd you no need to try: no more can ye make a stubbid, gritty cretur out o' Lowly. She's good as gold: but she's one o' them that hankers arter pleasantness, an' lovin', an' sich; they're vittles an' drink to her, I tell ye. You an' I can live on pork an' cabbage, and sass each other continooal, without turnin' a hair; but Lowly won't stan' it; 'nd, ef ye expect this next baby to git along, I tell ye it's got to be easy goin' with her. You want to keep your fight with the Lord up, I s'pose: you're sot on hevin' another Freedom Wheeler?"

"I be," was the curt response. But though Aunt Huldah turned her back upon him without further encouragement, and marched through the ranks of "garden-sass" back to the house, her apron over her head, and her nose high in air, like one who snuffeth the battle from afar, her pungent words fell not to the ground. Freedom perceived the truth of what she said, and his uneasy conscience goaded him considerably as to past opportunities; but he was an honest man, and, when he saw a thing was to be done, he did it. Next day he brought Lowly a new rocking-chair from the Centre. He modified his manners daily. He helped her lift the heavy milk-pails, he kept her wood-pile by the shed-door well heaped, and was even known to swing the great dinner-pot off the crane, if it was full and weighty.

"For the land sakes!" exclaimed Aunt Hannah, "what's a-comin' to Freedom? He does act halfway decent, Huldah."

Aunt Huldah shook her cap-ruffle up and down, and looked sagacious as an ancient owl. "That's me! I gin it to him, I tell ye, Hanner!

Lowly wants cossetin', 'nd handlin' tender-like, or we'll be havin' more dyin' babies 'round. I up an' told him so Wednesday mornin' out in the barn, 's true's I'm alive."

"I'm glad on't! I'm real glad on't!" exclaimed Aunt Hannah. "You done right, Huldy. But, massy to me! how darst ye?"

"Ho!" sniffed Aunt Huldah. "Ef you think I'm afeard o' Freedom, you're clean mistook. I've spanked him too often, 'n' I wish to goodness I'd ha' spanked him a heap more: he'd ha' ben a heap the better for't. You reklect I had the tunin' of him, Hanner? You was allus a-nussin' mother: Freedom come to us jest as she got bedrid. Land! what a besom he was! His folks never tuned him, nor never took him to do, a mite. I hed it all to do, 'nd my mind misgives me now I didn't half do it. 'Jest as the twig is bent the tree's inclined,' ye know it says in the Speller."

"But, Huldy, 'tain't so easy bending a white-oak staddle; 'specially ef it's got a six-years' growth."

"Well, I got the hang of him, anyhow; 'nd he'll hear to me most allus, whether he performs accordin', or not."

"Mabbe it's too late, though, now, Huldy."

"Law, don't ye croak, Hanner. The little cretur'l hev a pleasant spell anyhow, for a while."

And so she did. Lowly's ready heart responded to sunshine as a rain-drenched bird will, preening its feathers, shaking its weary wings, welcoming the warm gladness with faint chirps and tiny brightening eyes, and then—taking flight.

A long and peaceful winter passed away, and in early May another boy was born: alas, it was another waxen, delicate creature. The old parson was brought in haste to baptize it. The pallid mother grew more white all through the ceremony, but nobody noticed her. She took the child in her arms with a wan smile, and tried to call it by name: "Free," was all she said. Her arms closed about it with a quick shudder and stringent grasp; her lips parted wide. Lowly and her baby were both "free," for its last breath fluttered upward with its mother's; and in the family Bible there was another record:—

"Lowly Wheeler. Died May 3."

"Freedom Wheeler. Born May 3, died same day."

"Well," said Aunt Huldah, as they came back to the ghastly quiet of the shut and silent house, after laying Lowly and her boy under the ragged turf of Dorset graveyard, "I guess Freedom'll give up his wrastle with Providence now, sence the Lord's took wife, 'nd baby, 'nd all."

"I don't feel sure of that," answered Aunt Hannah, for once sarcastic.

II

AUNT HULDAH and Aunt Hannah took Love and Phœbe over to the red house to live with them; for they found a little note in Lowly's Bible requesting them to take charge of these two, and their father did not object. Phœbe was a baby still, hopelessly feeble: she could not stand alone, though she was more than two years old; and Love was devoted to her. Bub and Marah could "fend for themselves;" and the old woman, who came as usual in Lowly's frequent absences from the kitchen, had promised to stay all summer. But, before the summer was over, Phœbe faded away like a tiny snow-wreath in the sun, and made a third little grave at her mother's feet; and Lovey grieved for her so bitterly, that Aunt Hannah insisted she should stay with them still, and made her father promise she should be their little girl always; certain forebodings of their own as to the future, prompting them to secure her a peaceful home while they lived.

As for Freedom, if he mourned Lowly, it was with no soft or sentimental grief, but with a certain resentful aching in his heart, and a defiant aspect of soul toward the divine will that had overset his intentions and desires,—a feeling that deepened into savage determination; for this man was made of no yielding stuff. Obstinacy stood him in stead of patience, an active instead of a passive trait; and in less than six months after Lowly's death he was "published," according to the custom of those days; the first intimation his aunts or his children had of the impending crisis being this announcement from the pulpit by Parson Pitcher, that "Freedom Wheeler of this town, and Melinda Bassett of Hartland, intend marriage."

Aunt Huldah looked at Aunt Hannah from under her poke-bonnet with the look of an enraged hen; her cap-frill trembled with indignation: and Lovey shrank up closer to Aunt Hannah than before; for she saw two tears rise to her kind old eyes as they met Huldah's, and she loved Aunt Hannah with all her gentle little soul. As for Freedom, he sat bolt upright, and perfectly unmoved.

"Set his face as a flint!" raged Aunt Huldah as soon as she got out of church, and went to take her "noon-spell" in the graveyard, where the basket of doughnuts, cheese, pie, cake, and early apples, was usually unpacked on the stone wall on pleasant Sundays, and the aunts sitting on a tombstone, and the children on the grass, ate their lunch. To-day Lovey and Marah were left on the stone to eat their fill. Bub had gone to the spring for water, and Freedom nobody knew where; while the aunts withdrew to "talk it over."

"Yis," repeated Aunt Huldah, "set his face like a flint. I tell ye he hain't got no more feelin' than a cherub on a tombstone, Hanner! She ain't cold in her grave afore he's off to Hartland, buyin' calves. Calves! I guess likely, comin' home jest as plausible as a pass-nip: 'I sha'n't make no butter this year: so I bought a lot o' calves to raise.' Ho! heifer-calves every one on 'em, mind ye. Ef we hadn't ha' ben a pair o' fools, we should ha' mistrusted suthin'. Ef that gal's Abigail Bassett's darter, things'll fly, I tell ye." And here Aunt Huldah blew a long breath out, as if her steam was at high pressure, and could not help opening a valve for relief; and wise Aunt Hannah seized the chance to speak.

"Well, Huldy, I declare I'm beat myself; but we can't help it. I must say I looked forrard to the time when he would do it; but I didn't reely expect it jest yet. We've got Lovey anyway; and, if Melindy ain' a pootty capable woman, she'll hev her hands full with Bub and Marah."

"Thet's a fact," returned Aunt Huldah, whose inmost soul rejoiced at the prospect of Bub's contumaciousness under new rule; for he was not a small boy any more, and shingles were in vain, though he still made a certain outward show of obedience. Marah, too, was well calculated to be a thorn in the flesh of any meek step-mother, with her high spirits, untamed temper, and utter wilfulness; and Aunt Huldah, whose soul was sore,— not because of Freedom's marriage, for she recognized its necessity, but because of its indecent haste, which not only seemed an insult to gentle Lowly, whom Aunt Huldah had loved dearly, but a matter of talk to all the town where the Wheelers had been respected for many a long year,—

Aunt Huldah rejoiced in that exasperated soul of hers at a prospect of torment to the woman who stepped into Lowly's place quite unconscious of any evil design or desire on the part of her new relatives.

But it was no meek step-mother whom Freedom brought home from a very informal wedding, in his old wagon, some three weeks after. Melinda Bassett was quite capable of holding her own, even with Aunt Huldah,—a strapping, buxom, rosy-faced girl, with abundant rough dark hair, and a pair of bright, quick, dark eyes, an arm of might in the dairy, and a power of work and management that would have furnished forth at least five feeble pieces like Lowly. Freedom soon found he had inaugurated Queen Stork. Bub was set to rights as to his clothes, and "pitched into," as he sulkily expressed it, in a way that gave him a new and unwilling respect for the other sex; and Marah entered at once into an alliance, offensive and defensive, with the new "mammy;" for Melinda was pleasant and cheerful when things went right, and generally meant they should go right. She was fond of children, too, when they were "pretty behaved;" and Marah was bright enough to find out, with the rapid perception of a keen-witted child, that it was much better for her to *be* pretty behaved than otherwise.

But Freedom—it was new times to him to have his orders unheeded, and his ways derided. He had been lord and master in his house a long time; but here was a capable, plucky, courageous, and cheery creature, who made no bones of turning him out of her dominions when he interfered, or ordering her own ways without his help at all.

"Land of Goshen!" said Melinda to the wondering Aunt Hannah, "do you s'pose I'm goin' to hev a man tewin' round in my way all the time, jest cos he's my husband? I guess not. I know how to 'tend to my business, and I expect to 'tend right up to it: moreover I expect he'll tend to his'n. When I get a-holt of his plough, or fodder his team, or do his choppin', 'll be time enough for him to tell me how to work butter, 'n' scald pans. I ain't nobody's fool, I tell ye, Aunt Hanner."

"I'm glad on't, I'm dredful glad on't!" growled Aunt Huldah, when she heard of this manifesto.

"That's the talk: she'll straighten him out, I'll bet ye! Ef poor Lowly'd had that spunk she might ha' been livin' to-day. But I guess she's better off," suddenly wound up Aunt Huldah, remembering her Catechism, no doubt, as she walked off muttering, "Are at their death made perfect in holiness, and do immediately pass into glory,"—an assurance that has upheld many a tried and weary soul more conversant with the language of the Assembly of Divines than that of their Lord and Head; for in those old days this formula of the faith was ground into every infant memory, though the tender gospel words were comparatively unknown.

So the first year of the new reign passed on; and in the next February Freedom was mastered by a more stringent power than Melinda, for he fell ill of old-fashioned typhus-fever, a malign evil that lights down here and there in lonely New-England farmhouses, utterly regardless of time or place; and in a week this strong man was helpless, muttering delirious speech, struggling for life with the fire that filled his veins and consumed his flesh. Aunt Hannah came to his aid, and the scarce neighbors did what they could for him. Brother-farmers snored away the night in a chair beside his bed, and said that they had "sot up with Freedom Wheeler last night,"—ministrations worse than useless, but yet repeated as a sort of needful observance. And at the end of the first week Aunt Hannah was called away to the "up-chamber" room, where Melinda slept now, and a big boy was introduced into the Wheeler family; while Moll Thunder, an old woman skilled in "yarbs," as most of her race are,—for she was a half-breed Indian,—was sent for from Wingfield, and took command of the fever-patient, who raged and raved at his will, dosed with all manner of teas, choked with lukewarm porridge, smothered in blankets, bled twice a week, and kept as hot, as feeble, and as dirty, as the old practice of medicine required, till disease became a mere question of "the survival of the fittest." Our grandfathers and grandmothers are vaunted to this day as a healthy, hard-working race, because the weakly share of each generation was neatly eliminated according to law.

But, if Freedom was helpless and wandering, Melinda was not. A week was all she spared to the rites and rights of the occasion; and when she first appeared in the kitchen, defying and horrifying Aunt Huldah, there ensued a brief and spicy conversation between the three women concerning this new baby, who lay sucking his fist in the old wooden cradle, looking round, hard, and red as a Baldwin apple, and quite unconscious what a firebrand he was about to be.

"It's real bad, ain't it?" purred Aunt Hannah, "to think Freedom shouldn't know nothin' about the baby? He'd be jest as tickled!"

"I don' know what for," snapped Melinda. "I should think there was young uns enough round now to suit him."

"But they wasn't boys," answered Aunt Hannah. "Freedom is sot on havin' a boy to be called for him. There's allus ben a Freedom Wheeler amongst our folks, as well as a Shearjashub, and I never see him more pestered by a little thing than when them two babies died, both on 'em bein' baptized Freedom; and he's had a real controversy with Providence, Parson Pitcher sez, his mind's so sot on this business."

"Well, this little feller isn't a-goin' to be called Freedom, now, I tell ye," uttered Melinda, with a look of positiveness that chilled Aunt Hannah to the heart. "He's jest as much my baby's he is his pa's, and a good sight more, I b'lieve. Sha'n't I hev all the trouble on him? an' jest as quick as he's big enough to help, instead o' hinder, won't he be snaked off inter the lots to work? I've seen men-folks afore; and I tell ye, Aunt Hanner, you give 'em an inch, 'n' they take a harf a yard certain."

"Well, Melindy," interfered Aunt Huldah, for once in her life essaying to make peace, "Freedom's dreadful sick now: reelly he's dangerous." [This is New-England vernacular for in danger.] "What ef he should up 'n' die? Wouldn't ye feel kind o' took aback to think on't?"

"Things is right 'n' wrong jest the same ef everybody dies; everybody doos, sooner or later. I don't see what odds that makes, Aunt Huldy. I ain't a-goin' to make no fuss about it. Fust Sunday in March is sacrament day, and childern is allers presented for baptism then. I'll jest fix it right; and, ef his pa gits well, why, there 'tis, 'nd he'll hev to git used to't; and, ef he don't, it ain't no matter, he won't never know. I guess I've got folks as well as you, and names too. There's old Grandsir Bassett: he sot a sight by me, 'nd he was ninety years old 'n' up'ards when he died. Why, he fit the British out to Ticonderogy long o' Ethan Allen! He was a dredful spry man, and had a kind o' pootty name too, smart-soundin'; and I'm a-goin' to call the boy for him. Freedom! Land o' Goshen! 'tain't a half a name anyhow; sounds like Fourth o' July oh-rations, 'nd Hail Columby, 'nd fire-crackers, 'nd root-beer, 'nd Yankee Doodle thrown in! Now Grandsir Bassett's name was Tyagustus. That sounds well, I tell ye!——kinder mighty an' pompous, 's though it come out o' them columns o' long proper names to the end of the Speller."

Here Melinda got out of breath; and dismayed Aunt Huldah followed Aunt Hannah, who had stolen off to Freedom's room with a certain instinct of protecting him, as a hen who sees the circling wings of a hawk in the high blue heavens runs to brood her chicks.

Moll Thunder was smoking a clay pipe up the wide chimney; and Freedom lay on the bed with half-shut eyes, drawn and red visage, parched lips, and restless, tossing head, murmuring wild words,—here and there calls for Lowly, a tender word for Love (whom he scarce ever noticed in health), or a muttered profanity at some balky horse or stupid ox-team.

"Kinder pootty sick," grunted Moll Thunder, nodding to the visitants. "Plenty much tea-drink drown him ole debbil fever clear out 'fore long. He, he, he! Moll knows: squaw-vine, pep'mint, cohosh, fever-wort; pootty good steep." And from a pitcher of steaming herbs, rank of taste and evil of smell, she proceeded to dose her patient, a heroic remedy that might have killed or cured, but that now Aunt Hannah was no more needed up stairs, and could resume her place by Freedom. And Moll was sent home to Wingfield with a piece of pork, a bag of meal, and a jug of cider-brandy,—a professional fee she much preferred to money.

But even Aunt Hannah could not arrest the fever: it had its sixty days of fight and fire. While yet it raged in Freedom's gaunt frame with unrelenting fierceness, Melinda carried out her programme, and had her baby baptized Tyagustus Bassett. Parson Pitcher came now and then to visit the sick man; but, even when recovery had proceeded so far that the reverend divine thought fit to exhort and catechise his weak brother in reference to his religious experience, the old gentleman shook his head, and took numerous pinches of snuff at the result.

"There seems to be a root of bitterness,—a root of bitterness remaining, Huldy. His speritooal frame is cold and hard. There is a want of tenderness,—a want of tenderness."

"He didn't never have no great," dryly remarked Aunt Huldah.

"Grace has considerable of a struggle, no doubt, with the nateral man; it is so with all of us: but after such a dispensation, an amazing dispensation,—brought into the jaws of death,—Huldy, where death got hold of him, and destruction made him afraid, in the words of Scripter, I should expect, I did expect, to find him in a tender frame. But he seems to kick against the pricks,—to kick against the pricks."

"Well, Parson Pitcher, folks don't allus do jest as ye calc'late to have 'em here below; and grace doos have a pootty hard clinch on't with Freedom, I'm free to confess. He's dredful sot, dredful; and I don't mind tellin' ye, seein' we're on the subject, that he's ben kinder thwarted in suthin' whilst he was sick, an' he hain't but jest found it out, and it doos rile him peskily: he dono how on airth to put up with't."

"Indeed, indeed! Well, Huldy, the heart knoweth its own bitterness. I guess I will pray with the family now, and set my face homeward without dealing with Freedom further to-day."

"I guess I would," frankly replied Aunt Huldah. "A little hullsome lettin' alone's good for grown folks as 'tis for children; and after a spell he'll kinder simmer down: as Hanner sez, when ye can't fix a thing your way, you've got to swaller it some other way; but it doos choke ye awful sometimes."

There is no doubt that "Tyagustus" did choke Freedom, when he found that sonorous name tacked irremediably on to the great hearty boy he had hoped for so long, but never seen till it was six weeks' old, and solemnly christened after Grandsir Bassett. A crosser and a more disagreeable man than this convalescent never made a house miserable. The aunts went delicately, in bitterness of soul, after Agag's fashion; Bub fled from before the paternal countenance, and almost lived in the barn; Marah had been for two months tyrannizing over Lovey at the Red House, as happy and as saucy as a bobolink on a fence-post; while Melinda, quite undaunted by the humors of her lord and master, went about her work with her usual zeal and energy, scolding Bub, working the hired man up to his extremest capacity, scrubbing, chattering, and cheery, now and then stopping to feed and hug the great good-tempered baby, or fetching some savory mess to Freedom, whose growls and groans disturbed her no more than the scrawks and croaks of the gossiping old hens about the doorstep.

By June he was about again, and things had found their level. If this were not a substantially true story, I should like to branch off here from the beaten track, and reform my hero,—make the gnarly oak into a fluent and facile willow-tree, and create a millennial peace and harmony in the old farmhouse, just to make things pleasant for dear Aunt Hannah and gentle Lovey: but facts are stubborn things; and, if circumstances and the grace of God modify character, they do not change it. Peter and Paul were Paul and Peter still, though the end and aim of life were changed for them after conversion.

So Freedom Wheeler returned to his active life unchastened, indeed rather exasperated, by his illness. The nervous irritation and general unhinging of mind and body that follow a severe fever, added, of course, to his disgust and rebellion against the state of things about him. His heart's desire had been refused him over and over; but it grew up again like a pruned shrub, the stronger and sturdier for every close cutting; and, grinding his teeth against fate,—he dared not say against God,—he went his bitter way.

Melinda never feared him, but he was a terror to the children; and, had there been any keen observer at hand, it would have been painful to see how "father" was a dreadful word, instead of a synonyme for loving protection and wise guidance. Aunt Hannah was shocked when Marah refused to say the Lord's Prayer one night. "Me won't! Me don't want Father in heaven: fathers is awful cross. Me won't say it, aunty."

"Now, you jest clap down 'nd say, 'Now I lay me' quick as a wink!" interposed Aunt Huldah. "Hanner, don't ye let that child talk so to ye. I'd tune her, afore I would, I tell ye."

But, in the secrecy of her own apartment, Aunt Huldah explained, "You see, Hanner, I've took the measure of that young un's foot. She's pa all over,—no more like Lowly'n chalk is like cheese. Ef you'd ha' battled it out with her, she'd ha' got the better of ye, 'nd more'n likely gone home an' told the hull story; and then Freedom would nigh about ha' slartered her; 'nd I don't want the leetle cretur's sperit broke. Fact is, I feel jes' so myself. He is so all-fired ugly, seems as though I should bust sometimes. Moreover, 'nd above all, 'tain't never best to let childern git the better of ye. They don't never go back on their tracks ef they do. I put in my finger that time so's't she shouldn't querrel with you, 'nd she said t'other thing jest like a cosset lamb: she was sort o' surprised into't, ye see."

"I presume likely, I presume likely, Huldy. She's a masterful piece,

Marah is. I'm afeard she'll taste trouble afore she dies. Sech as she has to have a lot of discipline to fetch 'em into the kingdom."

"Don't seem to be no use to Freedom, 'flictions don't, Hanner. Sometimes, I declare for't, I have my doubts ef he ever got religion, anyhow."

"Why, Huldy Wheeler!" Aunt Hannah's eyes glowed with mild wrath,—"'nd he's ben a professor nigh on to thirty year. How can ye talk so? I'm clean overcome."

"Well, I can't help it. There's some things stand to reason, ef they be speritooal things; 'nd one on 'em is, that, ef a man's born again, he's a new cretur. You're paowerful on Bible-texts; so I won't sling no Catechism at ye this time: but there's suthin', somewhere 'long in some o' the 'Pistles, about 'love, joy, peace, gentleness, goodness, meekness,' 'nd so on, for quite a spell; and, if that cap fits Freedom, why, I'm free to say I don't see it."

"Well, Huldy, we must make allowances: ye see, he's dreadful disapp'inted."

"That's so. You'd better believe *he* don't say the Lord's Prayer no more'n Marah; or, ef he doos, it goes, 'My will be done:' he hain't learnt how to spell it t'other way." Aunt Hannah sighed. She was getting old now; and Freedom was as dear to her as an only child, wayward and wilful though it be, to a loving mother; but she rested her heart on its lifelong comfort,—a merciful presence that was her daily strength,—and hoped for the best, for some future time, even if she did not live to see it, when this stubborn heart of her boy's should become flesh, and his soul accept a divine Master, with strong and submissive faith.

Poor Aunt Hannah! She had shed countless tears, and uttered countless prayers, to this end, but as yet in vain. Next year only brought fresh exasperation to Freedom in the birth of a daughter, as cross, noisy, and disagreeable as she was unwelcome. He flung out of the house, and went to ploughing the ten-acre lot, though the frost was only out of the surface: he broke his share, goaded his oxen till even those patient beasts rebelled, and at last left the plough in the furrow, and took a last year's colt out to train. Melinda escaped a great deal through that poor colt; for what he dared not pour on her offending head in the way of reviling, he safely hurled at the wild creature he found so restive in harness; and many a kick and blow taught the brute how superior a being man is—particularly when he is out of temper.

"Keep that brat out o' my sight, Aunt Hanner," was his first greeting to the child. "Don't fetch it 'round here: it's nothin' but a noosance."

Aunt Hannah retreated in dismay; but she dared not tell Melinda, whose passion for fine-sounding names was mightily gratified at the opportunity to select a girl's appellation. Before she issued from her sick-room made up her mind to call this child Chimera Una Vilda.

Dear reader, give me no credit for imagination here. These are actual names, registered on church records and tombstones, with sundry others of the like sort, such as Secretia, Luelle, Lorilla Allaroila, Lue, Plumy, Antha, Loruhama, Lophelia, Bethursda, and a host more. But it mattered little to Freedom: the child might have any name, or no name, as far as he cared. It was a naughty baby, and rent the air with cries of temper in a manner that was truly hereditary.

"I never see such a piece in all my days!" sighed Aunt Hannah, whose belief in total depravity became an active principle under this dispensation. "I declare for't, Huldy, you can hear her scream way over here."

"Well, I b'lieve you, Hanner: the winders is wide open, and we ain't but jest acrost the road. I guess you could hear her a good mile. An' she keeps it up the hull endurin' time. Makes me think o' them cherubims the Rev'lations tells about, that continooally do cry: only she ain't cryin' for praise."

"I expect she'd cry for suthin' besides crossness ef she knew how her pa feels about her. It's awful, Huldy, it is awful, to see him look at the child once in a while."

"She knows it in her bones, I tell ye. Talk about 'riginal sin! I guess she won't want no sin more 'riginal than what's come down pootty straight from him. She's jest another of 'em, now I tell ye."

But Melinda was equal to the situation, whether she picked up the last maple-twig Marah brought in from driving the cows, or pulled the stiff wooden busk from her maternal bosom, or "ketched off her shoe," or even descended upon that chubby form with her own hard hand, and pungently "reversed the magnetic currents," as they say in Boston. Those currents were reversed so often, it might have been matter of doubt which way they originally ran after a year or two. But the old Adam was strong; and when

Chimera—no chimera to them, but a dreadful reality—was sent over to stay a while at the red house, the aunts were at their wits' ends, and Lovey both tired and tormented.

This time, for Chimera's visit to the aunts was occasioned by the immediate prospect of another baby, Aunt Hannah was not able to take care of Melindy. The dear old woman was getting old: a "shockanum palsy," as Aunt Huldah called a slight paralytic stroke, had given her warning; her head shook perpetually, and her hands trembled. She could still do a little work about the house; but her whole failing body was weary with the perpetual motion, and she knew life was near its end for her. So they sent to Dorset Centre for the village nurse,—a fat, good-natured creature; and one morning, early, a boy—a rosy, sturdy, big boy—appeared on the stage.

Now Freedom exulted: he strode over to the red house to tell the news. "Fact, Aunt Hannah! I've got him now,—a real stunner too. You won't see no tricks played now, I tell ye! By jingo! I'm goin' off for Parson Pitcher quicker'n lightnin'. I'll bet ye Melindy won't git ahead o' me this time. That leetle feller'll be Freedom Wheeler in two hours' time, sure's ye live."

"Providence permitting," put in Aunt Hannah softly, as if to avert the omen of this loud and presumptuous rejoicing. But, soft as the prayer was, Freedom heard it, and, as he opened the door, turned on his heel, and answered, "Whether or no, this time."

Aunt Hannah lay back in her chair, utterly shocked. This was rank blasphemy in her ears: she did not remember the illustrative story Aunt Huldah told Freedom, on a time long past, about a certain old woman's intention to go to Hartford, or she might, perhaps, have been less horrified. Still it was bad enough; for, if the words were lightly spoken, the spirit within the man accorded fully with his tone, and never was keener triumph rampant in any conqueror's heart than in this rough, self-willed farmer's as he drove his horse, full tilt, down the long hills, and up the sharp ascents, that lay between him and the parsonage. But Parson Pitcher had been called up higher than Freedom Wheeler's. That very morning he had fallen asleep in his bed, weak and wasted with a long influenza; and, being almost ninety years old, the sleep of weakness had slipped quietly into the deeper calm of death.

He had for a year past been obliged to have a colleague: so Freedom hunted the young man up at his boarding-place, and took him instead,—a little aggrieved, indeed, for long custom made Parson Pitcher seem the only valid authority for religious observances of this kind; and, years after he ceased to preach, the little children were always brought to him for baptism.

"But I s'pose one on 'em's reelly as good as t'other for this puppus," hilariously remarked Freedom to the old lady who lodged the colleague, receiving a grim stare of disapproval for his answer, as he deserved. However, there was one advantage in having Mr. Brooks instead of the parson. Freedom was but slightly acquainted with the new-comer: so he poured out all his troubles, his losses, and his present rejoicing, all the way home, with a frankness and fluency strange enough; for New-Englanders as a race are reticent both of their affairs and their feelings, and Freedom Wheeler was more so by nature than by race. This exultation seemed to have fused his whole character for the time into glowing, outpouring fervor: a deep and ardent excitement fired his eye, and loosed his tongue; and Mr. Brooks, who had a tinge of the metaphysical and inquisitive about him, was mightily interested in the man; and being, as he phrased it, a "student of character,"—which is, being interpreted, an impertinent soul who makes puppets of his fellows to see how their wires work, and discover the thoughts of their hearts for his own theories and speculations,—he gently drew out this intoxicated man, "drunken, but not with wine," as he was, with judicious suggestions and inquiries, till he knew him to the core; a knowledge of use to neither party, and to the young clergyman only another apple off the tree from which Eve plucked sin and misery, and a sour one at that.

Once more the old china punch-bowl that had been a relic in the Wheeler family beyond their record, and would have crazed a china-fancier with the lust of the eye, was filled from the spring, and set on the claw-footed round table in the parlor, the door left open into Melinda's room so she could see all the ceremony, the aunts and nurse assembled in solemn array (all the children being sent over to Lovey's care at the red house); and with due propriety the new baby, squirming and kicking with great vigor in his father's arms, was baptized Freedom Wheeler.

Why is it that "the curse of a granted prayer" comes sometimes immediately? Why do we pant and thirst, and find the draught poisonous? or, after long exile, come home, only to find home gone? Alas! these are the conditions of humanity, the questions we all ask, the thwarting and despair we all endure, and also the mystery and incompleteness which tell us in hourly admonition that this life is a fragment and a beginning, and that its ends are not peace and rapture, but discipline and education. Freedom Wheeler was no apt pupil, but his sharpest lesson came to-day.

Full of exultation over fate, Melinda, and the aunts, chuckling to himself with savage satisfaction at the conscious feeling that it was no use for anybody—even the indefinite influence he dared not call God—to try to get the better of him, he strode across the room to give his boy back to Melinda, stumbled over a little stool that intruded from below the sofa, fell full-length on the floor, with the child under him; and when he rose to his feet, dazed with the jar of the fall, it was but just in time to see those baby eyelids quiver once, and close forever. The child was dead.

Melinda rose up in the bed with a dreadful face: shriek on shriek burst from her lips. The women crowded about Freedom, and took the limp little body from his arms. He leaned against the door-way like a man in a dream. The torrents of reproach and agony that burst from Melinda's lips seemed not to enter his ears: "Now, you've done it! you've killed him! you have! you have!" But why repeat the wild and bitter words of a mother bereft of her child in the first hours of its fresh, strong life? Melinda was not a cruel or ungenerous woman naturally; but now she was weak and nervous, and the shock was too much for her brain.

In this sudden stress Mr. Brooks forgot his metaphysics, and fell back on the old formulas, which, after all, do seem to wear better than metaphysics in any real woe or want. He drew near to Freedom, and put his hand on the wretched man's shoulder. "My brother," said he gently, "this evil is from the hand of the Lord: bear it like a Christian."

"He ain't no Christian!" shouted Melinda, with accents of concentrated bitterness. "Christians ain't that sort, growlin' and scoldin', and fightin' with the Lord that made him, cos he couldn't hev his own way, and uplifted sky-high when he got it: 'nd now look to where 'tis! The hypocrite's hope is cut off, cut off! Oh, my baby, my baby, my baby!" Here she fell into piteous wailing and fainting; and Mr. Brooks led the passive, stricken man away; while Aunt Huldah despatched Reuben Stark for the doctor, and Aunt Hannah and the nurse tried to calm and restore Melinda.

But it was idle to try to draw Freedom from his silent gloom. He would neither speak nor hear, apparently; and Mr. Brooks, seeing Reuben hitching the horse to the wagon, took his hat to leave. Aunt Huldah followed him to the door for politeness.

"Send for me when you are ready for the funeral, Miss Huldah," said he in taking leave. "I feel deeply for you all, especially for brother Wheeler. The Lord seems to have a controversy with him indeed."

"That's so," curtly replied Aunt Huldah; "an' I don't see but what he's kep' up his end on't pootty well. But I guess he's got to let go. This makes three on 'em; and its an old sayin', 'three times an' out.'"

A suddenly subdued smile curled the corners of Mr. Brooks's mouth for a second. Poor man, he had a keen sense of the ludicrous, and was minister in a country parish.

"Good-day," nodded Aunt Huldah, quite unaware that she had said any thing peculiar; and then she returned to Freedom. But he had gone out of the kitchen; nor did any one know where he was, till the horn called to supper, when he came in, swallowed a cup of tea, and went speechless to bed, not even asking about Melinda, whom the doctor found in the first stage of fever, and pronounced "dangerous."

But Melinda was strong, and could bear a great deal yet. She was comparatively a young woman; and, after a month's severe illness, she began to improve daily, and in another month was like her old self again,— perhaps a trifle less cheery, but still busy, vivacious, and unsparing of herself or others. But Freedom was a changed man. The scornful and bitter words Melinda had uttered in her frantic passion burnt deep into his soul, though he gave no sign even of hearing them.

Kingsley speaks of "the still, deep-hearted Northern, whose pride breaks slowly and silently, but breaks once for all; who tells to God what he never will tell to man, and, having told it, is a new creature from that day forth forever;" and something after this fashion was Freedom Wheeler shaped. He had been brought up in the strictest Calvinism, had his "experience" in due form, and then united with the church. But Parson Pitcher never preached to anybody but unconverted sinners: hell-fire drove him on to save from the consequences of sin. Its conditions, people who were once converted must look out for themselves. And Freedom's strong will, sullen temper, and undisciplined character, grew up like the thorns in the parable, and choked the struggling blades of grain that never reached an ear. Melinda's accusations were the first sermon that ever awoke his consciousness. He had always prided himself on his honesty, and here he saw that he had been an utter hypocrite.

With all his faults, he had a simple faith in the truths of the Bible, and a conscientious respect for ordinances; and now there fell upon him a deep conviction of heinous sin, a gloom, a despair, that amounted almost to insanity. But he asked no counsel, he implored no divine aid: with the peculiar sophistry of religious melancholy, he considered that his prayers would be an abomination to the Lord. So he kept silence, poring more and more over his Bible, appropriating its dreadful texts all to himself, and turning his eyes away from every gracious and tender promise, as one unworthy to read them.

He worked more faithfully than ever,—worked from day's first dawn into the edge of darkness, as if the suffering of a worn-out body had a certain counter-irritation for the tortured mind. There are many rods of stone wall on that old farm to-day, laid up of such great stones, made so wide and strong and close, that the passer-by looks at it with wonder, little knowing that the dreadful struggles of a wandering and thwarted soul mark the layers of massive granite, and record the exhaustion of flesh mastered by strong and strenuous spirit.

When Melinda was herself again, it was yet some time before she noticed the change in Freedom. There was a certain simple selfishness about her that made her own grief hide every other, and impelled her to try with all her might to forget her trouble, to get rid of the sharp memory that irked her soul like a rankling thorn. She hid all her baby-clothes away in the garret; she sent the cradle out to the shed-loft, and never opened her lips about that lost boy, whose name Aunt Huldah had recorded in the same record with the two who had preceded him, and whose little body lay under the mulleins and golden-rods, beside the others, at Lowly's feet.

But, as time wore on, Melinda began to see that some change had passed over her husband. She had quite forgotten her own mad words, spoken in the first delirium of her anguish, and followed by the severe fever that had almost swept away life as well as memory. No remorse, therefore, softened her heart; but it was not needed. Though Melinda was an incisive, stirring, resolute woman, with her warm temper she had also a warm heart: she could not live in the house with a dog or a cat without feeling a certain kindly affection for the creature. Her step-children never suffered at her hands, but shared in all the care she gave her own, and loved her as well as shy, careless children of a healthy sort love anybody. She loved her husband truly. Her quick, stormy words meant no more than the scolding of a wren: in her heart she held Freedom dear and honored, only he did not know it.

But she began now, in her anxiety about his sad and gloomy ways, to soften her manner toward him daily. She remembered the things he liked to eat, and prepared them for the table; she made him a set of new shirts, and set the stitches in them with scrupulous neatness; she kept the house in trim and pleasant order, and sat up at night to mend his working-clothes, so that they were always whole,—homely services and demon-strations, no doubt, but having as much fitness to place and person as the scenic passion of a novel in high life, or a moral drama where the repentant wife throws herself into a stern husband's arms, and, with flying tresses and flowing tears, vows never to vex or misunderstand his noble soul again.

Freedom's conscious controversy with his Maker still went on within him, and raged between doubt and despair; but he was human, and the gentle ray of affection that stole from Melinda's "little candle" did its work in his "naughty world." He felt a certain comfort pervading home when he came in at night sad and weary: the children's faces were clean, the hearth washed, the fire bright; warmth and peace brooded over the old kitchen, crackled softly from the back-log, purred in the cat, sang from the kettle-nose; Melinda's shining hair was smooth, her look quiet and wistful; the table was neatly spread,—little things, surely; but life is made up of them, and hope and happiness and success.

The dark cloud in this man's soul began to lift imperceptibly; and he was called out of himself presently to stand by Aunt Hannah's bed and see her die. A second shock of paralysis suddenly prostrated her, and she was laid on the pillows speechless and senseless. Twenty-four hours of anxiety and tears passed, and then she seemed to revive: she stirred her hand, her face relaxed, her eyes opened; but the exhaustion was great, and she was unable to speak. Conscious and patient, she endured through a few days more, and then the final message came. Another paralysis, a longer silence, and those grouped about her bed in the old red house, thinking every moment to see the shadow of death fall over those beloved features, beheld with surprise the soft brown eyes open, and fix upon Freedom such a look of longing, tender, piteous affection as might have broken the heart of a stone; a long, long gaze, a very passion of love, pity, and yearning, and then those eyes turned heavenward, grew glorious with light and peace, and closed slowly,—closed forever.

Freedom went out and wept bitterly: he had denied his Lord too; and it was a look that smote him to the heart, as that divine glance did Peter. But no man knew or saw it. Hidden in the barn, a dim and fragrant oratory that has seen more than one struggle of soul in the past and unknown records of New England, Freedom "gave up," and gave up finally.

He was no longer a young man, and he was not the stuff that saints are made of; but he had a stern honesty, an inward uprightness, that held him to his new resolve like hooks of steel. If his temper softened a little, his obstinacy yielded here and there, his manner gave out now and then some scanty spark of affection and consideration, these were the outward signs of a mighty change within; for an old and weather-beaten tree does not bloom in its spring resurrection with the flowers and promise of a young and vigorous growth: it is much if the gnarled boughs put out their scanty share of verdure, if there is a blossom on a few branches, and shelter enough for a small bird's nest from sun or rain. Lovey, grown by this time a tall and helpful girl, with her mother's delicate sweetness in face and figure, was first perhaps to feel this vital change in her father. Aunt Hannah's death was a woeful loss to her tender, clinging nature; and she turned to him with the instinct of a child, and found a shy and silent sympathy from him that was strangely dear and sweet, and bound them together as never before. Aunt Huldah, too, noticed it. "Dear me!" said she to herself, as she sat alone by the fire, knitting red stockings for Chimera, who had begun to mend her ways a little under the steady birch-and-shingle discipline,— "dear me, I'm real afraid Freedom ain't long for this world. He is kinder mellerin', like a stone-apple in June: it's onnateral. I expect he's struck with death, Hanner, don't you? Oh, my land, what a old fool I be! Hanner's gone, 'nd here I be a-talkin' to her jest as though"—Aunt Huldah wiped her dimmed eyes with a red silk handkerchief, and rubbed her misty glasses before she went on, still leaving the sentence unfinished. "Mabbe it's a triumph o' grace. I s'pose grace can get the better o' Freedom: seems kinder doubtful, I must confess; but I don't see nothin' else that could fetch him, and he is a-growin' soft, sure as ye live."

But Melinda, less sensitive or perceptive, perceived only that her efforts had "kinder sorter slicked him down," as she said.

It was reserved for the birth of another child to demonstrate how Freedom had laid down his arms, and gone over to the king at last. Yes, two years after Aunt Hannah's death, another fine and hearty boy entered the family, but not this time with such acclaim and welcome as the last. Melinda, weak and happy, grew gentler than ever before, between present bliss and future fear: and Freedom, hiding his face in his hard brown hands, thanked God with shame and trembling for this undeserved mercy; and even while he shuddered, naturally enough, at the possibilities the past recalled, he could say humbly and fervently, "Thy will be done."

Nobody spoke of sending for the minister now, nor was even a name for baby suggested till two months after, when Melinda said to Freedom one night, when the children were all in bed, and they sat alone by the fire, waiting for the last brand to fall in two before it could be raked up, "Next Sunday but one is sacrament Sunday, Freedom. It's good weather now: hadn't the little feller better be presented for baptism?"

"I guess so," answered he.

"What do ye calkerlate to call him?" asked Melinda shyly, after a pause.

"Thet's for you to say, Melinda: I wish ye to do jest as ye're a mind to," he said gently, with a stifled sigh.

"That's easy settled then," she replied, a pretty smile about her red lips, and laying her hand on her husband's knee: "I don't want to call him nothin' more nor less than Freedom."

He put his hand on hers for a moment, looked the other way, and then got up and went out silently.

So one bright June day baby was taken to the meeting-house, and received his name, and was duly recorded in the family Bible, but with no ominous monosyllable added to his birth-date; and Aunt Huldah, as she went out of church, said to Mr. Brooks, by no means inaudibly, "I guess Freedom's gin up his controversy finally. He did keep up his end on't quite a spell; but he's gin up for good now, I expect."

"Yes," answered the young parson, with a smile of mingled feeling and reverence. "The Lord was in the still small voice."

MRS. FLINT'S MARRIED EXPERIENCE

"WELL, Mindwell, I have counselled a good deal about it. I was happy as the day is long with your father. I don't say but what I cleaved to this world consider'ble more than was good for my growth in grace. He was about the best. But it pleased the Lord to remove him, and it was quite a spell before I could reely submit: the nateral man rebelled, now I tell you! You can't never tell what it is to lose a companion till you exper'ence it."

A faint color, vanishing as rapidly as it came, almost as if ashamed that it bore witness to the emotion within her, rose to Mindwell Pratt's face as her mother spoke. She was a typical New-England woman,—pale, serious, with delicate features, grave dark eyes, a tall, slight, undeveloped figure, graceful from mere unconsciousness, awkward and angular otherwise. You could compare her to nothing but some delicate and slender tree of the forest that waves its fragile but hardy branches fresh and green in spring-time, and abides undaunted the worst blast of winter, rooted in the fissures of the rock, fed by the bitterest showers, the melting snows, the furious hail that bends but never breaks it; perfect in its place, fitted utterly to its surroundings. Her mother, the Widow Gold, was externally like her; but deep in Mindwell's heart lay a strength of character, and acuteness of judgment, the elder woman did not possess, and a reticence that forbade her to express sympathy, even with her mother's sorrow, further than by that reluctant blush; for sympathy implied an expression of her love for her husband,—a hidden treasure she could not profane by speech, which found its only demonstration in deeds, and was the chief spring of her active and devoted life as wife and mother.

Mrs. Gold had been a happy woman, as she said, while her husband lived, and had not yet ceased to reproach herself for mourning him so bitterly. The religion of New England at that time was of a stern type: it demanded a spiritual asceticism of its followers, and virtually forbade them to enjoy the blessings of this life by keeping them in horrid and continual dread of "the pains of hell forever," as their Catechism expresses it. It was their purpose to work out their own salvation with fear and trembling under the curse of the law. The gospel was a profound and awful mystery, to be longed for afar off, no more daily bread than the show-bread of the Temple.

They lived and worked, and suffered and died, with few exceptions, in an awful sense of flying time, brief probation, an angry God, a certain hell, but a very uncertain heaven. No wonder that they were austere and hard: the wonder was that even natural temperament and mental organization should ever resist this outside pressure, and give play to humor, or fancy, or passion of any sort. Yet in this faithless faith lay elements of wonderful strength. The compelling force of duty made men nobly honest, rigidly upright, just, as far as their narrow views allowed, and true to the outward relations of this life, however they violated their inner principle and meaning. Speculation, defalcation, divorce, were crimes they called by other names than these, and abhorred. Can we say as much for ourselves? However we may sneer at Puritanism, it had its strong virtues; and its outgrowth was honesty, decency, and respect for law. A share of such virtues would be worth much to us now.

Mrs. Gold was "a professor," and it behooved her to submit to the will of God when her husband died. He had been a strong, generous, warm-hearted man; and, though undemonstrative as his race, his wife had been loved and cherished as the very blossom of his life. She was a sweet, fair girl when Ethan Gold married her, clinging and dependent by nature, though education had made her a hard worker; but her fragile beauty and soft temper had attracted the strength and fervor of the man, and their short life together had been exceptionally happy. Then fever struck him down in his full prime; and their only child, a girl of six, could but just remember all her life that she once had a father whose very memory was sacred. Fifteen years of mourning, at first deeply, then steadily, at last habitually, and rather as a form than a feeling, passed away.

Ethan had left his wife with "means;" so that poverty did not vex her. And now Mindwell was a grown woman, and married to Samuel Pratt, a well-to-do young farmer of Colebrook, a hearty, jovial young fellow, whose fun and animal spirits would bubble over in spite of reproving eyes and tongues, and who came into Mindwell's restrained and reserved life like a burst of sunshine. Are the wild blossoms grateful to the sun that draws them with powerful attraction from the cold sod,

> "Where they together,
> All the cold weather,
> Keep house alone"?

Perhaps their odor and color are for him who brings them to light and delight of life. Mindwell's great fear was that she made an idol of her husband, yet he certainly had not an idea that she did.

If the good soul had stopped to analyze the relation between them, his consciousness would have been found, when formulated, to be, that his wife bore with him as saints do with rather amusing sinners; while he worshipped her as even the most humorous of sinners do sometimes secretly worship saints. But what the wife did not acknowledge, or the husband perceive, became in a few years painfully perceptible to the mother's feminine and maternal instinct. Mindwell treated her with all possible respect and kindness, but she was no longer her first object. There is a strange hunger in the average female heart to be the one and only love of some other heart, which lies at the root of fearful tragedies and long agonies of unspoken pain,—a God-given instinct, no doubt, to make the monopoly of marriage dear and desirable, but, like all other instincts, fatal if it be not fulfilled or followed. Utterly wanting in men, who grasp the pluralities of passion as well as of office, this instinct niches itself deepest in the gentlest of women, and was the ruling yet unrecognized motive in the Widow Gold's character. If Mindwell had not had children, perhaps her mother would have been more necessary to her, and more dear; but two babies had followed on her marriage within three years, and her mother-love was a true passion. This the grandmother perceived with a tender jealousy fast growing acute. She loved the little girls, as grandmothers do, with unreasoning and lavish fondness. If there had been a maiden aunt in the family,—that unconsidered maid-of-all-work, whose love is felt to be intrusive, while yet the demands on it are insatiable,—the Widow Gold would have had at least one sympathetic breast to appeal to; but as it was she became more and more uneasy and unhappy, and began to make herself wretched with all the commonplaces she could think of,—about her "room being better than her company," "love runs down, not up," and the like,—till she was really pining, when just at this moment an admirer came upon the scene, and made known the reason of his appearance in a business-like way.

"Deacon Flint's in the keepin'-room, mother, wishful to see you," said Mindwell one day, about five years after her marriage. Deacon Flint was an old acquaintance, known to Mrs. Gold ever since she was a girl in Bassett. When she married, and moved to Denslow, the acquaintance had been partly dropped, though only nine miles lay between them; but she had then her family cares, and Ethan Gold and Amasa Flint were as unlikely to be friends as a Newfoundland dog and a weasel. Since she had come to Colebrook to live with her daughter, she was a little farther still from her Bassett friends, and therefore it was a long time since she had seen the deacon. Meanwhile he had lost his wife, a silent and sickly woman, who crept about and worried through her daily duties for years, spent and fainting when the last supper-dish was washed, and aching at early dawn when she had to get up to milk. She did not complain: her duty lay there, in her home, and she did it as long as she could—then she died. This is a common record among our barren hills, which count by thousands their unknown and unsung martyrs. It was a year after her death when Deacon Flint made his first visit to Widow Gold. He was tired of paying Aunt Polly Morse seventy-five cents a week to do housework, though she spun and wove, and made and mended, as faithfully as his wife had done, confiding only to one trusty ear her opinion of her employer.

"He's a professor, ye know, Isr'el, and I make no doubt but what he's a good man; but he is dreadful near. Seems as if he reelly begrutched me my vittles sometimes; and there ain't a grain o' salt in that house spilt without his findin' of it out. Now, I don't calc'late *to* spill no salt, nor nothin' else, to waste it; but, land's sakes! I can't see like a fly, so's to scare up every mite of sugar that's left onto the edges of the paper he fetches it hum in. I wish to gracious he'd get somebody else. I'd ruther do chores for Mirandy Huff than for the deacon."

Old Israel's wrinkled face, puckered mouth, and deep-set eyes, twitched with a furtive laugh. He was the village fool, yet shrewder than any man who stopped to jest with him, and a fool only in the satiric sense of jester; for though he had nothing of his own but a tiny brown house and pig-pen, and made his living, such as it was, by doing odd jobs, and peddling yeast from the distilleries at Simsbury, he was the most independent man in Bassett, being regardless of public opinion, and not at all afraid of Parson Roberts.

"Well, Aunt Polly," he answered, "you stay by a spell: the deacon won't want ye too long. He's got a sharp eye, now I tell ye, and he's forehanded as fury. Fust you know, Miss Flint'll *come* home, and you'll *go* home."

"Miss Flint!" screamed Aunt Polly. "Why, Isr'el Tucker, you give me such a turn! Poor cretur, she's safe under the mulleins this year back. I guess I shall go when she comes, but 'twon't be till the day o' judgment."

"Then the day o' judgment's near by, Aunt Polly; and I reckon it is for one poor cretur. But you don't somehow seem to take it in. I tell ye the deacon's gone a-courtin'."

"Courtin'! *Isr'el!* you be a-foolin' of me now, certain sure."

"Not a mite on't. I see him a-'ilin' up his old harness yesterday, and a-rubbin' down the mare, and I mistrusted he was up to suthin. And Squire Battle he met him a'most to Colebrook this mornin': I heerd him say so. I put this 'n' that together, and drawed my own influences; and I figgered out that he's gone to Colebrook to see if Widder Gold won't hev him. A wife's a lot cheaper than hired help, and this one's got means."

"For mercy's sakes! You don't suppose Sarepty Gold would look at him, do ye?"

"I never see the woman yet that wouldn't look at a man when he axed her to," was the dry answer. But Aunt Polly was too stunned with her new ideas to retort. She went on, as if the sneer at her sex had not reached her ear,—

"Why, she ha'n't no need to marry him: she's got a good home to Sam Pratt's. And there's that farm here that Hi Smith runs on shares, and money in Har'ford bank, they do say. She won't have him: don't ye tell me so."

"Women are mortal queer," replied old Israel.

"If they wa'n't, there wouldn't no men get married," snapped Aunt Polly, who was a contented old maid, and never suspected she was "queer" herself.

"That's so, Aunt Polly. Mabbe it's what Parson Roberts calls a dispensation, and I guess it is. I say for't, a woman must be extry queer to marry Amasy Flint, ef she's even got a chance at Bassett poor-house."

Yet Israel was right in his prophecy. At that very moment Deacon Flint was sitting bolt-upright in a high-backed chair in Sam Pratt's keeping-room, discoursing with the Widow Gold.

Two people more opposite in aspect could hardly be found. Mrs. Gold was not yet fifty, and retained much of her soft loveliness. Her cheek was still round and fair, her pale brown hair but slightly lined with gray, and the mild light of her eyes shone tenderly yet; though her figure was a little bent, and her hands knotted with work.

She looked fair and young in comparison with the grizzled, stern, hard-favored man before her. A far-off Scotch ancestry had bequeathed to him the high cheek-bones and deep-set eyes that gave him so severe an aspect; and to these an aquiline nose, a cruel, pinched mouth, a low forehead, and a sallow, wrinkled skin, added no charms. But the charm of old association brought him a welcome here. Bassett was the home of Mrs. Gold's childhood, and she had a great many questions to ask. Her face gathered color and light as she recalled old affections and sympathies; and the deacon took a certain satisfaction in looking at her. But this was a mere ripple above his serious intention. He meant business, and could not waste time: so, as soon as there came a little lull in Mrs. Gold's fluent reminiscences, he curtly began,—

"I came over to-day on an arrand, Miss Gold,—I may say quite a ser'ous arrand. I lost my companion, I suppose ye know, a year ago come September the 10th. She was a good woman, Miss Flint was, savin' and reasonable as ever was."

"I always heard her well spoke of," modestly rejoined the widow.

"Yes, her children praise her in the gates,—or they would hev, if she'd had any. I feel her loss. And Scripter says, 'It is not good for man to be alone.' Scripter is right. You are a woman that's seen affliction too, Miss Gold: you've passed under the rod. Well, folks must be resigned: professors like you and me have got to set example. We can't fault the Lord when he takes our companions away, and say, 'Why do ye so?' as though 'twas a man done it. We've got this treasure in earthen vessels. Well, to come to the p'int, I come over to-day to see ef you wa'n't willin' to consider the subject of uniting yourself to me in the bonds of marriage."

"Oh!" said the astonished widow.

"I don't want to hurry ye none," he went on: "take time on't. I should like to get my answer right off; but I can make allowance for bein' onexpected. I'll come agin next week—say this day week. I hope you'll make it a subject of prayer, and I expect you'll get light on your duty by that time. I've got a good house and a good farm, and I'll do well by ye. And, moreover and besides, you know Mr. Pratt's folks are pressed some for room, I expect. I guess they won't stand in the way of your goin' to Bassett. Good-day, good-day."

And the widow received a calm up-and-down handshake, with which decorous caress the deacon—for we cannot call him the lover—departed, leaving Mrs. Gold in a state of pleased amazement, partly because she was a woman and a widow, partly because it was Deacon Flint who had asked her to marry him; for the deacon was a pillar in Bassett church, owned a large farm and a goodly square house, and was a power in the State, having twice been sent to the General Assembly. She could not but be gratified by the preference, and as she pondered on the matter it grew more feasible. Her girl was hers no longer, but a wife and mother herself; and she who had been all in all to Mindwell was now little more than "grandma" in the house,—a sort of suffered and necessary burden on Samuel's hands. But here a home of her own was offered her, a place of dignity among other women,—a place where she could ask her children to come to her, and give rather than receive.

There is nothing so attractive to a woman who is no longer young as the idea of a home. The shadow of age and its infirmities affrights her; loneliness is a terror in the future; and the prospect of drifting about here and there, a dependent, poor, proud, unwelcome, when flesh and heart fail, and the ability to labor is gone, makes any permanent shelter a blessed prospect, and draws many a woman into a far more dreadful fate than the work-house mercies or the colder charity of relatives.

This terror was strong in Mrs. Gold's feeble heart. She was one of the thousands of women who cannot trust what they do not see, and she misjudged her daughter cruelly. Mindwell felt that to-day, as her mother avowed to her Deacon Flint's offer and her own perplexities. When Mrs. Gold asserted that her daughter could never understand what it was to lose a husband, Mindwell felt a sure but unspoken conviction that the terror of such a bereavement, which confronted her whenever her heart leaped up to meet Samuel, was experience enough for her to interpret thereby the longings of a real bereavement; but she only colored faintly, and answered,—

"Well, mother, I don't see my way clear to offer you any advice. You must use your own judgment. You know Samuel and me think every thing of having you here; and the children just begin to know grandma by heart. But I don't want to be self-seeking: if it's for your best good, why, we sha'n't neither of us say a word. I don't skerce know how to speak about it, it's so strange like and sudden. I can't say no more than this: if you're going to be happier and better off with Deacon Flint than with your own folks, we haven't no right to hinder you, and we won't."

Mindwell turned away with trembling lips, silent, because strong emotion choked her. If she had fallen on her mother's neck and wept, and begged her to stay, with repeated kisses and warm embrace, Mrs. Gold never would have become Mrs. Flint; but she could not appreciate Mindwell's feeling. She took her conscientious self-control and candor for indifference, and her elderly lover loomed through this mist in grander proportions than ever. She resolved then and there that it was her duty to accept him.

Mindwell had gone down stairs to find her husband, who sat by the fire, fitting a rake-tail more firmly into a hay-rake. He had been caught in a distant field by a heavy shower, and was steaming now close to the fireplace, where a heap of chips was lighted to boil the kettle for tea. Mindwell stole up to him, and laid one hand on his handsome head. He looked up, astonished at the slight caress, and saw his wife's eyes were full of tears.

"What's the matter, darling?" he said in his cheery voice. It was like a kiss to her to have him say "darling," for sweet words were rare among their class; and this was the only one he ever used, kept sacredly, too, for Mindwell.

"O Sam!" she answered, with a quiver in her delicate voice, "don't you think, Deacon Flint wants to marry mother!"

"Thunder an' guns! You don't mean it, wife? Haw, haw, haw! It's as good as a general trainin'. Of all things! What doos she say to't?"

"Well, I'm 'most afraid she favors him a little. He's given her a week's time to consider of it; but, someway, I can't bear to have it thought of."

"Don't pester your head about it, Miss Pratt: you can't make nor meddle in such things. But I'm free to own that I never was more beat in all my days. Why, Amasy Flint is town-talk for nearness an' meanness. He pretends to be as pious as a basket o' chips, but I hain't no vital faith in that kind o' pious. I b'lieve in my soul he's a darned old hypocrite."

"O Sam, Sam! you hadn't ought to judge folks."

"I suppose I hadn't, reelly; but you know what Scripter says somewhere or 'nother, that some folks's sins are open, an' go to judgment beforehand, and I guess his'n do. I should hate to have mother take up with him."

"What can we do, Sam?"

"Nothin', strenoously. I don't know what 'tis about women-folks in such matters: they won't bear no more meddlin' with than a pa'tridge's nest; you'll spile the brood if you put in a finger. I'd say jest as much as I could about her bein' always welcome here. I'll do my part of that set piece o' music; and that's all we can do. If she's set on havin' him, she will; and you nor me can't stop it, Miss Pratt." With which sound advice, Sam rose from the milking-stool with his reconstructed rake, took down a coarse comb from the clock-case, ran it through his hair by way of toilet, and sat down to supper at the table with the three other hay-makers. Mindwell and her mother were going out to tea, so they did not sup with the men.

After they came home, Sam expressed himself in a succinct but forcible manner to Mrs. Gold on the subject of her marriage, and Mindwell attempted a faint remonstrance again; but her morbid fear of selfishness shut the heart-throbs she longed to express to her mother back into their habitual silence. She and Sam both, trying to do their best, actually helped, rather than hindered, this unpropitious marriage.

Mrs. Gold, in her heart, longed to stay with her children, but feared and disliked so heartily to be a burden on their hands, that she was unjust to herself and them too. A little less self-inspection, and a little more simple honesty of speech, would have settled this matter in favor of Mindwell and Colebrook: as it was, Deacon Flint carried the day. On the Friday following he arrived for his answer; his gray hair tied in a long cue, his Sunday coat of blue, and brass buttons, his tight drab pantaloons, ruffled shirt, and low boots, all indicating a ceremonial occasion.

"Gosh," said old Israel Tucker, jogging along in his yeast-cart, as he met the gray mare in clean harness, whipped up by the deacon in this fine raiment, the old wagon itself being for once washed and greased,—"gosh! it's easy tellin' what he's after. I should think them mulleins an' hardbacks in the buryin'-ground would kinder rustle round. I don't know, though; mabbe Miss Flint's realized by now that she's better off under them beauties of natur' than she ever was in Amasy Flint's house. Good land! what fools women-folks be! They don't never know when they're well off. She's had an easy time along back; but she's seen the last on't, she's seen the last on't.—Get up, Jewpiter."

Nothing daunted by any mystic or magnetic sense of this vaticination by the highway, Deacon Flint whipped up his bony steed still more, and to such good purpose that he arrived in Colebrook before the widow had taken down the last pinned-up curl on her forehead, or decided which of her two worked collars she would put on, and whether it would be incongruous to wear a brooch of blue enamel with a white centre, on which was depicted (in a fine brown tint produced by grinding up in oil a lock of the deceased Ethan Gold's hair) a weeping-willow bending over a tomb, with an urn, and a date on the urn. This did seem a little personal on such an occasion: so she pinned on a blue bow instead, and went down to receive the expecting deacon.

"I hope I see you well, ma'am," said Mr. Flint.

"Comfortably well, I'm obleeged to you," was the prim answer.

But the deacon was not to be daunted at this crisis: he plunged valiantly into the middle of things at once. "I suppose you've took into consideration the matter in hand, Miss Gold?"

The widow creased her handkerchief between her finger and thumb, and seemed to be critical about the hemming of it; but she pretty soon said softly, "Yes, I can't say but what I have thought on't a good deal. I've counselled some with the children too."

"Well, I hope you're fit and prepared to acknowledge the leadin's of Providence to this end, and air about ready to be my companion through the valley of this world up to them fields beyond the swellin' flood stands dressed in livin' green. Amen."

The deacon forgot he was not in a prayer-meeting, and so dropped into the hymn-book, as Mr. Wegg did into secular poetry.

"H'm, well there's a good deal to be thought of for and ag'inst it too," remarked Mrs. Gold, unwilling to give too easy an assent, and so cheapen herself in the eyes of her acute adorer. But, when her thoughts were sternly sifted down, they appeared to be slight matters; and the deacon soon carried his point. He wasted no time in this transaction. Having "shook hands on it," as he expressed himself, he proceeded at once to arrange the programme.

"Well, Sarepty, we're both along in years, and to our time o' life delays is dangerous. I think we'd better get married pretty quick. I'm keepin' that great lazy Polly Morse, and payin' out cash right along; and you no need to fix up any, you've got good clothes enough: besides, what's clothes to worms of the dust sech as we be? The Catechism says 'Man's chief end is to glorify God and enjoy him forever;' and if that's so,—and I expect '*tis* so,—why, 'tain't nothin' to be concerned about what our poor dyin' bodies is clothed in."

Mrs. Gold did not agree with him at all. She liked her clothes, as women ought to; but his preternatural piety awed her, and she said meekly enough, "Well, I don't need no great of gowns. I sha'n't buy but one, I don't believe."

A faint color stole to her cheek as she said it, for she meant a wedding-dress; and Deacon Flint was acute enough to perceive it, and to understand that this was a point he could not carry.

"One gown ain't neither here nor there, Sarepty; but I aim to fix it on your mind, that, as I said afore, delays is dangerous. I purpose, with the divine blessin', to be married this day two weeks. I suppose you're agreeable?" The widow was too surprised to deny this soft impeachment; and he went on, "Ye see, there's papers to be drawed up: you've got independent means, and so have I, and it's jest as well to settle things fust as last. Did Ethan Gold leave you a life-int'rest in your thirds, or out an' out?"

The widow's lip trembled: her dead husband had been careful of her, more careful than she knew, till now.

"He didn't will me no thirds at all: he left me use an' privilege, for my nateral life, of every thing that was his'n, and all to go to Mindwell when I'm gone."

"Do tell! He was forehanded, I declare for't!" exclaimed the deacon, both pleased and displeased; for, if his wife's income was to be greater than he supposed, in case of her death before his there would be no increase to his actual possessions.

"Well, I always calc'lated you had your thirds, an' prob'ly, knowin' Ethan was free-handed, you had 'em out an' out. This makes some difference about what papers I'll have to have drawed up. Now, I guess the best way is to have a agreement like this: I agree not to expect to hev an' to hold none of your property, an' you don't none of mine; but I to have the use of your'n, and you to have your livin' out o' mine. You see, you don't have no more'n your livin' out of your'n now: that's all we any of us get in this here world. 'Hevin' food an' raiment, let us therewith be content,' as Scripter says. You agree to this, don't ye?"

Bewildered with the plausible phrases ballasted by a text, unaware that even the Devil can quote Scripture to serve his turn, Mrs. Gold did not see that she was putting herself entirely into the hands of this man, and meekly agreed to his arrangement. If this story were not absolutely true, I should scarce dare to invent such a character as Deacon Flint. But he was once a living man, and hesitating to condemn him utterly, being now defenceless among the dead, we can but hope for him and his like that there are purifying fires beyond this life, where he may be melted and refined into the image of Him who made him a man, and gave him a long life here to develop manhood. Not till after he was gone did Mrs. Gold begin to think that he had left her to explain his arrangements to Mindwell and Sam, and instinctively she shrank from doing so. Like many another weak woman, she hated words, particularly hard words. Her life had flowed on in a gentle routine, so peacefully that she had known but one sorrow, and that was so great, that, with the propensity we all have to balance accounts with Providence, she thought her trouble had been all she could bear. But there was yet reserved for her that sharp attrition of life which is so different from the calm and awful force of sorrow,—so much more exasperating, so much more educating. Some instinct warned her to avoid remonstrance by concealing from her children the contract she was about to make, and she felt, too, the uncertainty of a woman unaccustomed to business, about her own clear understanding of the situation. So she satisfied herself with telling Mindwell of the near approach of her marriage.

"O mother, so soon!" was all Mindwell said, though her eyes and lips spoke far more eloquently.

"Well, now the thing's settled, I don't know but what it may as well be over with. We ain't young folks, Mindwell. 'Tain't as if we had quite a spell to live."

Tears stood in her eyes as she said it. A certain misgiving stole over her: just then it seemed a good thing that she could not live long.

Mindwell forced back the sob that choked her. A woman of single heart, she did not consider a second marriage sacred. For herself, she would rather have taken her children to the town-farm, cold as corporative charity is, than married another man than Samuel, even if he had been dead thirty years; and she bitterly resented this default of respect to her father's memory. But her filial duty came to the rescue.

"Dear mother, I can't bear to think of it. What shall I do? What will the children say? I did hope you would take time to consider."

"It ain't real dutiful in you to take me to do, Mindwell: I'm full old to be lessoned, seems to me. As for you and the children, I don't feel no great distress: love runs down, not up, folks say; and I don't believe you'll any of ye pine a long spell."

This weak and petulant outburst dismayed Mindwell, who had never seen her mother otherwise than gentle and pleasant; but, with the tact of a great heart, she said nothing, only put her arms about the elder woman's neck, and kissed her over and over. At this, Mrs. Gold began to cry; and, in soothing her distress, Mindwell forgot to ask any further questions, but set herself to divert both their minds from this brief and bitter outburst by inquiring what preparation her mother meant to make in the fortnight.

"I don't look to no great preparation," sighed the widow. "I have always had good clothes enough, and there's a piece of linen I wove before we come here that'll do for all I want. I suppose I had ought to have a new gown to be married in. When I was married to Ethan, I had a white dimity gown and a blue levantine petticoat; and if he didn't fetch me a big bunch of sand-violets—they was blossoming then—for to match my eyes and my skirt, he said. But that's past and gone, as the hymn-book says. I do want to have one good gown, Mindwell; and, now I'm a little along in years, I guess I'll have a dark one. T'other night, when we was up to Squire Barnes's to tea, Miss Barnes was telling about a piece of plum-colored paduasoy Mr. Battle bought in Har'ford for 'Leety's weddin'-gown, and she wouldn't hev it. She said 'twasn't lively enough, and so she's set her mind on a blue levantine. But I should think the plum-color would become me real well."

So the plum-colored silk was bought; and arrayed in its simple folds, with a new worked collar and a white satin bow, the Widow Gold was dressed for her second wedding.

Did she think, as she looked into her oval mirror that morning, what a different vision was this quiet, elderly, sober woman, in decent but not festal garments, from the smiling, blushing, blue-eyed creature in her spotless dimity gown opening over a blue petticoat, and clasped at the throat with a bunch of still bluer violets? What does a woman think who is married the second time? A man is satisfied that now his house will be kept once more, his clothes mended, his whims humored, his table spread to his taste, and his children looked after. If it is needful, he can marry six wives one after the other. They are a domestic necessity: the Lord himself says it is not good for *man* to be alone. But it is quite another thing for the woman. Such a relation is not a movable feast to her: it is once for all; and, if circumstance or pique betray her into this faithlessness, what does she think of herself when it becomes inevitable?

The Widow Gold did not tell. She was paler when she turned from the glass than when she looked into it: and she trembled as she went down stairs to sign the papers before Parson Roberts should arrive.

The best parlor was opened to-day. The high-backed chairs with old brocade cushions, that had belonged to Sam Pratt's grandmother, were ranged along the wall like a row of stiff ghosts; the corner-cupboards were set open to display the old china and glass that filled them; there was a "bow-pot" of great red peonies, abundant and riotous with color and fatness, set under the chimney in the well-whited fireplace; and a few late roses glowed in a blue china jar on the high mantelpiece. On a square table with a leaf lay a legal paper that Sam was reading, with his hands supporting his head as if it was hard to understand the document.

The deacon, in his Sunday garments, was looking at him askance; and Mindwell, with the little girls Ede and Sylvia clinging to her gown, was staring out of the window, down the road,—staring, but not seeing; for the spendid summer day that lavished its bloom and verdure and odor on these gaunt New-England hills, and hid their rude poverty with its royal mantle, was all a dim blur to the heart-wrung woman.

"Mother," said Sam Pratt, raising his head, "do you know what's the sum and substance of these here papers? and do you agree to't?"

The widow glanced aside at Deacon Flint, and caught his "married eye," early as it was to use that ocular weapon.

"Why, yes, Samwell: I don't know but what I do," she said slowly and rather timidly.

"Well," said Sam, rising, and pushing the paper away, "if you do, why, then you're going right into't, and it's right, I s'pose; but, by Jinks! I think it's the d—"

Mindwell's touch on his arm arrested the sentence. 'There's Parson Roberts, Samwell. You jest help him out of the gig, will you? He's quite lame, I see."

Sam Pratt went, with the half-finished sentence on his lips. He was glad his wife had stopped him, on many accounts; but he did long to give Deacon Flint his own opinion of that preliminary contract.

He indulged himself for this deprivation, after the stiff and somewhat melancholy wedding was over, and the staid couple had departed for Bassett in the deacon's wagon, by freeing his mind to his wife.

"Miss Pratt, I was some riled to hev you stop me when I was a-goin' to tell the deacon what I thought about that there contrack; but I don't never stay riled with you, marm, as you'd ought to know by this time." And Sam emphasized this statement with a hearty kiss. "Besides, I will own on second thoughts I was glad you did stop me; for it's no use pinchin' your fingers in a pair o' nippers. But I do say now and here, it was the darndest piece o' swindlin' I ever see,—done under a cover of law an' gospel, you may say; for the deacon had stuck in a bit of Scripter so's to salt it like. He's got the best of the bargain, I tell ye, a long sight. I'm real glad your father went and fixed that prop'ty so she has the use on't only; for she wouldn't have two cents in two years' time, if she'd had it to do with what she's a mind to."

"I am glad he did," said Mindwell. "I have felt as though mother would be better suited if she did have it to do what she liked to with; but if this was to happen, why, it's as good she is provided for. She can't want for nothing now."

"I guess she'll want for more'n money, and mabbe for that too. The paper says she's to have her livin'. Now, that's a wide word. Folks can live on bread and water, I expect; and he can't be holden for no more than he's a mind to give."

"O Sam, you don't think Deacon Flint would grudge her a good living? Why, if he is near, as folks tell he is, he's a professor of religion."

"I'd a durned sight ruther he was a practiser on't, Miss Pratt. Religion's about the best thing there is, and makin' believe it is about the wust. I b'lieve in Amasy Flint's religion jest so far forth as I hear him talk, an' not a inch farther. I know he'll pinch an' shave an' spare to the outside of a cheese-rind; and I haven't no great reason to think he'll do better by Mother Gold than he does by himself." Mindwell turned away, full of foreboding; and Sam, following her, put his arm about her, and drew her back to the settle.

"Don't worry, dear. She's made her bed, and she's got to lie on't. But, after all, it's the Lord who lets folks do that way, so's to show 'em, I expect, that beds ain't always meant to sleep on, but sometimes to wake folks up. We're kind of apt to lie long an' get lazy on feathers. I expect that's what's the matter with me. I'll get my husks by and by, I guess."

Mindwell looked up at him, with all her heart in her eyes; but she said nothing, and he gave a shy laugh. Their deep love for each other was "a fountain shut up;" and so far no angel had rolled away the stone, and given it visible life. It was still voiceless and sleeping.

Before her wedding-day was over, Mrs. Flint's new life began; for Polly Morse had been sent off the night before, being the end of an even week, lest she might charge ninepence for an extra day. So her successor without wages had to lay aside her plum-colored silk, put on a calimanco petticoat and short-gown, and proceed to get supper; while Polly, leaning over the half-door of the old red house which she shared with the village tailoress, exchanged pungent remarks with old Israel on the topic of the day in Bassett.

"No, they didn't make no weddin', Isr'el. There wa'n't nobody asked, nor no loaf-cake made for her: he wouldn't hear to't, noway. I'd have staid and fixed up for her to-day; but he was bound I shouldn't. As for me, I'm most amazin' glad to get hum, now I tell ye. I'd a sight ruther be in Simsbury prison for a spell, if it wa'n't for the name on't."

"Say, Polly, do you call to mind what I said three weeks back about Miss Flint comin' home? Oh! ye do, do ye? Well, I ain't nobody's fool, be I? I guess I can see through a millstone, providin' the hole's big enough, as well as the next man. I'm what ye may call mighty obsarvin', now. I can figger consider'ble well on folks, ef I can't on 'rithmetic; and I know'd jest as well, when I see him rigged up in his sabba'-day go-to-meetin's, and his nose p'inted for Colebrook, what he was up to, as though I heerd him a-askin' her to hev him."

"Well, I never did think Sarepty Gold would demean herself to have him. She's got means and a real good home; and Mindwell sets a sight by her, and so does Sam Pratt: but here she's ben an' gone an' done it. I wouldn't ha' thought it, not if th' angel Gabriel had have told me on't."

"Guess he's in better business than goin' round with Bassett gossip, anyhow. But what was you so took back by? Lordy! I should think you was old enough to git over bein' surprised at women-folks: them and the weather is two things I don't never calc'late on. You can't no more tell what a woman'll do, 'specially about marryin', than you can tell which way in the road a pig'll go, unless you work it back'ard, same as some folks tell they drive a pig; and then 'tain't reel reliable: they may go right ahead when you don't a mite expect it."

"That is one thing about men, I allow, Isr'el: you can always tell which way they'll go for sartain; and that is after their own advantage, an' nobody else's, now an' forever."

"Amen! They'd be all fools, like me, if they didn't," assented the old man, with a dry chuckle, as he drove off his empty cart. Yet, for all his sneers and sniffs, neither Polly nor the new Mrs. Flint had a truer friend than Israel. Rough as he was, satiric as a chestnut burr that shows all its prickles in open defiance, conscious of a sweet white heart within, his words only were bitter: his nature was generous, kindly, and perceptive. He had become the peripatetic satirist and philosopher that he was out of this very nature,

"Dowered with a scorn of scorn, a love of love," [1]

and free with the freedom of independent poverty to express pungently what he felt poignantly, being in his own kind and measure the "salt of the earth" to Bassett.

But, in spite of comment and pity, the thing was a fixed fact. Mrs. Flint's married life had begun under new auspices, and it was not a path of roses upon which she had entered. Her housekeeping had always been frugal, with the thrift that is or was characteristic of her race; but it had been abundant for the wants of her family. The viands she provided were those of the place and period, simple and primitive enough; but the great brick oven was well filled with light bread of wheat and rye both; pies of whatever material was in season, whose flaky crust and well-filled interiors testified to her knowledge of the art; deep dishes of baked beans; jars of winter pears; pans of golden-sweet apples; and cards of yellow ginger-bread, with rows of snowy and puffy biscuit. Ede and Sylvia knew very well where to find crisp cookies and fat nut-cakes; and pie was reiterated three times a day on Sam Pratt's table.

It was part of her "pride of life" that she was a good housekeeper; and Mindwell had given her the widest liberty. But now the tide had changed. She soon found that Deacon Flint's parsimony extended into every detail. Her pies were first assailed.

"Sarepty, don't make them pies o' your'n so all-fired rich. They ain't good for the stomach: besides, they use up all the drippin's, and you had ought to make soap next month. Pie is good, and I think it's savin' of meat. But it pompers up the flesh, too good livin' does; and we hev got to give an account, ye know. I don't mean to have no wicked waste laid to my account."

So she left out half the shortening from her crust, and felt ashamed to see the tough substance this economy produced. Next came the sugar question.

"We buy too much sweetenin', Sarepty. There's a kag of tree-molasses down cellar. I expect it's worked some; but you jest take an' bile it up, an' stir consider'ble saleratus into't, an' it'll do. I want to get along jest as reasonable as we can. Wilful waste makes woful want, ye know."

Yet in his own way the deacon was greedy enough. He had the insatiable appetite that belongs to people of his figure far more often than to the stout.

"He's a real racer," said Uncle Israel, reverting to his own experience in pigs,—"slab-sided an' lank. I bet you could count his ribs this minnit; and that's the kind you can feed till the day after never, and they won't do ye no credit. I never see a man could punish vittles the way he can; but there ain't no more fat to him than there is to a hen's forehead."

Mrs. Flint was not "hungry nor hankering," as she expressed it, but a reasonable eater of plain food; but the deacon's mode of procedure was peculiar.

"Say, Sarepty, don't bile but a small piece o' pork with that cabbage to-day. I've got a pain to my head, an' I don't feel no appetite; an' cold pork gets eat up for supper when there ain't no need on't."

Obeying instructions, the small piece of fat pork would be cooked, and, once at the table, transferred bodily to the deacon's plate. "Seems as though my appetite had reelly come back. I guess 'twas a hungry head-ache." And the tired woman had to make her dinner from cabbage and potatoes seasoned with the salt and greasy water in which they had been cooked.

There were no amusements for her out of the house. The younger people had their berrying frolics, sleigh-rides, kitchen-dances, nuttings, and the like; and their elders, their huskings, apple-bees, and sewing-societies: but against all these the deacons set his hard face.

"It's jest as good to do your own extry chores yourself as to ask folks to come an' help. That costs more'n it comes to. You've got to feed 'em, and like enough keep a big fire up in the spare room. I'd ruther be diligent in business, as Scripter says, than depend on neighbors."

The sewing society, too, was denied to poor Mrs. Flint, because they had to have tea got for them. Prayer-meetings he could not deny her; for they cost nothing, and officially he attended them. Meeting on Sunday was another outlet, when she could see friendly faces, receive kind greetings, and read in many eyes a sympathy and pity that at once pleased and exasperated her.

Another woman in her place might have had spirit or guile enough to have resisted the pressure under which she only quailed and submitted. She was one of those feeble souls to whom a hard word is like a blow, and who will bear any thing and every thing rather than be found fault with, and who necessarily become drudges and slaves to those with whom they live, and are despised and ill-treated simply because they are incapable of resentment. There are some persons who stand in this position not so much from want of strength as from abounding and eager affection for those whom they serve; and their suffering, when they discover how vain has been their labor and self-sacrifice, is known only to Him who was

> "At once denied, betrayed, and fled
> By those who shared his daily bread."

But Mrs. Flint had no affection for her husband: she married him because it seemed a good thing to do, and obeyed him because he was her husband, as was the custom in those days. So she toiled on dumbly from day to day, half fed, overworked, desperately lonely, but still uncomplaining; for her constitution was naturally strong, and nerves were unrecognized then.

Her only comfort was the rare visits of her children. Mindwell found it hard to leave home; but, suspicious of her mother's comfort, she made every effort to see her as often as possible, and always to carry her some little present,—a dozen fresh eggs, which the poor woman boiled privately, and ate between her scanty meals, a few peaches, or a little loaf of cake,—small gifts, merely to demonstrate her feeling. She did not know what good purpose they served, for Mrs. Flint did not tell her daughter what she endured. She remembered too well how Mindwell had begged her to delay and consider her marriage; and she would not own to her now that she had made any mistake: for Mrs. Flint had as much human nature in her composition as the rest of us; and who does like to hear even their dearest friend say, "I told you so"?

Matters went on in this way for five years, every day being a little more weary and dreary than the preceding. The plum-colored paduasoy still did duty as the Sunday gown, for none of her own money ever passed into Mrs. Flint's hands. By this time she understood fully what her ante-nuptial contract meant. She had her living, and no more. People could live without finery, even without warmth. A stuff gown of coarse linsey-woolsey for winter wear replaced the soft merinoes she had always bought for that purpose; and homespun linen check was serviceable in summer, though it kept her busy at flax-wheel and loom many an hour. She had outlived the early forbearances of her married life, and learned to ask, to beg, to persist in entreating, for what she absolutely needed; for only in this way could she get her "living." Her only vivid pleasure was in occasional visits from Ede and Sylvia,—lovely little creatures in whom their mother's beauty of character and their father's cheery, genial nature seemed to combine, and with so much of Mindwell's delicate loveliness, her sweet, dark eyes contrasted with the fair hair of their father's family, that to grandmotherly eyes they seemed perfectly beautiful. For them the poor woman schemed and toiled, and grew secretive. She hid a comb of honey sometimes, when the deacon's back was turned, and kept it for Sylvia, who loved honey like a real bee-bird; she stored up red pearmains in the parlor-closet for Ede; and when Sam Pratt went into Hartford with a load of wool, and brought the children as far as Bassett to stay at Deacon Flint's over night, the poor woman would make for them gingerbread such as they remembered, and savory cookies that they loved, though she encountered hard looks, and hard words too, for wasting her husband's substance on another man's children.

Ede, who had a ready memory and a fluent tongue, was the first to report to Mindwell these comments of "Grandsir Flint," as they were taught to call him.

"O mother," she exclaimed, "I do think grandsir is real mean!"

"Edy, Edy, you mustn't talk so about your elders and betters."

"I can't help it," chattered on the irrepressible child. "What did he want to come into the kitchen for when granny was giving us supper, and scold because she made cookies for us? Granny 'most cried; and he kept tellin' how he'd said before she shouldn't do it, and he wouldn't have it."

"Don't talk about it, Edy," said her mother, full of grief and indignation.

"Mother, it's true. I heard him too," interposed Sylvia, who thought Ede's word was doubted; for the voluble and outspoken child was a little apt to embellish her reports.

"Well, Sylvy dear, it isn't best to talk about a good many things that are true."

But, for all that, Mindwell did discuss the matter with Sam before she slept, in that "grand committee of two" which is the strength and comfort of a happy marriage.

"What ever can we do about it, Sam?" she said, with tears in her voice. "I can't bear to keep the children to home,—mother sets by 'em like her life; but, if they're going to make trouble between her and Deacon Flint, don't you think I had ought to prevent their going there?"

"Well, it does seem hard on mother every way; but I guess I can fix it. You know we had a heap of wheat off that east lot last year, and I've sent it to mill to be ground up for us. I guess I'll take and send a barrel on't over to mother for a present. The deacon won't mistrust nothing; nor he can't say nothing about her usin' on't for the children."

"That's the very thing," said Mindwell. And so it was, for that small trouble; yet that was only a drop in the bucket. After a few years of real privation, and a worse hunger of spirit, Mrs. Flint's health began to fail. She grew nervous and irritable, and the deacon browbeat her more than ever. Her temper had long since failed under the hourly exasperation of her husband's companionship, and she had become as cross, as peevish, and as exasperating herself as a feeble nature can become under such a pressure.

"I never see nobody so changed as Miss Flint is," confided Aunt Polly to old Israel. "I've always heerd tell that 'flictions was sent for folks's good; but her'n don't seem to work that way a mite."

"Well, Polly, I expect there's a reel vital differ'nce in 'flictions, jest as there is in folks. She picked her'n up, as you may say, when she married him. 'Twan't reelly the Lord's sendin'. She no need to ha' married him, if she hadn't ben a min' to."

"I sorter thought the Lord sent every thing't happened to folks."

"Well, in a manner mabbe he doos. But don't ye rek'lect what David said,—how't he'd ruther fall inter the hands of the Lord than inter men's? I expect we're to blame for wilful sins, ain't we? And I guess we fetch 'flictions on ourselves sometimes."

"I don't see how you make them idees jibe with 'lection and fore-ordination," rejoined Aunt Polly, who was a zealous theologian, and believed the Saybrook Platform and the Assembly's Catechism to be merely a skilful abridgment and condensation of Scripture.

"I don't know as I'm called to, Polly. I don't believe the Lord's ways is jest like a primer, for everybody to larn right off. I shouldn't have no great respect for a ruler an' governor, as the Confession sez, that wa'n't no bigger'n I was. Land! ef I was to set sail on them seas o' divinity, I should be snooped up in the fust gale, an' drownded right off. I b'lieve He is good, and doos right, anyhow. Ef I can't see the way on't, why, it's 'cause my spiritooal eyes ain't big enough. I can't see into some littler things than him, and I don't hold to takin' up the sea in a pint cap: 'twon't carry it, nohow." With which aphorism old Israel travelled off with his barrow, leaving Polly amazed and shocked, but perhaps a little wiser after all.

Just about this time a cousin of Deacon Flint's died "over in York State," as he said, and left him guardian of her only daughter, a girl of eighteen. A couple of thousand dollars was all the property that the Widow Eldridge had to give her child; for they had both worked hard for their living after the husband and father left them, and this money was the price of the farm, which had been sold at his death. It was something to get so much cash into his own hands; and the deacon accordingly wrote at once to Mabel, and offered her a home in his house, intimating, that, the interest of her money not being enough to board and clothe her, he would, out of family affection, supply these necessities for that inadequate sum, if she was willing to help a little about the house. Mabel was friendless enough to grasp eagerly this hope of a home; and very soon the stage stopped at Deacon Flint's door, and a new inmate entered his house.

Mabel Eldridge was a capable, spirited, handsome girl, and, before she had been a week in the Flint family, understood her position, and resolved only to endure it till something better could be found. In her heart she pitied Aunt Flint, as she called her, as much as she detested the deacon; and her fresh girlish heart fairly ached with compassion and indignation over the poor woman. But she was a great comfort and help while she staid; though she made that stay as short as possible, and utterly refused to give up her savings-bank book to the deacon, who was unable legally to claim it, since her mother left no will, having only asked him, in a letter written just before her death, to act as Mabel's guardian. Her three months' sojourn in the house made her thoroughly aware of Deacon Flint's character and his wife's sufferings. She could not blame Mrs. Flint that she snapped back at the deacon's snarls, or complained long and bitterly of her wants and distresses.

"You don't know nothing what it is, Mabel," she said one day, sobbing bitterly. "I'm put upon so hard! I want for clothes, and for vittles, and for some time to rest, so's't I don't know but what 'twill clean kill me: and, if 'twa'n't for the childern, I'd wish to die; but I do cleave to them amazingly."

Indignant tears filled Mab's eyes. "I don't know how you bear it, aunty," she said, putting her arms about the old lady's neck. "Can't you get away from him anyhow?"

"I could, but I suppose I hadn't ought to. There's a house on my farm that ain't goin' to be in use come next April. Hiram Smith—him that's rented it along back—wants some repairin' done on't, and Mr. Flint won't hear to't: so Hi he's been and gone and bought a piece of ground acrost the road, an' put up a buildin' for himself. He's got a long lease of the land; but he don't want the house no more, and he won't pay for't. I s'pose I might move over there for a spell, and have some peace. There's enough old furnitoor there that was father's. But then, agin, I do suppose I haven't no right to leave my husband."

"Haven't you got any right to save your life?" indignantly asked Mabel.

"It ha'n't come to that, not quite," said Mrs. Flint sadly.

But before April she began to think it was a matter of life and death to stay any longer with the man. Mabel had left her some months before, and gone into the family of Sam Pratt's mother, in Colebrook, promising her aunt, that, if ever the time came when she needed her in another home, she would come and take care of her.

Toward the middle of February Mrs. Flint was seized with congestion of the lungs, and was very ill indeed. A fear of public opinion made Deacon Flint send for the doctor; but nothing could induce him to let a nurse enter the house, or even to send for Mindwell Pratt. He was able to do for his wife, he said, and nobody could interfere.

Mrs. Flint's Married Experience

It was the depth of winter; and the communication between Bassett and Colebrook was not frequent in the best weather, neither place being dependent on the other for supplies; and now the roads were blocked with heavy drifts, and the inhabitants of both places had hibernated, as New-Englanders must in winter. It was a matter of congratulation with Deacon Flint that he had no out-door work to do just now, and so was spared the expense of a woman to care for his wife. He could do it, too, more economically than a nurse. It did not matter to him that the gruel was lumpy, or burned, or served without flavoring. Sick folks, particularly with serious sickness, ought not to pamper the flesh: their souls were the things to be considered. He did not want to have Sarepta die, for she had an income that helped him much; but he did not want her to be a "bill of expense," as he phrased it. So while he read the Bible to her twice a day, and prayed to, or rather at, her by the hour, he fed her on sloppy gruel and hard bread, sage-tea, and cold toast without butter, and just kept life flickering within her till she could get about and help herself, unknown to him, to draughts of fresh milk, and now and then a raw egg.

But she did not get well: she was feeble, and wasted a long time. The village doctor, knowing what Deacon Flint was, and filled with pity for his wife, called often, carefully stating that his visits were those of a friend, but urging, also, that Mrs. Flint should have a generous diet, and a glass of wine daily, to restore her strength. The deacon heard him through in silence, and when he left began to growl.

"Well, fools a'n't all dead yet. Wine! I guess not. A good drink o' thoroughwort-tea's wuth all the wine in creation. 'Wine's a mocker, an' strong drink is ragin'.' Dr. Grant don't read his Bible as he'd ought to."

"There ain't nothin' in the Bible aginst beef-tea, I guess," feebly piped his wife. "I do feel as though that would fetch me up. Can't you get a piece o' meat down to the slaughter, deacon?"

"I don't see no need on't, Sarepty: you're doin' reasonable well. Meat is reel costly; an' pomperin' the flesh is sinful. I'll git another cod-fish next time I go to the store: that's nourishin'. I don't hold to Grant's idees entire. Besides, 'twa'n't nothin' what he said: he come as a friend."

The poor woman burst into tears. Indignation gave her momentary strength: she did not hear the shed-door open behind her; but she rose in her chair like a spectre, and looked at him with burning eyes.

"Amasy Flint, I b'lieve you'd a sight rather I'd die than live. I hain't had decent vittles since I was took sick, nor no care whatever. You're a loud pray-er an' reader; but, if 'twa'n't for the name of it, I b'lieve you'd kill me with the axe instead of starvation. I've a good mind to send for Squire Battle, and swear the peace against ye."

Deacon Flint at this moment saw a shocked face behind his wife's chair: it was Polly Morse. His acuteness came to the rescue. "She's a leetle out," he said, nodding to the unexpected guest. "Come right along, Polly."

This was too much for the weak woman to bear. She fell back, and fainted. Her indignation had overborne her weakness for a moment, but exhausted it also. And, when she awoke to life, Polly was rubbing her, and crying over her; but her husband had gone. Those tears of sympathy were more than she could endure silently. She put her arms round Polly's neck, and, sobbing like a child, poured out the long list of her sorrows into that faithful ear.

"Bless your dear soul!" said Polly, wiping her eyes, "you can't tell me nothing new about him. Didn't I summer an' winter him, so to speak, afore you come here? Don't I know what killed the fust woman? 'Twa'n't no fever, ef they did call it so. 'Twas livin' with him—want o' food, an' fire, an' lovin'-kindness. Don't tell me. I pitied ye afore ye was married, an' I hain't stopped yit."

But Polly's words were not words only. From that day on, many a cup of broth, vial of currant-wine, or bit of hot stewed chicken, found its way surreptitiously to Mrs. Flint; and her strength of mind and body returned fast, with this sympathy for one, and food for the other. She made up her mind at last that she would leave her husband, at least for a time, and in her own house endeavor to find the peace and rest necessary to her entire recovery. If she could have seen Mindwell and Sam, and taken counsel with them, her course might have been different; but the roads were now well-nigh impassable from deep mud, and she could not get to Colebrook, and in sheer desperation she resolved to leave her present home as soon as Hiram Smith moved from the farmhouse. Fortunately for her, the deacon had to attend town-meeting, three miles off, on the first Monday in April; and, with Polly and Israel to help her, Mrs. Flint was established in the other house before he returned, and found her flown. His wrath was great but still. He said and did nothing, never went near her, and, for very shame's sake, did not speak of her—for what could he say?

Perhaps in that solitary house, whose silence was like balm to her weary and fevered soul, she might have starved but for the mercy of her neighbors. Polly Morse had a tongue of swiftness, and it never wagged faster than in Mrs. Flint's behalf. Dr. Grant sent half a barrel of flour to that destitute dwelling, and Israel, a bushel of apples. Polly, out of her poverty, shared her kit of pork with the poor woman; and Hiram Smith brought in a barrel of potatoes and a bag of meal, which he duly charged against her account with the farm. But there were many who dared not help her; for the deacon held notes and mortgages on many a house and of many a man in Bassett who could not afford to offend him. And old Parson Roberts was just then shut up with an attack of low fever: so he knew nothing about the matter. However, the deacon was not long to be left nursing his wrath. Food and fire are not enough for life sometimes. The old house was leaky, damp, comfortless; and in a few weeks Mrs. Flint was taken again with disease of the lungs, and Polly Morse found her in her bed, unable to speak loud, her fire gone out, and the rain dripping down in the corner of her bedroom. Polly had come to tell her that Israel was going to Colebrook to buy a pig, and would take any message. She did not tell her, but, stepping to the door, called to him across the yard to tell Sam Pratt he must come over to Bassett directly. This done, she hunted about for something to make a fire, and then looked for the tea; but there was none. Nothing like food remained but a half-loaf of bread and some cold potatoes: so she had to break the bread up in some hot water, and feed the exhausted woman slowly, while she chafed her icy feet, and covered her closely with her own shawl. The next day Sam and Mindwell came over, shocked and indignant, their wagon loaded with provisions; and the old house was soon filled with odors of beef-broth, milk-porridge, fragrant tea and toast, and the sharp crackle of a great fire in two rooms; while, best of all, tender hands fed and soothed the poor woman, and soft filial kisses comforted her starved soul.

Mindwell could not stay,—there was a little baby at home,—but Sam would be left behind while old Israel drove her back to Colebrook, and fetched Mabel Eldridge to take her place.

Mab burst into a passion of tears when she entered the kitchen.

"I knew it!" she sobbed: "I knew that old wretch would kill her!" And it was long before Sam could calm her anger and grief, and bring her in to the invalid.

In the course of two or three weeks, however, Mab's faithful nursing, and Sam's care and providing, brought back life and some strength to the perishing woman. And meanwhile Polly's tongue had wagged well: it flew all over Bassett that Deacon Flint's wife had left him, and almost died of cold and hunger.

To-day such a rumor would have had some direct effect on its object; but then to find fault with authorities was little less than a sin, and for a wife to leave her husband, a fearful scandal. In spite of the facts and all their witnesses, the sentiment of Bassett went with the deacon. Conjugal sub-jection was the fashion, or rather the principle and custom, of the day, and was to be upheld in spite of facts. However, Parson Roberts by this time had heard of the matter, and called Deacon Flint to account, thinking it to be his duty.

"This is the hull sum and substance on't, parson," explained the deacon: "Miss Flint is a miser'ble hystericky female, a dreadful weak vessel, and noways inclined to foller Scripter in the marriage-relation. I've gin her the same livin' I had myself. I hain't denied her food an' raiment wherewith she had ought to be content, as the 'Postle Poll says. But she is real pernickity, and given to the lusts of the flesh about her eatin'; and I feel it to be my dooty to be a faithful stooard of my substance, and not pomper up our poor perishin' bodies, while there is forty million more or less o' heathen creturs lyin' in wickedness in foreign parts. Ye know, parson, I hain't never stented my contributions to them things: I've ben constant to means of grace allus, and I may say a pillar—mabbe a small and creaky one, but still a pillar—in the temple sech as 'tis. I don't know as I had ought to be disturbed by this strife of tongues."

Parson Roberts was a little confounded. He himself loved a bit of good eating,—a cantle of chicken-pie, a tender roast pig, a young chicken broiled on hickory coals, or a succulent shad from the Connecticut, washed down with sparkling cider or foaming flip,—and the conscious-ness of this mild weakness gave undue exaltation to Deacon Flint's boasted asceticism. The parson was too honestly humble to see that Deacon Flint loved money with a greed far surpassing that of any epicure; that his own fault was but a failing, while the other was a passion. Besides, he considered that Mrs. Flint had made light of the sacred ordinance of marriage, and set an awful example to the wives of the parish: so he went away from this interview convinced that the deacon was a stern saint, and his wife a weak sinner.

Next day, however, the deacon himself was surprised by another visit. Pale and worn, clinging tight to Sam Pratt's arm, and followed by Mabel carrying a cushion, his wife entered the kitchen, where he sat devouring salt pork and potatoes with the zest of a dog who gnaws his bone unmolested.

"I come back, Amasy, to see if we couldn't agree to get along together agin," she said weakly and meekly. "I hear there's ben consider'ble talk about my leavin' on ye, and I don't want to cast no reflections. I was tired all out, an' I wanted to rest a spell. Sam an' Mab has nursed me up, so't I could get along now, I guess."

The man turned his cold green-gray eyes on her slowly. "I don't know what you want to come back for now," he said.

"Why, I want for to do my duty so far as I can."

"You had oughter have considered that afore you went off," was the dogged answer.

Tears ran down the poor woman's face: she could not speak. Mabel's beautiful eyes blazed with wrath: she made a step forward; but Sam Pratt gently put her back, and said,—

"Look here, Deacon Flint. Mother left you because she hadn't food, nor care, nor nothing she needed, nyther when she was sick, nor when she was gettin' better. She thought a spell o' rest would do her good. She knowed by that smart contrack you got out of her that you owed her a livin' anyhow; and you hain't done a thing to'rds it sence she went to her own house. Now, I don't call that conduct honest, by no means, much less Christian."

"Jedge not, Samwell Pratt. Scripter, no less'n statoot law, commands a wife to be subjeck to her husband. Sarepty had what I had. I done what I jedged best for her; and, instead of submittin' to her head, she up and went off to live by herself, and lef' me to git along as I could. I wa'n't noway bound by no law nor no contrack to supply her with means, so long as she went away from her dooties, and made me an astonishment an' a hissin' in Israel, so to speak."

"Stop right there!" broke in Mabel, furious. "I've heard say the Devil could fetch Scripter to further his own purposes, and I b'lieve it. Didn't you have no duties to your wife? Don't the Bible say you've got to love and cherish her? Don't tell me! I lived here long enough to see you starve and browbeat and torment her. I know your mean, hateful, crabbed ways; and I don't know how she lived with you so long. She ought to have run away years ago; and, if folks do hiss at you, it's more'n time they did. Christian!—*you* a Christian! You're a dyed-in-the-wool hypocrite. If you're pious, I hope I shall be a reprobate."

"I ha'n't no doubt but what you will be, young woman," answered the deacon with cold fury. "You'd ought to be put under the pump this minnit, for a common scold. Get out of my house, right off!"

And with this he advanced upon her. But Sam Pratt, lifting the old lady in his arms, carried her away, and gently shoved Mabel, glowing with rage, before them till they reached the wagon. Then he himself went back, and tried to make terms with the deacon. At last, moved by the worldly wisdom of Sam's argument, that it would put him in a bad light before people if he refused to do any thing for his wife, he did agree to let her have half of his share of the produce from her farm, if Sam and Mindwell would provide for her other wants. And, making the best of a bad bargain, the poor woman retired to the old house, which Sam had repaired, so that most of it was habitable; and Mabel, who had agreed to teach the district school the next year, took up her abode with her.

Now the deacon had a clear field, and appeared in the arena of Bassett in the character of an injured and forsaken husband. His prayers at meeting were longer and more eloquent than ever; and the church, sympathizing with his sorrows,—the male members especially deprecating Mrs. Flint's example, lest it should some time be followed by their own wives,—unanimously agreed to withdraw their fellowship from Mrs. Flint,—a proceeding in kind, if not in degree, like the anathema of the papacy. The poor old woman quivered under the blow, imparted to her by Parson Roberts, awful in the dignity of his office and a new wig. But the parson was human; and the meek grief of the woman, set off by Mab's blazing indignation, worked upon his honest soul, and caused him to doubt a little the church's wisdom. Mab had followed him across the door-yard to the gate in order to "free her mind."

"I want to know what you wanted that poor woman to do, Parson Roberts. She was dyin' by inches for want of vittles fit to eat, and the care most folks would give a sick ox. Do you think, now, honest, she'd ought to have staid with that old wretch?"

"Speak not evil of dignities, young woman. Amasy Flint is a deacon of Bassett church. It does not become you so to revile him."

This glittering generality did not daunt Mab a moment.

"I don't care if he was deacon in the New Jerusalem, or minister either. If he was the angel Gabriel, and acted the way he did act, I shouldn't have no faith in his piety, nor no patience with his prayers."

Parson Roberts glared at her over his spectacles with pious horror. "What, what, what!" he sternly cried. "Who be you that set in judgment on your elders and betters?"

"I'm one that's seen him where you haven't, anyway, nor your church-members. I've lived to his house, and I know him like a book."

Was it possible, the parson thought, that brother Flint might have been in fault,—just a little? But he was faithful to his dogmas and his education.

"Do not excuse the woman's sin. She has left her lawful husband, threatened to swear the peace against a Christian man whom she was bound by human and divine law to obey, and caused a scandal and a disturbance in the fold of Christ. Is this a light matter, you daughter of Belial?"

Mab laughed,—laughed in the parson's face, in full front of his majestic wig, his awful spectacles, his gold-headed cane uplifted in the heat of argument. He could not see that she was a little hysterical. He grew red with ungodly rage, but Mab did not care a pin.

"You ain't a fool, Parson Roberts," she said undauntedly. "You've got eyes in your head; and you'd know, if you'd use 'em, that Aunt Flint is a weak sister anyway. She wouldn't turn no sooner'n the least worm that ever was; but *they* will turn, if you tread right on 'em. And, whatever you say, you know, jest as well as I do, that Amasy Flint drove her into leavin' him, and drove her with a whip of scorpions, as the Bible tells about."

"Woman, do you mean to say I lie?" thundered the parson.

"Well, yes—if you don't tell the truth," returned Mab, completely at bay now. An audible chuckle betrayed some listener; and the parson, turning round, beheld old Israel silently unloading a wheelbarrow-load of potatoes at the corner of the fence, and wondered in his soul how long the man had been there, but considered it the better part of valor to leave the scene, now that it had ceased to be a *tête-à-tête*; so he waved his hand at Mab with a gloomy scowl, and went his way.

"Land o' liberty!" ejaculated the old man, drawing the back of his hand across his mouth to smother a laugh. "Didn't you give him jesse! I swan you're the gal for a free fight, now. He's heerd the fac's in the case, if he never did afore. Of all things! What be you a-cryin' for now, eh?" For Mab, a real woman, had flung her apron over her face, and was sobbing violently. Uncle Israel gently tried to pull the check screen away; but she held on to it.

"Let me cry," she said. "I ain't sorry: I'm mad, and I've got to cry it out."

"Well," said Israel, returning to his potatoes, and slowly shaking his head, "women-folks air the beateree. I don't know nothing about 'em, and I'm five an' sixty year old come Friday. Lordy! there ain't no riddles nor Chinese puzzle-rings to compare with 'em. I've hed a wife, an' lost a wife, praise the Lord! but I never was sure o' her even. I wouldn't no more try it agin than I'd slip down into a bee-tree; for there's full as much stings as honey to 'em, and, take an everidge, I guess there's more."

Whether or not the parson's silent ideas coincided with those Israel expressed is not for the ignorant chronicler to say; but it is certain that his candid and generous soul was so far moved by Mab's tirade, however he denied and defied it during its delivery, that the next day he resolved to call in a council of his neighboring brethren to discuss the matter, and indorse or reprobate the action of his own church.

So he wrote to the Rev. Ami Dobbins of Dorset, and the Rev. Samuel Jehoram Hill of Bassington, better known as Father Hill; and, in compliance with his request, they repaired to Bassett, and investigated the matter. Being advised of the pastor, who had had his experiences, they went to Mrs. Flint's during school-hours; and Mabel had no chance to pour out her soul before them. They encountered only a pale, depressed, weak woman, who was frightened out of what little heart was left her by past trials, when these two august personages came into her presence, and with severe countenances began their catechism of her life with Deacon Flint. As in the case of many another woman, her terror, her humiliation, and a lingering desire to shield her husband from his own misdeeds, all conspired against her. Her testimony was tearful, confused, and contradictory; though through it all she did feebly insist on her own sufferings, and depicted them in honest colors. From her they went to the deacon, whom they found resigned, pious and loftily superior to common things; then he was a man, and a deacon! Is it to be wondered at that their letter to the church at Bassett was in the deacon's favor? They did indeed own that Mrs. Flint had "peculiar trials," but went on to say,—

"Nevertheless, she cannot be fully justified, but has departed from meekness and a Christian spirit . . . particularly in indulging angry and passionate expressions, tending to provoke and irritate her husband; and, however unjustifiable his conduct may be, that doth not exculpate her. We think that it would be proper and suitable for her to make suitable reflections, acknowledge she hath given her brethren and sisters of the church occasion of stumbling and to be dissatisfied; and, upon her manifesting a becoming spirit of meekness and love, we think they ought to restore her; but if she should refuse to make such reflections, they cannot consistently receive her."

And with a few added remarks on the perplexity of the case, and advising the church to call the ecclesiastical council, the Rev. Ami Dobbins and Father Hill retired for the present.

But Bassett was not content. Weeks passed, and no act of confession or contrition came from this poor old offender. To tell the truth, Mabel stood behind her now, afire with honest rage at the way she had been put upon.

"You sha'n't do it, aunty!" she said, with all her native vehemence.

"You confess! I like that! It is that old hypocrite's place to confess. He drove you out, now when you get down to it; and he hain't asked you to come back, that I've heard tell. I'd let him and the church, and Bassett too, go to thunder, if they're a mind to. If you make 'suitable reflections,' they'll reflect on old Flint and Bassett church-members. Dear me! I know one thing: I'd rather be an old maid ten times over than married to that man."

A faint smile crept over the old woman's pale face. From her high pillows she had a good outlook, and more than once she had seen an interview by the little gate that did not augur long maidenhood for Mab.

"Well, Mabel, if that's your say, why, it behooves you to be real cautious, though I don't know as Sam Pratt's brother could be anyways other than good."

Mab blushed like a Provence rose, but said nothing, yet day after day kept hardening her aunt's heart as well as she knew how; and Parson Roberts, receiving no "reflections" from the offender, and having great faith in Father Hill's power of persuasion, invited him to come again by himself, and hold a conversation with sister Flint on the subject of her trials and her contumacy.

Father Hill was a quaint, gentle, sweet-natured old man, steeped, however, in the prejudices of his time and his faith. He, too, went to the house mailed with his fixed assurance of ecclesiastical dignity and marital supremacy. Sympathy, pity, comprehension of her side of the case, would have disarmed Mrs. Flint completely; she would have sobbed, confessed, laid her hand on her mouth, and her mouth in the dust, and been ready to own herself the chief of sinners: but to be placed in the wrong from the first, reproved, admonished, and treated as an impenitent and hardened culprit, made it easier for her weak nature to accept the situation than to defy or to deny it. Nothing Father Hill could say moved her, but her dull and feeble obstinacy stirred his tender heart to its depths: he felt a despair of human means and a yearning tenderness that could find no outlet but in prayer. He fell on his knees before the chair in which he had been sitting, and lifted his earnest face to heaven.

"O dear Lord and Master," he said, speaking even as a man unto his friend, "thou hast borne our griefs, and carried our sorrows. Thou knowest by heart every pain and woe that we feel. A stranger cannot intermeddle, but, O thou Hope of Israel, why shouldst thou be as a stranger that passeth by, and a wayfaring man that tarrieth but a night, in this dwelling of thy handmaid? Dear Lord, it is not in man that walketh to direct his own steps, how much less the steps of others! Come thou in the might of thy great gentleness and thine all-knowing sympathy and love, and show this child of thine the right way, saying, 'Walk ye in it.' Thou knowest every sorrow she has passed through, every bitter draught she has drunk, every sin she has been led into: yea, when she said there was no comforter, thine eye pitied and thine arm waited to save her, though the eye of flesh saw it not. Come now, and place beneath her weary heart and failing flesh the everlasting arms of thy overflowing love and care; give her peace and rest; give her an understanding heart; above all, with thy love and pity redeem her, as thou didst the elder Israel, and bring her with tender leading and divine affection, not only into thy fold on earth, but to the general assembly and church of the first-born in heaven. And to thee shall be praise and love and glory forever. Amen."

When he arose, his old face fair with the shining of the mount from whence he came down, the poor woman, who had dropped her head on her hand, lifted it, and tried to thank him; but streaming tears choked her, and behind the door into the shed a stifled sob betrayed some hidden auditor.

"Farewell!" said Father Hill, and with a look of heavenly benignity went out from the house. His deep and earnest piety had got the better of his dogmas; and, so strange is human nature, he was a little ashamed of it. But on his departing steps the shed-door opened, and Mab came in, her face all washed with tears.

"*That* man's got religion," she said decisively. "I never heerd a mortal creature pray like that: seemed as though he see right into glory, and talked face to face with the Lord. If that's bein' pious, I wish I was as pious as fury myself."

"He's a good man," sobbed Mrs. Flint; "one of the Lord's an'inted, I make no doubt. And, Mabel, I don't know but what I have did wrong. I ain't noways heavenly-minded like him: mabbe I had ought to have put up with every thing."

"No, you hadn't: that ain't so. But if it's goin' to make you easier, aunty, to 'make reflections,' as old Parson Roberts says, why, make 'em: only don't tell no lies to the church because you've got into a heavenly mood all to once. Folks that ain't just to themselves don't never get justice elsewheres, now I tell you."

Father Hill, despairing of having impressed Mrs. Flint, had cast the matter into his Master's hands, and from his study in Bassington sent a letter to Parson Roberts, running thus:—

"Rev'd and dear Brother,—I have had Opportunity with Mrs. Flint, and find that she conceived her leaving the Deacon was a real duty at that time; that her Recovery under Providence turned upon it; that she did not then foresee the Consequences that such a step would issue in her final Separation. . . . She stands ready to reflect upon herself as far as she can be convinced she ought to do so, but thinks the fault is not on her Side as things are now.

"I feel unable to direct or advise further. The cause of Religion, the cause of the Christian Church, you are very sensible, is of more Consequence than the Honor or Pease of any individual. If such a settlement can be made as may secure Religion from suffering, it must be an object to be desired. . . . Sensible of the Embarrassments you and the church labor under, and desirous to contribute my mite, I use this Freedom.

"This from your affectionate Brother,

"Samuel J. Hill.

To Rev'd Mr. Roberts.

"To be communicated if you think expedient."

But, while the ministers were in this strait about their obstinate parishioner, the Lord had answered Father Hill, unknown to himself, while he was yet speaking. Moved, and indeed melted, by the love and sympathy that prayer showed, Mrs. Flint, no longer hindered by Mabel, prepared herself to write "proper reflections" to the church; but in doing so was also perpetually prompted by Mabel not to traitorously deny her own cause, or slip aside from the truth in a voluntary humility; and in due time the following confession was laid before that august body:—

"I, the subscriber, Sarepta Flint, a member of the church of Christ in Bassett, sensible that the Church are dissatisfied with me on account of the Separation that has taken place between Deacon Flint and myself, and that they are Apprehensive that I have not been innocent as to measures which have led to this unhappy Event, whereby Religion is wounded and the Pease of the Church disturbed, take this opportunity to publickly acknowledge myself a poor, imperfect Creture, and to own that under my Weak state of Body and weakness of mind, with which I was attended at one Time or another, I no doubt manifested on certain Occasions an unsuitable Temper of mind, said and Did things which under other Circumstances I should not have said or done. I am far from justifying myself in all my conduct. Particular I would reflect on myself for that Expresion in regard to swearing the Pease against Deacon Flint. . . . I ask the Forgivness of God and this church, and of all others who are aggrieved, and request the prayers of my Christian Brethren and Sisters that I henceforth conduct as a true and faithful Disciple of Christ, and adorn the Solem Vocation by which I am called.

"SAREPTA FLINT.

"P.S.—I stand ready also to return to my Husband as soon as a suitable Door opens for that Purpose."

Perhaps something in the self-respecting yet honest humility of this document touched the heart of Bassett church; or perhaps only their self-love and pride of place was soothed by it. Be that as it may, the confession was accepted; and Parson Roberts, with a valor and persistence that did him honor, insisted that Deacon Flint should go with him to inform his wife of her release from interdict, and also to open that "Door" of reconciliation to which she had so pathetically alluded. The parson's wig was fresh buckled, the deacon's cue new wound and tied, and their sabbath-day garments prim and speckless, as the next morning they opened the door of the old house where Sarepta Flint had taken refuge from her oppressor. A scene they little expected met their eyes. On the low bed, covered with its rough blue homespun spread, lay an evidently dying figure. A more "Solem Vocation" than life had called Deacon Flint's wife, and she was about to obey. Mindwell and Sam Pratt upheld her as she gasped for breath, and the two children clung together sobbing at her feet; while Mabel, with Joe Pratt's arm about her, and her face streaming with tears she did not feel, stood by the bedside gazing at her friend. Her face blazed as the deacon and Parson Roberts entered; but, roused by the click of the latch, Mrs. Flint opened her eyes, and looked at the youthful pair with a gentle smile. They had been the one bright outlook of her latter life, and to them she gave her last smile; for, as her eyes turned toward her husband, a cold terror filled them, the lids fell, her head drooped on Mindwell's shoulder, and with one long, shuddering sigh she escaped forever. The forgiveness of the church and the condescension of her husband came too late: she was already safe where the wicked cease from troubling, and the Consoler dries all mortal tears.

Deacon Flint stood like a stone. Did remorse trouble him? Was regret busy at his heart? Or did he feel a bitter and deep chagrin at the loss of so much income?

Mabel's tears ceased: she withdrew from Joe's arm, and went round to where Deacon Flint stood. "Are you proper pleased now?" she said in a low voice of concentred contempt and rage. "You've got her turned out of church, and into heaven. You won't never see her again,—no, never! not to all eternity. But you've killed her as good as if you took an axe to her. You can take that hum to sleep on."

"Hush!" said Parson Roberts, with all the dignity a little man could give to his voice and manner. "When the Lord giveth quietness, who, then, can make trouble?"

But even as he spoke, Joe Pratt—his face full of black wrath—set his hand to the deacon's collar, and walked him summarily into the road. Mabel had spoken truth: never again did he see his wife's face, not even in the fair peace of death. Whether ever, in that far world of souls, they met again, is perhaps doubtful: let us pray not. Mrs. Flint's married experience was over in this world a hundred years ago, and in the next "they neither marry nor are given in marriage."

HOW CELIA CHANGED HER MIND

※※※※※

"IF THERE'S anything on the face of the earth I *do* hate, it's an old maid!"

Mrs. Stearns looked up from her sewing in astonishment.

"Why, Miss Celia!"

"Oh, yes! I know it. I'm one myself, but all the same, I hate 'em worse than p'ison. They ain't nothing nor nobody; they're cumberers of the ground." And Celia Barnes laid down her scissors with a bang, as if she might be Atropos herself, ready to cut the thread of life for all the despised class of which she was a notable member.

The minister's wife was genuinely surprised at this outburst; she herself had been well along in life before she married, and though she had been fairly happy in the uncertain relationship to which she had attained, she was, on the whole, inclined to agree with St. Paul, that the woman who did not marry "doeth better." "I don't agree with you, Miss Celia," she said gently. "Many, indeed, most of my best friends are maiden ladies, and I respect and love them just as much as if they were married women."

"Well, I don't. A woman that's married is somebody; she's got a place in the world; she ain't everybody's tag; folks don't say, 'Oh, it's nobody but that old maid Celye Varnes;' it's 'Mis' Price,' and 'Mis' Simms,' or 'Thomas Smith's wife,' as though you was somebody. I don't know how 't is elsewheres, but here in Bassett you might as well be a dog as an old maid. I allow it might be better if they all had means or eddication: money's 'a dreadful good thing to have in the house,' as I see in a book once, and learning is sort of comp'ny to you if you're lonesome; but then lonesome you be, and you've got to be, if you're an old maid, and it can't be helped noway."

Mrs. Stearns smiled a little sadly, thinking that even married life had its own loneliness when your husband was shut up in his study, or gone off on a long drive to see some sick parishioner or conduct a neighborhood prayer-meeting, or even when he was the other side of the fireplace absorbed in a religious paper or a New York daily, or meditating on his next sermon, while the silent wife sat unnoticed at her mending or knitting. "But married women have more troubles and responsibilities than the unmarried, Miss Celia," she said. "You have no children to bring up and be anxious about, no daily dread of not doing your duty by the family whom you preside over, and no fear of the supplies giving out that are really needed. Nobody but your own self to look out for."

"That's jest it," snapped Celia, laying down the boy's coat she was sewing with a vicious jerk of her thread. "There 't is! Nobody to home to care if you live or die; nobody to peek out of the winder to see if you're comin', or to make a mess of gruel or a cup of tea for you, or to throw ye a feelin' word if you're sick nigh unto death. And old maids is just as li'ble to up and die as them that's married. And as to responsibility, I ain't afraid to tackle that. Never! I don't hold with them that cringe and crawl and are skeert at a shadder, and won't do a living thing that they had ought to do because they're 'afraid to take the responsibility.' Why, there's Mrs. Deacon Trimble, she durst n't so much as set up a prayer-meetin' for missions or the temp'rance cause, because 't was 'sech a reesponsibility to take the lead in them matters.' I suppose it's somethin' of a responsible chore to preach the gospel to the heathen, or grab a drinkin' feller by the scruff of his neck and haul him out of the horrible pit anyway, but if it's dooty it's got to be done, whether or no; and I ain't afraid of pitchin' into anything the Lord sets me to do!"

"Except being an old maid," said Mrs. Stearns.

Celia darted a sharp glance at her over her silver-rimmed spectacles, and pulled her needle through and through the seams of Willy's jacket with fresh vigor, while a thoughtful shadow came across her fine old face. Celia was a candid woman, for all her prejudices, a combination peculiarly characteristic of New England, for she was a typical Yankee. Presently she said abruptly, "I had n't thought on 't in that light." But then the minister opened the door, and the conversation stopped.

Parson Stearns was tired and hungry and cross, and his wife knew all that as soon as she saw his face. She had learned long ago that ministers, however good they may be, are still men; so to-day she had kept her husband's dinner warm in the under-oven, and had the kettle boiling to make him a cup of tea on the spot to assuage his irritation in the shortest and surest way; but though the odor of a savory stew and the cheerful warmth of the cooking-stove greeted him as he preceded her through the door into the kitchen, he snapped out, sharply enough for Celia to hear him through the half-closed door, "What do you have that old maid here for so often?"

"There!" said Celia to herself,—"there 't is! *He* don't look upon't as a dispensation, if she doos. Men-folks run the world, and they know it. There ain't one of the hull caboodle but what despises an onmarried woman! Well, 't ain't altogether my fault. I would n't marry them that I could; I could n't—not and be honest; and them that I would hev had did n't ask me. I don't know as I'm to blame, after all, when you look into 't."

And she went on sewing Willy's jacket, contrived with pains and skill out of an old coat of his father's, while Mrs. Stearns poured out her husband's tea in the kitchen, replenished his plate with stew, and cut for him more than one segment of the crisp, fresh apple-pie, and urged upon him the squares of new cheese that legitimately accompany this deleterious viand of the race and country, the sempiternal, insistent, flagrant, and alas! also fragrant pie.

Celia Barnes was the tailoress of the little scattered country town of Bassett. Early left an orphan, without near relatives or money, she had received the scantiest measure of education that our town authorities deal to the pauper children of such organizations. She was ten years old when her mother, a widow for almost all those ten years, left her to the tender mercies of the selectmen of Bassett. The selectmen of our country towns are almost irresponsible governors of their petty spheres, and gratify the instinct of oligarchy peculiar to, and conservative of, the human race. Men must be governed and tyrannized over,—it is an inborn necessity of their nature; and while a republic is a beautiful theory, eminently fitted for a race who are "non Angli, sed Angeli," it has in practice the effect of producing more than Russian tyranny, but on smaller scales and in far and scattered localities. Nowhere are there more despots than among village selectmen in New England. Those who have wrestled with their absolute monarchism in behalf of some charity that might abstract a few of the almighty dollars made out of poverty and distress from their official pockets know how positive and dogmatic is their use of power—*experto crede*.[1] The Bassett "first selectman" promptly bound out little Celia Barnes to a hard, imperious woman, who made a white slave of the child, and only dealt out to her the smallest measure of schooling demanded by law, because the good old minister, Father Perkins, interfered in the child's behalf.

As she was strong and hardy and resolute, Celia lived through her bondage, and at the "free" age of eighteen apprenticed herself to old Miss Polly Mariner, the Bassett tailoress, and being deft with her fingers and quick of brain, soon outran her teacher, and when Polly died, succeeded to her business.

She was a bright girl, not particularly noticeable among others, for she had none of that delicate flower-like New England beauty which is so peculiar, so charming, and so evanescent; her features were tolerably regular, her forehead broad and calm, her gray eyes keen and perceptive, and she had abundant hair of an uncertain brown; but forty other girls in Bassett might have been described in the same way; Celia's face was one to improve with age; its strong sense, capacity for humor, fine outlines of a rugged sort, were always more the style of fifty than fifteen, and what she said of herself was true.

She had been asked to marry an old farmer with five uproarious boys, a man notorious in East Bassett for his stinginess and bad temper, and she had promptly declined the offer. Once more fate had given her a chance. A young fellow of no character, poor, "shiftless," and given to cider as a beverage, had considered it a good idea to marry some one who would make a home for him and earn his living. Looking about him for a proper person to fill this pleasant situation, he pounced on Celia—and she returned the attention!

"Marry *you* ? I wonder you've got the sass to ask any decent girl to marry ye, Alfred Hatch! What be you good for, anyway? I don't know what under the canopy the Lord spares you for,—only He doos let the tares grow amongst the wheat, Scripter says, and I'm free to suppose He knows why, but I don't. No, *sir!* Ef you was the last man in the livin' universe I would n't tech ye with the tongs. If you'd got a speck of grit into you, you'd be ashamed to ask a woman to take ye in and support ye, for that's what it comes to. You go 'long! I can make my hands save my head so long as I hev the use of 'em, and I have n't no call to set up a private poor-house!"

So Alfred Hatch sneaked off, much like a cur that has sought to share the kennel of a mastiff, and been shortly and sharply convinced of his presumption.

Here ended Celia's "chances," as she phrased it. Young men were few in Bassett; the West had drawn them away with its subtle attraction of unknown possibilities, just as it does to-day, and Celia grew old in the service of those established matrons who always want clothes cut over for their children, carpet rags sewed, quilts quilted, and comfortables tacked. She was industrious and frugal, and in time laid up some money in the Dartford Savings' Bank; but she did not, like many spinsters, invest her hard-earned dollars in a small house. Often she was urged to do so, but her reasons were good for refusing.

"I should be so independent? Well, I'm as independent now as the law allows. I've got two good rooms to myself, south winders, stairs of my own and outside door, and some privileges. If I had a house there'd be taxes, and insurance, and cleanin' off snow come winter-time, and hoein' paths; and likely enough I should be so fur left to myself that I should set up a garden, and make my succotash cost a dollar a pint a-hirin' of a man to dig it up and hoe it down. Like enough, too, I should be gettin' flower seeds and things; I'm kinder fond of blows in the time of 'em. My old fish-geran'um is a sight of comfort to me as 't is, and there would be a bill of expense again. Then you can't noway build a house with only two rooms in't, it would be all outside; and you might as well try to heat the universe with a cookin'-stove as such a house. Besides, how lonesome I should be! It's forlorn enough to be an old maid anyway, but to have it sort of ground into you, as you may say, by livin' all alone in a hull house, that ain't necessary nor agreeable. Now, if I'm sick or sorry, I can just step down-stairs and have aunt Nabby to help or hearten me. Deacon Everts he did set to work one time to persuade me to buy a house; he said 't was a good thing to be able to give somebody shelter 't was poorer'n I was. Says I,

'Deacon, I've worked for my livin' ever sence I remember, and I know there 's no use in anybody bein' poorer than I be. I have n't no call to take any sech in and do for 'em. I give what I can to missions,—home ones,— and I'm willin', cheerfully willin', to do a day's work now and again for somebody that is strivin' with too heavy burdens; but as for keepin' free lodgin' and board, I sha'n't do it.' 'Well, well, well,' says he, kinder as if I was a fractious young one, and a-sawin' his fat hand up and down in the air till I wanted to slap him, 'just as you'd ruther, Celye,—just as you'd ruther. I don't mean to drive ye a mite, only, as Scripter says, "Provoke one another to love and good works."'

"That did rile me! Says I: 'Well, you've provoked me full enough, though I don't know as you've done it in the Scripter sense; and mabbe I should n't have got so fur provoked if I had n't have known that little red house your grandsir' lived and died in was throwed back on your hands just now, and advertised for sellin'. I see the "Mounting County Herald," Deacon Everts.' He shut up, I tell ye. But I sha'n't never buy no house so long as aunt Nabby lets me have her two south chambers, and use the back stairway and the north door continual."

So Miss Celia had kept on her way till now she was fifty, and to-day making over old clothes at the minister's. The minister's wife had, as we have seen, little romance or wild happiness in her life; it is not often the portion of country ministers' wives; and, moreover, she had two step-daughters who were girls of sixteen and twelve when she married their father. Katy was married herself now, this ten years, and doing her hard duty by an annual baby and a struggling parish in Dakota; but Rosabel, whose fine name had been the only legacy her dying mother left the day-old child she had scarce had time to kiss and christen before she went to take her own "new name" above, was now a girl of twenty-two, pretty, headstrong, and rebellious. Nature had endowed her with keen dark eyes, crisp dark curls, a long chin, and a very obstinate mouth, which only her red lips and white even teeth redeemed from ugliness; her bright color and her sense of fun made her attractive to young men wherever she encountered one of that rare species. Just now she was engaged in a serious flirtation with the station-master at Bassett Centre,—an impecunious youth of no special interest to other people and quite unable to maintain a wife. But out of the "strong necessity of loving," as it is called, and the want of young society or settled occupation, Rosa Stearns chose to fall in love with Amos Barker, and her father considered it a "fall" indeed. So, with the natural clumsiness of a man and a father, Parson Stearns set himself to prevent the matter, and began by forbidding Rosabel to see or speak or write to the youth in question, and thereby inspired in her mind a burning desire to do all three. Up to this time she had rather languidly amused herself by mild and gentle flirtations with him, such as looking at him sidewise in church on Sunday, meeting him accidentally on his way to and from the station, for she spent at least half her time at her aunt's in Bassett Centre, and had even taught the small school there during the last six months. She had also sent him her tintype, and his own was secreted in her bureau drawer. He had invited her to go with him to two sleigh-rides and one sugaring-off, and always came home with her from prayer-meeting and singing-school; but like a wise youth he had never yet proposed to marry her in due form, not so much because he was wise as because he was thoughtless and lazy; and while he enjoyed the society of a bright girl, and liked to dangle after the prettiest one in Bassett, and the minister's daughter too, he did not love work well enough to shoulder the responsibility of providing for another those material but necessary supplies that imply labor of an incessant sort.

Rosabel, in her first inconsiderate anger at her father's command, sat down and wrote a note to Amos, eminently calculated to call out his sympathy with her own wrath, and promptly mailed it as soon as it was written. It ran as follows:—

> DEAR FRIEND,—Pa has forbidden me to speak to you any more, or to correspond with you. I suppose I must submit so far; but he did not say I must return your picture [the parson had not an idea that she possessed that precious thing], so I shall keep it to remind me of the pleasant hours we have passed together.
> > "Fare thee well, and if forever,
> > Still forever fare thee well!"
> > Your true friend, ROSABEL STEARNS
> P.S.—I think pa is *horrid!*

So did Amos as he read this heart-rending missive, in which the postscript, according to the established sneer at woman's postscripts, carried the whole force of the epistle.

Now Amos had made a friend of Miss Celia by once telegraphing for her trunk, which she had lost on her way home from the only journey of her life, a trip to Boston, whither she had gone, on the strength of the one share of B.&A.R.R. stock she held, to spend the allotted three days granted to stockholders on their annual excursions, presumably to attend the annual meeting. Amos had put himself to the immense trouble of sending two messages for Miss Celia, and asked her nothing for the civility, so that ever after, in the fashion of solitary women, she held herself deeply in his debt. He knew that she was at work for Mrs. Stearns when he received Rosa's epistle, for he had just been over to Bassett on the train—there was but a mile to traverse—to get her to repair his Sunday coat, and not found her at home, but had no time to look her up at the parson's, as he must walk back to his station. Now he resolved to take his answer to Rosa to Miss Celia in the evening, and so be sure that his abused sweetheart received it, for he had read too many dime novels to doubt that her tyrannic father would intercept their letters, and drive them both to madness and despair. That well-meaning but rather dull divine never would have thought of such a thing; he was a puffy, absent-minded, fat little man, with a weak, squeaky voice, and a sudden temper that blazed up like a bunch of dry weeds at a passing spark, and went out at once in flattest ashes. It had been Mrs. Stearns's step-motherly interference that drove him into his harshness to Rosa. She meant well and he meant well, but we all know what good intentions with no further sequel of act are good for, and nobody did more of that "paving" than these two excellent but futile people.

Miss Celia was ready to do anything for Amos Barker, and she considered it little less than a mortal sin to stand in the way of any marriage that was really desired by two parties. That Amos was poor did not daunt her at all; she had the curious faith that possesses some women, that any man can be prosperous if he has the will so to be; and she had a high opinion of this youth, based on his civility to her. It may be said of men, as of elephants, that it is lucky they do not know their own power; for how many more women would become their worshipers and slaves than are so to-day if they knew the abject gratitude the average woman feels for the least attention, the smallest kindness, the faintest expression of affection or good will. We are all, like the Syrophenician woman,[2] glad and ready to eat of the crumbs which fall from the children's table, so great is our faith— in men.

Miss Celia took the note in her big basket over to the minister's the very next day after that on which we introduced her to our readers. She was perhaps more rejoiced to contravene that reverend gentleman's orders than if she had not heard his querulous and contemptuous remark about her through the crack of the door on the previous afternoon; and it was with a sense of joy that, after all, an old maid could do something, that she slipped the envelope into Rosa's hands, and told her to put it quickly into her pocket, the very first moment she found herself alone with that young woman.

Many a hasty word had Parson Stearns spoken in the suddenness of his petulant temper, but never one that bore direr fruit than that when he called Celia Barnes "that old maid."

For of course Amos and Rosabel found in her an ardent friend. They had the instinct of distressed lovers to cajole her with all their confidences, caresses, and eager gratitude, and for once she felt herself dear and of importance. Amos consulted her on his plans for the future, which of course pointed westward, where he had a brother editing and owning a newspaper. This brother had before offered him a place in his office, but Amos had liked better the easy work of a station-master in a tiny village. Now his ambition was aroused, for the time at least. He wanted to make a home for Rosabel, but, alack! he had not one cent to pay their united expenses to Peoria, and a lion stood in the way. Here again Celia stepped in: she had some money laid up; she would lend it to them.

I do not say that at this stage she had no misgivings, but even these were set at rest by a conversation she had with Mrs. Stearns some six weeks after the day on which Celia had so fully expressed her scorn of spinsters. She was there again to tack a comfortable for Rosabel's bed, and bethought herself that it was a good time to feel her way a little concerning Mrs. Stearns's opinion of things.

"They do say," she remarked, stopping to snip off her thread and twist the end of it through her needle's eye, "that your Rosy don't go with Amos Barker no more. Is that so?"

"Yes," said Mrs. Stearns, with a half sigh. "Husband was rather prompt about it; he don't think Amos Barker ever'll amount to much, and he thinks his people are not just what they should be. You know his father never was very much of a man, and his grandfather is a real old reprobate. Husband says he never knew anything but crows come out of a crow's nest, and so he told Rosa to break acquaintance with him."

"Who does he like to hev come to see her?" asked Celia, with a grim set of her lips, stabbing her needle fiercely through the unoffending calico.

Mrs. Stearns laughed rather feebly. "I don't think he has anybody on his mind, Miss Celia. I don't think there are any young men in Bassett. I dare say Rosa will never marry. I wish she would, for she is n't happy here, and I can't do much to help it, with all my cares."

"And you can't feel for her as though she was your own, if you try ever so," confidently asserted Celia.

"No, I suppose not. I try to do my duty by her, and I am sorry for her; but I know all the time an own mother would understand her better and make it easier for her. Mr. Stearns is peculiar, and men don't know just how to manage girls."

It was a cautious admission, but Miss Celia had sharp eyes, and knew very well that Rosabel neither loved nor respected her father, and that they were now on terms of real if unavowed hostility.

"Well," said she, "I don' know but you will have to have one of them onpleasant creturs, an old maid, in your fam'ly. I declare for't, I'd hold a Thanksgiving Day all to myself ef I'd escaped that marcy."

"You may not always think so, Celia."

"I don't know what'll change me. 'T will be something I don't look forrard to now," answered Celia obstinately.

Mrs. Stearns sighed. "I hope Rosa will do nothing worse than to live unmarried," she said; but she could not help wishing silently that some worthy man would carry the perverse and annoying girl out of the parsonage for good.

After this Celia felt a certain freedom to help Rosabel; she encouraged the lovers to meet at her house, helped plan their elopement, sewed for the girl, and at last went with them as far as Brimfield when they stole away one evening, saw them safely married at the Methodist parsonage there, and bidding them good-speed, returned to Bassett Centre on the midnight train, and walked over to her own dwelling in the full moonshine of the October night, quite fearless and entirely exultant.

But she was not to come off unscathed. There was a scene of wild commotion at the parsonage next day, when Rosa's letter, modeled on that of the last novel heroine she had become acquainted with, was found on her bureau, as per novel aforesaid.

With her natural thoughtlessness she assured her parents that she "fled not uncompanioned," that her "kind and all but maternal friend, Miss Celia Barnes, would accompany her to the altar, and give her support and her countenance to the solemn ceremony that should make Rosabel Stearns the blessed wife of Amos Barker!"

It was all the minister could do not to swear as he read this astounding letter. His flabby face grew purple; his fat, sallow hands shook with rage; he dared not speak, he only sputtered, for he knew that profane and unbecoming words would surely leap from his tongue if he set it free; but he must—he really must—do or say something! So he clapped on his old hat, and with coat tails flying in the breeze, and rage in every step, set out to find Celia Barnes; and find her he did.

It would be unpleasant, and it is needless, to depict this encounter; language both unjust and unsavory smote the air and reverberated along the highway, for he met the spinster on her road to an engagement at Deacon Stiles's. Suffice it to say that both freed their minds with great enlargement of opinion, and the parson wound up with,—

"And I never want to see you again inside of my house, you confounded old maid!"

"There! that's it!" retorted Celia. "Ef I was n't an old maid, you would n't no more have darst to 'a' talked to me this way than nothin'. Ef I'd had a man to stand up to ye you'd have been dumber'n Balaam's ass a great sight,—afore it seen the angel, I mean. I swow to man, I b'lieve I'd marry a hitchin'-post if 't was big enough to trounce ye. You great lummox, if I could knock ye over you would n't peep nor mutter agin, if I be a woman!"

And with a burst of furious tears that asserted her womanhood Miss

Celia went her way. Her hands were clinched under her blanket-shawl, her eyes red with angry rain, and as she walked on she soliloquized aloud:—

"I declare for 't, I b'lieve I'd marry the Old Boy himself if he'd ask me. I'm sicker'n ever of bein' an old maid!"

"Be ye?" queried a voice at her elbow. "P'r'aps, then, you might hear to me if I was to speak my mind, Celye."

Celia jumped. As she said afterward, "I vum I thought 't was the Enemy, for certain; and to think 't was only Deacon Everts!"

"Mercy me!" she said now; "is 't you, deacon?"

"Yes, it's me; and I think 't is a real providence I come up behind ye just in the nick of time. I've sold my farm only last week, and I've come to live on the street in that old red house of grand-sir's, that you mistrusted once I wanted you to buy. I'm real lonesome sence I lost my partner" (he meant his wife), "and I've been a-hangin' on by the edges the past two year; hired help is worse than nothing onto a farm, and hard to get at that; so I sold out, and I'm a-movin' yet, but the old house looks forlorn enough, and I was intendin' to look about for a second; so if you'll have me, Celye, here I be."

Celia looked at him sharply; he was an apple-faced little man, with shrewd, twinkling eyes, a hard, dull red still lingering on his round cheeks in spite of the deep wrinkles about his pursed-up lips and around his eye-lids; his mouth gave him a consequential and self-important air, to which the short stubbly hair, brushed up "like a blaze" above his forehead, added; and his old blue coat with brass buttons, his homespun trousers, the old-fashioned aspect of his unbleached cotton shirt, all attested his frugality. Indeed, everybody knew that Deacon Everts was "near," and also that he had plenty of money, that is to say, far more than he could spend. He had no children, no near relations; his first wife had died two years since, after long invalidism, and all her relations had moved far west. All this Celia knew and now recalled; her wrath against Parson Stearns was yet fresh and vivid; she remembered that Simeon Everts was senior deacon of the church, and had it in his power to make the minister extremely uncom-fortable if he chose. I have never said Celia was a very good woman; her religion was of the dormant type not uncommon nowadays; she kept up its observances properly, and said her prayers every day, bestowed a part of her savings on each church collection, and was rated as a church-member "in good and regular standing;" but the vital transforming power of that Christianity which means to "love the Lord thy God with all thy heart, and mind, and soul, and strength, and thy neighbor as thyself," had no more entered into her soul than it had into Deacon Everts's; and while she would have honestly admitted that revenge was a very wrong sentiment, and entirely improper for any other person to cherish, she felt that she did well to be angry with Parson Stearns, and had a perfect right to "pay him off" in any way she could.

Now here was her opportunity. If she said "Yes" to Deacon Everts, he would no doubt take her part. Her objections to housekeeping were set aside by the fact that the house-owner himself would have to do those heavy labors about the house which she must otherwise have hired a man to do; and the cooking and the indoor work for two people could not be so hard as to sew from house to house for her daily bread. In short, her mind was slowly turning favorably toward this sudden project, but she did not want this wooer to be too sure; so she said: "W-e-ll, 't is a life sentence, as you may say, deacon, and I want to think on't a spell. Let's see,—to-day's Tuesday; I'll let ye know Thursday night, after prayer-meetin'."

"Well," answered the deacon.

Blessed Yankee monosyllable that means so much and so little; that has such shades of phrase and intention in its myriad inflections; that is "yes," or "no," or "perhaps," just as you accent it; that is at once preface and peroration, evasion and definition! What would all New England speech be without "well"? Even as salt without any savor, or pepper with no pungency.

Now it meant to Miss Celia assent to her proposition; and in accordance the deacon escorted her home from meeting Thursday night, and received for reward a consenting answer. This was no love affair, but a matter of mere business. Deacon Everts needed a housekeeper, and did not want to pay out wages for one; and Miss Celia's position she expressed herself as she put out her tallow candle on that memorable night, and breathed out on the darkness the audible aspiration, "Thank goodness, I sha'n't hev to die an old maid!"

There was no touch of sanctifying love or consoling affection, or even friendly comradeship, in this arrangement; it was as truly a *marriage de convenance* as was ever contracted in Paris itself, and when the wedding day came, a short month afterward, the sourest aspect of November skies threatening a drenching pour, the dead and sodden leaves that strewed the earth, the wailing northeast wind, even the draggled and bony old horse behind which they jogged over to Bassett Centre, seemed fit accompaniments to the degraded ceremony performed by a justice of the peace, who concluded this merely legal compact, for Miss Celia stoutly refused to be married by Parson Stearns; she would not be accessory to putting one dollar in his pocket, even as her own wedding fee. So she went home to the little red house on Bassett Street, and begun her married life by scrubbing the dust and dirt of years from the kitchen table, making biscuit for tea, washing up the dishes, and at last falling asleep during the deacon's long nasal prayer, wherein he wandered to the ends of the earth, and prayed fervently for the heathen, piteously unconscious that he was little better than a heathen himself.

It did not take many weeks to discover to Celia what is meant by "the curse of a granted prayer." She could not at first accept the situation at all; she was accustomed to enough food, if it was plain and simple, when she herself provided it; but now it was hard to get such viands as would satisfy a healthy appetite.

"You've used a sight of pork, Celye," the deacon would remonstrate. "My first never cooked half what you do. We shall come to want certain, if you're so free-handed."

"Well, Mr. Everts, there was n't a mite left to set by. We eat it all, and I did n't have no more'n I wanted, if you did."

"We must mortify the flesh, Celye. It's hull-some to get up from your victuals hungry. Ye know what Scripter says, 'Jeshurun waxed fat an' kicked.'"

"Well, I ain't Jeshurun, but I expect I shall be more likely to kick if I don't have enough to eat, when it's only pork 'n' potatoes."

"My first used to say them was the best, for steady victuals, of anything, and she never used but two codfish and two quarts of m'lasses the year round; and as for butter, she was real sparin'; she'd fry our bread along with the salt pork, and 't was just as good."

"Look here!" snapped Celia. "I don't want to hear no more about your 'first.' I'm ready to say I wish 't she'd ha' been your last too."

"Well, well, well! this is onseemly contention, Celye," sputtered the alarmed deacon. "Le' 's dwell together in unity so fur as we can, Mis' Everts. I have n't no intention to starve ye, none whatever. I only want to be keerful, so as we sha'n't have to fetch up in the poor-us."

"No need to have a poor-house to home," muttered Celia.

But this is only a mild specimen of poor Celia's life as a married woman. She did not find the honor and glory of "Mrs." before her name a compensation for the thousand evils that she "knew not of" when she fled to them as a desirable change from her single blessedness. Deacon Everts entirely refused to enter into any of her devices against Parson Stearns; he did not care a penny about Celia's wrongs; and he knew very well that no other man than dreamy, unpractical Mr. Stearns, who eked out his minute pittance by writing school-books of a primary sort, would put up with four hundred dollars a year from his parish; yet that was all Bassett people would pay. If they must have the gospel, they must have it at the lowest living rates, and everybody would not assent to that.

So Celia found her revenge no more feasible after her marriage than before, and, gradually absorbed in her own wrongs and sufferings, her desire to reward Mr. Stearns in kind for his treatment of her vanished; she thought less of his futile wrath and more of her present distresses every day.

For Celia, like everybody who profanes the sacrament of marriage, was beginning to suffer the consequences of her misstep. As her husband's mean, querulous, loveless character unveiled itself in the terrible intimacy of constant and inevitable companionship, she began to look woefully back to the freedom and peace of her maiden days. She learned that a husband is by no means his wife's defender always, not even against reviling tongues. It did not suit Deacon Everts to quarrel with any one, whatever they said to him, or of him and his; he "did n't want no enemies," and Celia bitterly felt that she must fight her own battles; she had not even an ally in her husband. She became not only defiant, but also depressed; the consciousness of a vital and life-long mistake is not productive of cheer or content; and now, admitted into the free-masonry of married women, she discovered how few among them were more than household drudges, the servants of their families, worked to the verge of exhaustion, and neither thanked nor rewarded for their pains. She saw here a woman whose children were careless of, and ungrateful to her, and her husband coldly indifferent; there was one on whom the man she had married wreaked all his fiendish temper in daily small injuries, little vexatious acts, petty tyrannies, a "street-angel, house-devil" of a man, of all sorts the most hateful. There were many whose lives had no other outlook than hard work until the end should come, who rose up to labor and lay down in sleepless exhaustion, and some whose days were a constant terror to them from the intemperate brutes to whom they had intrusted their happiness, and indeed their whole existence.

It was no worse with Celia than with most of her sex in Bassett; here and there, there were of course exceptions, but so rare as to be shining examples and objects of envy. Then, too, after two years, there came forlorn accounts of poor Rosabel's situation at the west. Amos Barker had done his best at first to make his wife comfortable, but change of place or new motives do not at once, if ever, transform an indolent man into an active and efficient one. He found work in his brother's office, but it was the hard work of collecting bills all about the country; the roads were bad, the weather as fluctuating as weather always is, the climate did not agree with him, and he got woefully tired of driving about from dawn till after dark, to dun unwilling debtors. Rosa had chills and fever and babies with persistent alacrity; she had indeed enough to eat, with no appetite, and a house, with no strength to keep it. She grew untidy, listless, hysterical; and her father, getting worried by her despondent and infrequent letters, actually so far roused himself as to sell his horse, and with this sacrificial money betook himself to Mound Village, where he found Rosabel with two babies in her arms, dust an inch deep on all her possessions, nothing but pork, potatoes, and corn bread in the pantry, and a slatternly negress washing some clothes in a kitchen that made the parson shudder.

The little man's heart was bigger than his soul. He put his arms about Rosa and the dingy babies, and forgave her all; but he had to say, even while he held them closely and fondly to his breast, "Oh, Rosy, I told you what would happen if you married that fellow."

Of course Rosa resented the speech, for, after all, she had loved Amos; perhaps could love him still if the poverty and malaria and babies could have all been eliminated from her daily life.

Fortunately the parson's horse had sold well, for it was strong and young, and the rack of venerable bones with which he replaced it was bought very cheap at a farmer's auction, so he had money enough to carry Rosa and the two children home to Bassett, where two months after she added another feeble, howling cipher to the miserable sum of humanity.

Miss—no, Mrs.—Celia's conscience stung her to the quick when she encountered this ghastly wreck of pretty Rosabel Stearns, now called Mrs. Barker. She remembered with deep regret how she had given aid and comfort to the girl who had defied and disobeyed parental counsel and authority, and so brought on herself all this misery. She fancied that Parson Stearns glared at her with eyes of bitter accusation and reproach, and not improbably he did, for beside his pity and affection for his daughter, it was no slight burden to take into his house a feeble woman with two children helpless as babies, and to look forward to the expense and anxiety of another soon to come. And Mrs. Stearns had never loved Rosa well enough to be complacent at this addition to her family cares. She gave the parson no sympathy. It would have been her way to let Rosabel lie on the bed she had made, and die there if need be. But the poor worn-out creature died at home, after all, and the third baby lay on its mother's breast in her coffin: they had gone together.

Celia felt almost like a murderess when she heard that Rosabel Barker was dead. She did not reflect that in all human probability the girl would have married Amos if she, Celia, had refused to help or encourage her. It began to be an importunate question in our friend's mind whether she herself had not made a mistake too; whether the phrase "single blessedness" was not an expression of a vital truth rather than a scoff. Celia was changing her mind no doubt, surely if slowly.

Meantime Deacon Everts did not find all the satisfaction with his "second" that he had anticipated. Celia had a will of her own, quite undisciplined, and it was too often asserted to suit her lord and master. Secretly he planned devices to circumvent her purposes, and sometimes succeeded. In prayer-meeting and in Sunday-school the idea haunted him; his malice lay down and rose up with him. Even when he propounded to his Bible class the important question, "How fur be the heathen *ree-*sponsible for what they dun know?" and asked them "to ponder on 't through the comin' week," he chuckled inwardly at the thought that Celia could not evade *her* responsibility; she knew enough, and would be judged accordingly: the deacon was not a merciful man.

At last he hit upon that great legal engine whereby men do inflict the last deadly kick upon their wives: he would remodel his will. Yes, he would leave those gathered thousands to foreign missions; he would leave behind him the indisputable testimony and taunt that he considered the wife of his bosom less than the savages and heathen afar off. He forgot conveniently that the man "who provideth not for his own household hath denied the faith, and is worse than an infidel." And in his delight of revenge he also forgot that the law of the land provides for a man's wife and children in spite of his wicked will. Nor did he remember that his life-insurance policy for five thousand dollars was made out in his wife's name, simply as his wife, her own name not being specified. He had paid the premium always from his "first's" small annual income, and agreed that it should be written for her benefit, but he supposed that at her death it had reverted to him. He forgot that he still had a wife when he mentioned that policy in his assets recorded in the will, and to save money he drew that evil document up himself, and had it signed down at "the store" by three witnesses.

Celia had borne her self-imposed yoke for four years, when it was suddenly broken. A late crop of grass was to be mowed in mid-July on the meadow which appertained to the old house, and the deacon, now some seventy years old, to save hiring help, determined to do it by himself. The grass was heavy and over-ripe, the day extremely hot and breathless, and the grim Mower of Man trod side by side with Simeon Everts, and laid him too, all along by the rough heads of timothy and the purpled feather-tops of the blue-grass. He did not come home at noon or at night, and when Celia went down to the lot to call him she heard no summons of hers; he had answered a call far more imperative and final.

After the funeral Celia found his will pushed back in the deep drawer of an old secretary, where he kept his one quill pen, a bottle of dried ink, a lump of chalk, some rat-poison, and various other odds and ends.

She was indignant enough at its tenor; but it was easily broken, and she not only had her "thirds," but the life policy reverted to her also, as it was made out to Simeon Everts's wife, and surely she had occupied that position for four wretched years. Then, also, she had a right to her support for one year out of the estate, and the use of the house for that time.

Oh, how sweet was her freedom! With her characteristic honesty she refused to put on mourning, and even went to the funeral in her usual gray

Sunday gown and bonnet. "I won't lie, anyhow!" she answered to Mrs. Stiles's remonstrance. "I ain't a mite sorry nor mournful. I could ha' wished he'd had time to repent of his sins, but sence the Lord saw fit to cut him short, I don't feel to rebel ag'inst it. I wish 't I'd never married him, that's all!"

"But, Celye, you got a good livin'."

"I earned it."

"And he's left ye with means too."

"He done his best not to. I don't owe him nothing for that; and I earned that too,—the hull on 't. It's poor pay for what I've lived through; and I'm a'most a mind to call it the wages of sin, for I done wrong, ondeniably wrong, in marryin' of him; but the Lord knows I've repented, and said my lesson, if I did get it by the hardest."

Yet all Bassett opened eyes and mouth both when on the next Thanksgiving Day Celia invited every old maid in town—seven all told— to take dinner with her. Never before had she celebrated this old New England day of solemn revel. A woman living in two small rooms could not "keep the feast," and rarely had she been asked to any family conclave. We Yankees are conservative at Thanksgiving if nowhere else, and like to gather our own people only about the family hearth; so Celia had but once or twice shared the turkeys of her more fortunate neighbors.

Now she called in Nabby Hyde and Sarah Gillett, Ann Smith, Celestia Potter, Delia Hills, Sophronia Ann Jenkins and her sister Adelia Ann, ancient twins, who lived together on next to nothing, and were happy.

Celia bloomed at the head of the board, not with beauty, but with gratification. "Well," she said, as soon as they were seated, "I sent for ye all to come because I wanted to have a good time, for one thing, and because it seems as though I'd ought to take back all the sassy and disagreeable things I used to be forever flingin' at old maids. 'I spoke in my haste,' as Scripter says, and also in my ignorance, I'm free to confess. I feel as though I could keep Thanksgivin' to-day with my hull soul. I'm so thankful to be an old maid ag'in!"

"I thought you was a widder," snapped Sally Gillett.

Celia flung a glance of wrath at her, but scorned to reply.

"And I'm thankful too that I'm spared to help ondo somethin' done in that ignorance. I've got means, and, as I've said before, I earned 'em. I don't feel noway obleeged to him for 'em; he did n't mean it. But now I can I'm goin' to adopt Rosy Barker's two children, and fetch 'em up to be dyed-in-the-wool old maids; and every year, so long as I live, I'm goin' to keep an old maids' Thanksgivin' for a kind of a burnt-offering, sech as the Bible tells about, for I've changed my mind clear down to the bottom, and I go the hull figure with the 'postle Paul when he speaks about the onmarried, 'It is better if she so abide.' Now let's go to work at the victuals."

MISS LUCINDA

BUT THAT Solomon is out of fashion, I should quote him here and now, to the effect that there is a time for all things; but Solomon is obsolete, and never—no, never—will I dare to quote a dead language, "for raisons I have," as the exiles of Erin say. Yet, in spite of Solomon and Horace, I may express my own less concise opinion, that even in hard times, and dull times, and war times, there is yet a little time to laugh, a brief hour to smile and love and pity; just as through this dreary easterly storm, bringing clouds and rain, sobbing against casement and door with the inarticulate wail of tempests, there comes now and then the soft shine of a sun behind it all, a fleeting glitter, an evanescent aspect of what has been.

But if I apologize for a story that is nowise tragic, nor fitted to "the fashion of these times," possibly somebody will say at its end that I should also have apologized for its subject, since it is as easy for an author to treat his readers to high themes as vulgar ones, and velvet can be thrown into a portrait as cheaply as calico; but of this apology I wash my hands. I believe nothing in place or circumstance makes romance. I have the same quick sympathy for Biddy's sorrows with Patrick that I have for the Empress of France and her august but rather grim lord and master. I think words are often no harder to bear than "a blue bating;" and I have a reverence for poor old maids as great as for the nine Muses. Commonplace people are only commonplace from character, and no position affects that. So forgive me once more, patient reader, if I offer to you no tragedy in high life, no sentimental history of fashion and wealth, but only a little story about a woman who could not be a heroine.

151

Miss Lucinda

Miss Lucinda Jane Ann Manners was a lady of unknown age, who lived in a place I call Dalton, in a State of these Disuniting States, which I do not mention for good cause. I have already had so many unconscious personalities visited on my devoted head, that, but for lucidity, I should never mention persons or places, inconvenient as it would be. However, Miss Lucinda did live, and lived by the aid of "means," which in the vernacular is money. Not a great deal, it is true,—five thousand dollars at lawful interest, and a little wooden house, do not imply many luxuries even to a single woman; and it is also true that a little fine sewing taken in helped Miss Manners to provide herself with a few small indulgences otherwise beyond her reach. She had one or two idiosyncrasies, as they are politely called, that were her delight. Plenty of dish-towels were necessary to her peace of mind; without five pair of scissors she could not be happy; and Tricopherous[1] was essential to her well-being: indeed, she often said she would rather give up coffee than Tricopherous, for her hair was black and wiry and curly, and caps she abhorred; so that, of a winter's day, her head presented the most irrelevant and volatile aspect, each particular hair taking a twist on its own responsibility, and improvising a wild halo about her unsaintly face, unless subdued into propriety by the aforesaid fluid.

I said Miss Lucinda's face was unsaintly; I mean unlike ancient saints as depicted by contemporary artists: modern and private saints are after another fashion. I met one yesterday, whose green eyes, great nose, thick lips, and sallow wrinkles, under a bonnet of fifteen years' standing, further clothed upon by a scant merino cloak and cat-skin tippet, would have cut a sorry figure in the gallery of the Vatican or the Louvre, and put the tranquil Madonna of San Sisto into a state of stunning antithesis. But if St. Agnes or St. Catharine was half as good as my saint, I am glad of it.

No, there was nothing sublime and dolorous about Miss Manners. Her face was round, cheery, and slightly puckered, with two little black eyes sparkling and shining under dark brows, a nose she unblushingly called pug, and a big mouth, with eminently white and regular teeth, which she said were such a comfort, for they never ached, and never would to the end of time. Add to this physiognomy a small and rather spare figure, dressed in the cleanest of calicoes, always made in one style, and rigidly scorning hoops, without a symptom of a collar, in whose place (or it may be over which) she wore a white cambric handkerchief knotted about her throat, and the two ends brought into subjection by means of a little angular-headed gold pin, her sole ornament, and a relic of her old father's days of widowhood, when buttons were precarious tenures. So much for her aspect. Her character was even more quaint.

She was the daughter of a clergyman, one of the old school, the last whose breeches and knee-buckles adorned the profession, who never "outlived his usefulness," nor lost his godly simplicity. Parson Manners held rule over an obscure and quiet village in the wilds of Vermont, where hard-handed farmers wrestled with rocks and forests for their daily bread, and looked forward to heaven as a land of green pastures and still waters, where agriculture should be a pastime, and winter impossible. Heavy freshets from the mountains, that swelled their rushing brooks into annual torrents, and snow-drifts that covered five-rail fences a foot above the posts, and blocked up the turnpike-road for weeks, caused this congregation fully to appreciate Parson Manners's favorite hymns,—

"There is a land of pure delight,"

and

"On Jordan's stormy banks I stand."

Indeed, one irreverent but "pretty smart feller," who lived on the top of a hill known as Drift Hill, where certain adventurous farmers dwelt for the sake of its smooth sheep-pastures, was heard to say, after a mighty sermon by Parson Manners about the seven-times heated furnaces of judgment reserved for the wicked, that "parson hadn't better try to skeer Drift-Hillers with a hot place: 'twouldn't more'n jest warm 'em through down there, arter a real snappin' winter."

In this out-of-the-way nook was Lucinda Jane Ann born and bred. Her mother was like her in many things,—just such a cheery, round-faced little body, but with no more mind than found ample scope for itself in superintending the affairs of house and farm, and vigorously "seeing to" her husband and child. So, while Mrs. Manners baked, and washed and ironed, and sewed and knit, and set the sweetest example of quiet goodness and industry to all her flock, without knowing she *could* set an example, or be followed as one, the parson amused himself, between sermons of powerful doctrine and parochial duties of a more human interest, with educating Lucinda, whose intellect was more like his own than her mother's. A strange training it was for a young girl,—mathematics, metaphysics, Latin, theology of the dryest sort; and after an utter failure at Greek and Hebrew, though she had toiled patiently through seven books of the "Æneid," Parson Manners mildly sniffed at the inferiority of the female mind, and betook himself to teaching her French, which she learned rapidly, and spoke with a pure American accent, perhaps as pleasing to a Parisian ear as the hiss of Piedmont or the gutturals of Switzerland. Moreover, the minister had been brought up himself in the most scrupulous refinement of manner: his mother was a widow, the last of an "old family;" and her dainty, delicate observances were inbred, as it were, in her only son. This sort of elegance is perhaps the most delicate test of training and descent, and all these things Lucinda was taught from the grateful recollection of a son who never forgot his mother through all the solitary labors and studies of a long life. So it came to pass, that, after her mother died, Lucinda grew more and more like her father; and, as she became a woman, these rare refinements separated her more and more from those about her, and made her necessarily solitary. As for marriage, the possibility of such a thing never crossed her mind: there was not a man in the parish who did not offend her sense of propriety, and shock her taste, whenever she met one; and though her warm, kind heart made her a blessing to the poor and sick, her mother was yet bitterly regretted at quiltings and tea-drinkings, where she had been so "sociable-like."

It is rather unfortunate for such a position as Lucinda's, that, as deacon Stowell one day remarked to her father, "Natur' will be natur' as much on Drift Hill as down to Bosting;" and when she began to feel that "strong necessity of loving," that sooner or later assails every woman's heart, there was nothing for it to overflow on when her father had taken his share. Now, Lucinda loved the parson most devoutly. Ever since the time when she could just remember watching through the dusk his white stockings as they glimmered across the road to evening meeting, and looked like a supernatural pair of legs taking a walk on their own responsibility, twilight concealing the black breeches and coat from mortal view, Lucinda had regarded her father with a certain pleasing awe. His long abstractions, his profound knowledge, his grave, benign manners, and the thousand daily refinements of speech and act that seemed to put him far above the sphere of his pastorate,—all these things inspired as much reverence as affection; and when she wished with all her heart and soul she had a sister or a brother to tend and kiss and pet, it never once occurred to her that any of those tender familiarities could be expended on her father. She would as soon have thought of caressing any of the goodly angels, whose stout legs, flowing curls, and impossible draperies, sprawled among the pictures in the big Bible, and who excited her wonder as much by their garments as their turkey-wings and brandishing arms. So she betook herself to pets, and growing up to the maidenhood of thirty-five before her father fell asleep, was by that time the centre of a little world of her own,—hens, chickens, squirrels, cats, dogs, lambs, and sundry transient guests of stranger kind; so that when she left her old home, and removed to the little house in Dalton that had been left her by her mother's aunt, and had found her small property safely invested by means of an old friend of her father's, Miss Manners made one more journey to Vermont to bring in safety to their future dwelling a cat and three kittens, an old blind crow, a yellow dog of the true cur breed, and a rooster with three hens, "real creepers," as she often said, "none of your long-legged, screaming creatures."

Lucinda missed her father, and mourned him as constantly and faithfully as ever a daughter could. But her temperament was more cheerful and buoyant than his; and when once she was quietly settled in her little house, her garden and her pets gave her such full occupation that she sometimes blamed herself for not feeling more lonely and unhappy. A little longer life, or a little more experience, would have taught her better: power to be happy is the last thing to regret. Besides, it would have been hard to be cheerless in that sunny little house, with its queer old furniture of three-legged tables, high-backed chairs, and chintz curtains, where red mandarins winked at blue pagodas on a deep yellow ground, and birds of insane ornithology pecked at insects that never could have been hatched, or perched themselves on blossoms totally unknown to any mortal flora. Old engravings of Bartolozzi, from the stiff elegances of Angelica Kaufman and the mythologies of Reynolds, adorned the shelf; and the carpet in the parlor was of veritable English make, older than Lucinda herself, but as bright in its fading, and as firm in its usefulness, as she. Up stairs the tiny chambers were decked with spotless white dimity, and rush-bottomed

chairs stood in each window, with a strip of the same old carpet by either
bedside; and in the kitchen the blue settle that had stood by the Vermont
fireside now defended this lesser hearth from the draught of the door, and
held under the seat thereof sundry ironing-sheets, the blanket belonging to
them, and a good store of ticking and worsted holders. A half-gone set of
egg-shell china stood in the parlor-closet,—cups and teapot rimmed with
brown and gold in a square pattern, and a shield without blazon on the
side; the quaint tea-caddy with its stopper stood over against the pursy
little cream-pot; and the three-legged sugar-bowl held amid its lumps of
sparkling sugar the oddest sugar-tongs, also a family relic; beside this, six
small spoons, three large ones, and a little silver porringer comprised all
the "plate" belonging to Miss Manners, so that no fear of burglars haunted
her, and, but for her pets, she would have led a life of profound and
monotonous tranquillity. But this was a vast exception: in her life her pets
were the great item now; her cat had its own chair in the parlor and
kitchen; her dog, a rug and a basket never to be meddled with by man or
beast; her old crow, its special nest of flannel and cotton, where it feebly
croaked as soon as Miss Lucinda began to spread the little table for her
meals; and the three kittens had their own playthings and their own saucer
as punctiliously as if they had been children. In fact, Miss Manners had a
greater share of kindness for beasts than for mankind. A strange compound
of learning and unworldliness, of queer simplicity, native penetration, and
common sense, she had read enough books to despise human nature as it
develops itself in history and theology, and she had not known enough
people to love it in its personal development. She had a general idea that all
men were liars, and that she must be on her guard against their propensity
to cheat and annoy a lonely and helpless woman; for, to tell the truth, in
her good father's over-anxiety to defend her from the snares of evil men
after his death, his teachings had given her opinion this bias, and he had
forgotten to tell her how kindly and how true he had found many of his
own parishioners, how few inclined to harm or pain him. So Miss Lucinda
made her entrance into life at Dalton, distrustful, but not suspicious; and,
after a few attempts on the part of the women who were her neighbors to
be friendly or intimate, they gave her up as impracticable: not because she
was impolite or unkind; they did not themselves know why they failed,
though she could have told them; for old maid as she was, poor and plain

and queer, she could not bring herself to associate familiarly with people who put their teaspoons into the sugar-bowl, helped themselves with their own knives and forks, gathered up bits of uneaten butter and returned them to the plate for next time, or replaced on the dish pieces of cake half eaten, or cut with the knives they had just introduced into their mouths. Miss Lucinda's code of minor morals would have forbidden her to drink from the same cup with a queen, and have considered a pitchfork as suitable as a knife to eat with; nor would she have offered to a servant the least thing she had touched with her own lips or her own implements of eating; and she was too delicately bred to look on in comfort where such things were practised. Of course these women were not ladies; and, though many of them had kind hearts and warm impulses of goodness, yet that did not make up to her for their social misdemeanors; and she drew herself more into her own little shell, and cared more for her garden and her chickens, her cats and her dog, than for all the humanity of Dalton put together.

Miss Manners held her flowers next dearest to her pets, and treated them accordingly. Her garden was the most brilliant bit of ground possible. It was big enough to hold one flourishing peach-tree, one Siberian crab, and a solitary egg-plum; while under these fruitful boughs bloomed moss-roses in profusion, of the dear old-fashioned kind, every deep pink bud, with its clinging garment of green, breathing out the richest odor. Close by, the real white rose, which fashion has banished to country towns, unfolded its cups of pearl, flushed with yellow sunrise, to the heart; and by its side its damask sister waved long sprays of bloom and perfume. Tulips, dark-purple and cream-color, burning scarlet and deep maroon, held their gay chalices up to catch the dew; hyacinths, blue, white, and pink, hung heavy bells beneath them; spiced carnations of rose and garnet crowded their bed in July and August; heart's-ease fringed the walks; May honey-suckles clambered over the board-fence; and monthly honeysuckles over-grew the porch at the back-door, making perpetual fragrance from their moth-like horns of crimson and ivory. Nothing inhabited those beds that was not sweet and fair and old-fashioned. Gray-lavender-bushes sent up purple spikes in the middle of the garden, and were duly housed in winter; but these were the sole tender plants admitted, and they pleaded their own cause in the breath of the linen-press and the bureau-drawers that held

Miss Lucinda's clothes. Beyond the flowers, utility blossomed in a row of bean-poles, a hedge of currant-bushes against the farther fence, carefully tended cauliflowers, and onions enough to tell of their use as sparing as their number. A few deep-red beets and golden carrots were all the vegetables beside. Miss Lucinda never ate potatoes or pork.

Her housekeeping, but for her pets, would have been the proper housewifery for a fairy. Out of her fruit she annually conserved miracles of flavor and transparence,—great plums like those in Aladdin's garden, of shining topaz; peaches tinged with the odorous bitter of their pits, and clear as amber; crimson crabs floating in their own ruby sirup, or transmuted into jelly crystal clear, yet breaking with a grain; and jelly from the acid currants to garnish her dinner-table, or refresh the fevered lips of a sick neighbor. It was a study to visit her tiny pantry, where all these "lucent sirops" stood in tempting array, where spices and sugar and tea in their small jars flanked the sweet-meats, and a jar of glass showed its store of whitest honey, and another stood filled with crisp cakes. Here always a loaf or two of home-made bread lay rolled in a snowy cloth, and another was spread over a dish of butter. Pies were not in favor here, nor milk,—save for the cats. Salt fish Miss Manners never could abide: her savory taste allowed only a bit of rich old cheese, or thin scraps of hung beef, with her bread and butter. Sauces and spices were few in her repertory; but she cooked as only a lady can cook, and might have asked Soyer[2] himself to dinner. For verily, after much meditation and experience, I have divined that it takes as much sense and refinement and talent to cook a dinner, wash and wipe a dish, make a bed as it should be made, and dust a room as it should be dusted, as goes to the writing of a novel, or shining in high society.

But because Miss Lucinda Manners was reserved and "unsociable," as the neighbors pronounced her, I did not, therefore, mean to imply that she was inhuman. No neighbor of hers, local or scriptural, fell ill, without an immediate offer of aid from her. She made the best gruel known to Dalton invalids, sent the ripest fruit and the sweetest flowers; and if she could not watch with the sick because it interfered with her duties at home in an unpleasant and inconvenient way, she would sit with them hour after hour in the day-time, and wait on all their caprices with the patient tenderness of a mother. Children she always eyed with strange wistfulness, as if she longed to kiss them, but didn't know how; yet no child was ever invited across her threshold, for the yellow cur hated to be played with, and children always torment kittens.

So Miss Lucinda wore on happily toward the farther side of the middle ages. One after another of her pets passed away, and was replaced; the yellow cur barked his last currish signal; the cat died, and her kittens came to various ends of time or casualty; the crow fell away to dust, and was too old to stuff; and the garden bloomed and faded ten times over, before Miss Manners found herself to be forty-six years old, which she heroically acknowledged one fine day to the census-taker. But it was not this consciousness, nor its confession, that drew the dark brows so low over Miss Lucinda's eyes that day: it was quite another trouble, and one that wore heavily on her mind, as we shall proceed to explain. For Miss Manners, being, like all the rest of her sex, quite unable to do without some masculine help, had employed for some seven years an old man by the name of Israel Slater to do her "chores," as the vernacular hath it. It is a mortifying thing, and one that strikes at the roots of women's rights terribly sharp blows, but I must even own it, that one might as well try to live without one's bread and butter as without the aid of the dominant sex. When I see women split wood, unload coal-carts, move wash-tubs, and roll barrels of flour and apples handily down cellar-ways or up into carts, then I shall believe in the sublime theories of the strong-minded sisters; but as long as I see before me my own forlorn little hands, and sit down on the top stair to recover breath, and try in vain to lift the water-pitcher at table, just so long I shall be glad and thankful that there are men in the world, and that half a dozen of them are my kindest and best friends. It was rather an affliction to Miss Lucinda to feel this innate dependence; and at first she resolved to employ only small boys, and never any one of them more than a week or two. She had an unshaped theory that an old maid was a match for a small boy, but that a man would cheat and domineer over her. Experience sadly put to flight these notions; for a succession of boys in this cabinet ministry for the first three years of her stay in Dalton would have driven her into a Presbyterian convent, had there been one at hand. Boy Number One caught the yellow cur out of bounds one day, and shaved his plumy tail to a bare stick, and Miss Lucinda fairly shed tears of grief and rage when Pink appeared at the door with the denuded appendage tucked between his little legs, and his funny yellow eyes casting sidelong looks of apprehension at his mistress. Boy Number One was despatched directly. Number Two did pretty well for a month; but his integrity and his appetite conflicted, and Miss Lucinda found him one moon-light night perched in her plum-tree devouring the half-ripe fruit. She shook him down with as little ceremony as if he had been an apple; and, though he lay at death's door for a week with resulting cholera-morbus, she relented not. So the experiment went on, till a list of casualties that numbered in it fatal accidents to three kittens, two hens, and a rooster, and at last Pink himself, who was sent into a decline by repeated drenchings from the watering-pot, put an end to her forbearance, and she instituted in her viziership the old man who had now kept his office so long,—a queer, withered, slow, humorous old creature, who did "chores" for some six or seven other households, and got a living by sundry "jobs" of wood-sawing, hoeing corn, and other like works of labor, if not of skill. Israel was a great comfort to Miss Lucinda: he was efficient counsel in the maladies of all her pets, had a sovereign cure for the gapes in chickens, and could stop a cat's fit with the greatest ease; he kept the tiny garden in perfect order, and was very honest, and Miss Manners favored him accordingly. She compounded liniment for his rheumatism, herb-sirup for his colds, presented him with a set of flannel shirts, and knit him a comforter; so that Israel expressed himself strongly in favor of "Miss Lucindy," and she said to herself he really was "quite good for a man."

But just now, in her forty-seventh year, Miss Lucinda had come to grief, and all on account of Israel, and his attempts to please her. About six months before this census-taking era, the old man had stepped into Miss Manners's kitchen with an unusual radiance on his wrinkles and in his eyes, and began, without his usual morning greeting,—

"I've got so'thin' for you naow, Miss Lucindy. You're a master-hand for pets; but I'll bet a red cent you ha'n't an idee what I've got for ye naow!"

"I'm sure I can't tell, Israel," said she: "you'll have to let me see it."

"Well," said he, lifting up his coat, and looking carefully behind him as he sat down on the settle, lest a stray kitten or chicken should pre-occupy the bench, "you see I was down to Orrin's abaout a week back, and he hed a litter o' pigs,—eleven on 'em. Well, he couldn't raise the hull on 'em,—'t a'n't good to raise more'n nine,—an' so he said ef I'd 'a' had a place o' my own, I could 'a' had one on 'em; but as 'twas he guessed he'd hev to send one to market for a roaster. I went daown to the barn to see 'em; an' there was one, the cutest little critter I ever sot eyes on,—an' I've seen more'n four pigs in my day,—'twas a little black-spotted one, as spry as an ant, and the dreffullest knowin' look out of its eyes. I fellowshipped it right off; and I said, says I, 'Orrin, ef you'll let me hev that 'ere little spotted feller, I'll git a place for him, for I do take to him consarnedly.' So he said I could, and I fetched him hum; and Miss Slater and me we kinder fed him up for a few days back, till he got sorter wonted, and I'm a-goin' to fetch him to you."

"But, Israel, I haven't any place to put him in."

"Well, that a'n't nothin' to hender. I'll jest fetch out them old boards out of the wood-shed, and knock up a little sty right off, daown by the end o' the shed, and you ken keep your swill that I've hed before, and it'll come handy."

"But pigs are so dirty!"

"I don't know as they be. They ha'n't no great conveniences for washin' ginerally; but I never heerd as they was dirtier'n other critters where they run wild. An' beside, that a'n't goin' to hender, nuther. I calculate to make it one o' the chores to take keer of him; 't won't cost no more to you, and I ha'n't no great opportunities to do things for folks that's allers a-doin' for me: so 't you needn't be afeard, Miss Lucindy: I love to."

Miss Lucinda's heart got the better of her judgment. A nature that could feel so tenderly for its inferiors in the scale could not be deaf to the tiny voices of humanity when they reached her solitude; and she thanked Israel for the pig so heartily, that the old man's face brightened still more, and his voice softened from its cracked harshness, as he said, clicking up and down the latch of the back-door,—

"Well, I'm sure you're as welcome as you are obleeged, and I'll knock up that 'ere pen right off. He sha'n't pester ye any, that's a fact."

Strange to say, yet perhaps it might have been expected from her proclivities, Miss Lucinda took an astonishing fancy to the pig. Very few people know how intelligent an animal a pig is; but, when one is regarded merely as pork and hams, one's intellect is apt to fall into neglect,—a moral sentiment which applies out of pigdom. This creature would not have passed muster at a county fair; no Suffolk blood compacted and rounded him: he belonged to the "racers," and skipped about his pen with the alacrity of a large flea, wiggling his curly tail as expressively as a dog's, and "all but speakin'," as Israel said. He was always glad to see Miss Lucinda, and established a firm friendship with her dog Fun,—a pretty, sentimental German spaniel. Besides, he kept tolerably clean by dint of Israel's care, and thrust his long nose between the rails of his pen for grass or fruit, or carrot and beet tops, with a knowing look out of his deep-set eyes, that was never to be resisted by the soft-hearted spinster. Indeed, Miss Lucinda enjoyed the possession of one pet who could not tyrannize over her. Pink's place was more than filled by Fun, who was so oppressively affectionate, that he never could leave his mistress alone. If she lay down on her bed, he leaped up and unlatched the door, and stretched himself on the white counterpane beside her with a grunt of satisfaction; if she sat down to knit or sew, he laid his head and shoulders across her lap, or curled himself up on her knees; if she was cooking, he whined and coaxed round her till she hardly knew whether she fried or broiled her steak; and if she turned him out, and buttoned the door, his cries were so pitiful, she could never be resolute enough to keep him in exile five minutes, for it was a prominent article in her creed that animals have feelings that are easily wounded, and are of "like passions" with men, only incapable of expression. Indeed, Miss Lucinda considered it the duty of human beings to atone to animals for the Lord's injustice in making them dumb and four-legged. She would have been rather startled at such an enunciation of her practice, but she was devoted to it as a practice. She would give her own chair to the cat, and sit on the settle herself; get up at midnight if a mew or a bark called her, though the thermometer was below zero; the tenderloin of her steak, or the liver of her chicken, was saved for a pining kitten or an ancient and toothless cat; and no disease or wound daunted her faithful nursing, or disgusted her devoted tenderness. It was rather hard on humanity, and rather reversive of Providence, that all this care and pains should be lavished on cats and dogs, while little morsels of flesh and blood, ragged, hungry, and immortal, wandered up and down the streets. Perhaps that they were immortal was their defence from Miss Lucinda. One might have hoped that her "other-worldliness" accepted that fact as enough to out-weigh present pangs, if she had not openly declared, to Israel Slater's immense amusement and astonishment, that *she* believed creatures had souls,—little ones perhaps, but souls, after all, and she did expect to see Pink again some time or other.

"Well, I hope he's got his tail feathered out ag'in," said Israel dryly. "I do'no' but what hair'd grow as well as feathers in a speretooal state, and I never see a pictur' of an angel but what hed consider'ble many feathers."

Miss Lucinda looked rather confounded. But humanity had one little revenge on her in the shape of her cat,—a beautiful Maltese with great yellow eyes, fur as soft as velvet, and silvery paws as lovely to look at as they were thistly to touch. Toby certainly pleaded hard for Miss Lucinda's theory of a soul: but his was no good one; some tricksy and malign little spirit had lent him his share of intellect, and he used it to the entire subjugation of Miss Lucinda. When he was hungry, he was as well-mannered and as amiable as a good child; he would coax and purr, and lick her fingers with his pretty red tongue, like a "perfect love:" but when he had his fill, and needed no more, then came Miss Lucinda's time of torment. If she attempted to caress him, he bit and scratched like a young tiger: he sprang at her from the floor, and fastened on her arm with real fury. If he cried at the window and was not directly let in, as soon as he had achieved entrance his first manœuvre was to dash at her ankles, and bite them if he could, as punishment for her tardiness. This skirmishing was his favorite mode of attack. If he was turned out of the closet, or off the pillow up stairs, he retreated under the bed, and made frantic sallies at her feet, till the poor woman got actually nervous, and if he was in the room made a flying leap as far as she could to her bed, to escape those keen claws. Indeed, old Israel found her more than once sitting in the middle of the kitchen-floor, with Toby crouched for a spring, under the table, his poor mistress afraid to move for fear of her unlucky ankles. And this literally cat-ridden woman was hazed about and ruled over by her feline tyrant to that extent that he occupied the easiest chair, the softest cushion, the middle of the bed, and the front of the fire, not only undisturbed, but caressed. This is a veritable history, beloved reader, and I offer it as a warning and an example. If you will be an old maid, or if you can't help it, take to petting children, or donkeys, or even a respectable cow, but beware of domestic tyranny in any shape but man's.

No wonder Miss Lucinda took kindly to the pig, who had a house of his own, and a servant as it were, to the avoidance of all trouble on her part,—the pig who capered for joy when she or Fun approached, and had so much expression in his physiognomy that one almost expected to see him smile. Many a sympathizing conference Miss Lucinda held with Israel over the perfections of piggy, as he leaned against the sty, and looked over at his favorite after this last chore was accomplished.

"I say for 't," exclaimed the old man one day, "I b'lieve that cre'tur' knows enough to be professor in a college. Why, he talks! he re'lly doos; a leetle through his nose, maybe, but no more'n Dr. Colton allers does,—'n' I declare he appears to have abaout as much sense. I never see the equal of him. I thought he'd 'a' larfed right out yesterday when I gin him that mess o' corn. He got up onto his forelegs on the trough, an' he winked them knowin' eyes o' his'n, an' waggled his tail, an' then he set off an' capered round till he come bunt up ag'inst the boards. I tell *you*, that sorter sobered him. He gin a growlin' grunt, an' shook his ears, an' looked sideways at me; and then he put to and eet up that corn as sober as a judge. I swan! he doos beat the Dutch!"

But there was one calculation forgotten, both by Miss Lucinda and Israel: the pig would grow, and in consequence, as I said before, Miss Lucinda came to grief; for, when the census-taker tinkled her sharp little door-bell, it called her from a laborious occupation at the sty,—no more and no less than trying to nail up a board that piggy had torn down in struggling to get out of his durance. He had grown so large, that Miss Lucinda was afraid of him; his long legs and their vivacious motion added to the shrewd intelligence of his eyes; and his nose seemed as formidable to this poor little woman as the tusk of a rhinoceros: but what should she do with him? One might as well have proposed to her to kill and cut up Israel as to consign piggy to the "fate of race." She could not turn him into the street to starve, for she loved him; and the old maid suffered from a constancy that might have made some good man happy, but only embarrassed her with the pig. She could not keep him forever, that was evident. She knew enough to be aware that time would increase his disabilities as a pet; and he was an expensive one now, for the corn-swallowing capacities of a pig, one of the "racer" breed, are almost incredible, and nothing about Miss Lucinda wanted for food, even to fatness. Besides, he was getting too big for his pen; and so "cute" an animal could not be debarred from all out-door pleasures, and tantalized by the sight of a green and growing garden before his eyes continually, without making an effort to partake of its delights. So, when Miss Lucinda endued herself with her brown linen sack and sun-bonnet to go and weed her carrot-patch, she was arrested on the way by a loud grunting and scrambling in piggy's quarter, and found, to her distress, that he had contrived to knock off the upper board from his pen. She had no hammer at hand: so she seized a large stone that lay near by, and pounded at the board till the twice-tinkling bell recalled her to the house; and, as soon as she had made confession to the census-taker, she went back—alas, too late! Piggy had redoubled his efforts, another board had yielded, and he was free. What a thing freedom is!—how objectionable in practice! how splendid in theory! More people than Miss Lucinda have been put to their wits' end when "hoggie" burst his bonds, and became rampant instead of couchant. But he enjoyed it. He made the tour of the garden on a delightful canter, brandishing his tail with an air of defiance that daunted his mistress at once, and regarding her with his small bright eyes as if he would before long taste her, and see if she was as crisp as she looked. She retreated forthwith to the shed, and caught up a broom, with which she courageously charged upon piggy, and was routed entirely; for, being no way alarmed by her demonstration, the creature capered directly at her, knocked her down, knocked the broom out of her hand, and capered away again to the young carrot-patch.

"Oh, dear!" said Miss Manners, gathering herself up from the ground, "if there only was a man here!"

Suddenly she betook herself to her heels; for the animal looked at her, and stopped eating: that was enough to drive Miss Lucinda off the field. And now, quite desperate, she rushed through the house, and out of the front-door, actually in search of a man. Just down the street she saw one. Had she been composed, she might have noticed the threadbare cleanliness of his dress, the odd cap that crowned his iron-gray locks, and the peculiar manner of his walk; for our little old maid had stumbled upon no less a person than Monsieur Jean Leclerc, the dancing-master of Dalton. Not that his accomplishment was much in vogue in the embryo city; but still there were a few who liked to fit themselves for firemen's balls and sleighing-party frolics, and quite a large class of children were learning betimes such graces as children in New England receive more easily than their elders. Monsieur Leclerc had just enough scholars to keep his coat threadbare, and restrict him to necessities; but he lived, and was independent. All this Miss Lucinda was ignorant of: she only saw a man; and, with the instinct of the sex in trouble or danger, she appealed to him at once.

"O sir! won't you step in and help me? My pig has got out, and I can't catch him, and he is ruining my garden!"

"Madame, I shall!" replied the Frenchman, bowing low, and assuming the first position.[3]

So Monsieur Leclerc followed Miss Manners, and supplied himself with a mop that was hanging in the shed as his best weapon. Dire was the battle between the pig and the Frenchman. They skipped past each other and back again as if they were practising for a cotillon. Piggy had four legs, which gave him a certain advantage; but the Frenchman had most brain, and in the long-run brain gets the better of legs. A weary dance they led each other; but after a while the pet was hemmed in a corner, and Miss Lucinda had run for a rope to tie him, when, just as she returned, the beast made a desperate charge, upset his opponent, and giving a leap in the wrong direction, to his manifest astonishment landed in his own sty. Miss Lucinda's courage rose: she forgot her prostrate friend in need, and, running to the pen, caught up hammer and nail-box on her way, and with unusual energy nailed up the bar stronger than ever, and then bethought herself to thank the stranger. But there he lay quite still and pale.

"Dear me!" said Miss Manners. "I hope you haven't hurt yourself, sir."

"I have fear that I am hurt, madame," said he, trying to smile. "I cannot to move but it pains me."

"Where is it? Is it your leg, or your arm? Try and move one at a time," said Miss Lucinda promptly.

The left leg was helpless, it could not answer to the effort; and the stranger lay back on the ground, pale with the pain. Miss Lucinda took her lavender-bottle out of her pocket, and softy bathed his head and face; then she took off her sack, and folded it up under his head, and put the lavender beside him. She was good at an emergency, and she showed it.

"You must lie quite still," said she. "You must not try to move till I come back with help, or your leg will be hurt more."

With that she went away, and presently returned with two strong men and the long shutter of a shop-window. To this extempore litter she carefully moved the Frenchman; and then her neighbors lifted him, and carried him into the parlor, where Miss Luncinda's chintz lounge was already spread with a tight-pinned sheet to receive the poor man; and, while her helpers put him to bed, she put on her bonnet, and ran for the doctor.

Dr. Colton did his best for his patient, but pronounced it an impossibility to remove him till the bone should be joined firmly, as a thorough cure was all-essential to his professional prospects. And now, indeed, Miss Lucinda had her hands full. A nurse could not be afforded; but Monsieur Leclerc was added to the list of old Israel's "chores," and what other nursing he needed Miss Lucinda was glad to do; for her kind heart was full of self-reproaches to think it was her pig that had knocked down the poor man, and her mop-handle that had twisted itself across and under his leg, and aided, if not caused, its breakage. So Israel came in four or five times a day to do what he could, and Miss Lucinda played nurse at other times to the best of her ability. Such flavorous gruels and porridges as she concocted! such *tisanes* after her guest's instructions! such dainty soups and sweetbreads and cutlets, served with such neatness! After his experience of a second-rate boarding-house, Monsieur Leclerc thought himself in a gastronomic paradise. Moreover, these tiny meals were garnished with flowers, which his French taste for color and decoration appreciated,—two or three stems of lilies-of-the-valley in their folded green leaves, cool and fragrant; a moss-rosebud and a spire of purple-gray lavender bound together with ribbon-grass; or three carnations set in glittering myrtle-sprays, the last acquisition of the garden.

Miss Lucinda enjoyed nursing thoroughly, and a kindlier patient no woman ever had. Her bright needle flew faster than ever through the cold linen and flaccid cambric of the shirts and cravats she fashioned, while he told her, in his odd idioms, stories of his life in France, and the curious customs, both of society and *cuisinerie*, with which last he showed a surprising acquaintance. Truth to tell, when Monsieur Leclerc said he had been a member of the Duc de Montmorenci's household, he withheld the other half of this truth,—that he had been his *valet-de-chambre*; but it was an hereditary service, and seemed to him as different a thing from common servitude as a peer's office in the bed chamber differs from a lackey's. Indeed, Monsieur Leclerc was a gentleman in his own way, not of blood, but of breeding; and while he had faithfully served the "aristocrats," as his father had done before him, he did not limit that service to their prosperity, but in their greatest need descended to menial offices, and forgot that he could dance and ride and fence almost as well as his young master. But a bullet from a barricade put an end to his duty there; and he hated utterly the democratic rule that had overturned for him both past and future: so he escaped, and came to America, the grand resort of refugees, where he had labored, as he best knew how, for his own support, and kept to himself his disgust at the manners and customs of the barbarians. Now, for the first time, he was at home and happy. Miss Lucinda's delicate fashions suited him exactly. He adored her taste for the beautiful, which she was unconscious of. He enjoyed her cookery; and though he groaned within himself at the amount of debt he was incurring, yet he took courage, from her kindness, to believe she would not be a hard creditor, and, being naturally cheerful, put aside his anxieties, and amused himself, as well as her, with his stories, his quavering songs, his recipes for *pot-au-feu*, *tisane*, and *pâtés*, at once economical and savory. Never had a leg of lamb or a piece of roast beef gone so far in her domestic experience. A chicken seemed almost to outlive its usefulness in its various forms of re-appearance; and the salads he devised were as wonderful as the omelets he superintended, or the gay dances he played on his beloved violin, as soon as he could sit up enough to manage it. Moreover,—I should say *most-over*, if the word were admissible,—Monsieur Leclerc lifted a great weight before long from Miss Lucinda's mind. He began by subduing Fun to his proper place by a mild determination that completely won the dog's heart. "Women and spaniels," the world knows, "like kicking;" and, though kicks were no part of the good man's Rareyfaction[4] of Fun, he certainly used a certain amount of coercion, and the dog's lawful owner admired the skill of the teacher, and enjoyed the better manners of the pupil thoroughly. She could do twice as much sewing now, and never were her nights disturbed by a bark; for the dog crouched by his new friend's bed in the parlor, and lay quiet there. Toby was next undertaken, and proved less amenable to discipline. He stood in some slight awe of the man who tried to teach him, but still continued to sally out at Miss Lucinda's feet, to spring at her caressing hand when he felt ill-humored, and to claw Fun's patient nose and his approaching paws, when his misplaced sentimentality led him to caress the cat. But, after a while, a few well-timed slaps, administered with vigor, cured Toby of his worst tricks: though every blow made Miss Lucinda wince, and almost shook her good opinion of Monsieur Leclerc; for in these long weeks he had wrought out a good opinion of himself in her mind, much to her own surprise. She could not have believed a man could be so polite, so gentle, so patient, and, above all, so capable of ruling without tyranny. Miss Lucinda was puzzled.

One day, as Monsieur Leclerc was getting better, just able to go about on crutches, Israel came into the kitchen, and Miss Manners went out to see him. She left the door open; and along with the odor of a pot of raspberry-jam scalding over the fire, sending its steams of leaf-and-insect fragrance through the little house, there came in also the following conversation.

"Israel," said Miss Lucinda, in a hesitating and rather forlorn tone, "I have been thinking,—I don't know what to do with Piggy. He is quite too big for me to keep. I'm afraid of him, if he gets out; and he eats up the garden."

"Well, that *is* a consider'ble swaller for a pig, Miss Lucindy; but I b'lieve you're abaout right abaout keepin' on him. He *is* too big, that's a fact; but he's so like a human cre'tur', I'd jest abaout as lieves slarter Orrin. I declare, I don't know no more'n a taown-house goose what to do with him!"

"If I gave him away, I suppose he would be fatted and killed, of course?"

"I guess he'd be killed, likely; but, as for fattenin' on him, I'd jest as soon undertake to fatten a salt codfish. He's one o' the racers, an' they're as holler as hogsheads. You can fill 'em up to their noses, ef you're a mind to spend your corn, and they'll caper it all off their bones in twenty-four haours. I b'lieve, ef they was tied neck an' heels, an' stuffed, they'd wiggle thin betwixt feedin-times. Why, Orrin, he raised nine on 'em, and every darned critter's as poor as Job's turkey to-day. They a'n't no good. I'd as lieves ha' had nine chestnut-rails, an' a little lieveser'; cause they don't eat nothin'."

"You don't know of any poor person who'd like to have a pig, do you?" said Miss Lucinda wistfully.

"Well, the poorer they was, the quicker they'd eat him up, I guess,—ef they could eat such a razorback."

"Oh, I don't like to think of his being eaten! I wish he could be got rid of some other way. Don't you thing he might be killed in his sleep, Israel?"

This was a little too much for Israel. An irresistible flicker of laughter twitched his wrinkles, and bubbled in his throat.

"I think it's likely 'twould wake him up," said he demurely. "Killin's killin', and a cre'tur' can't sleep over it's though 'twas the stomach-ache. I guess he'd kick some, ef he *was* asleep—and screech some too!"

"Dear me!" said Miss Lucinda, horrified at the idea. "I wish he could be sent out to run in the woods. Are there any good woods near here, Israel?"

"I don't know but what he'd as lieves be slartered to once as to starve, an' be hunted down out in the lots. Besides, there a'n't nobody as I knows of would like a hog to be a-rootin' round amongst their turnips and young wheat."

"Well, what I shall do with him I don't know!" despairingly exclaimed Miss Lucinda. "He was such a dear little thing when you brought him, Israel! Do you remember how pink his pretty little nose was,—just like a rose-bud,—and how bright his eyes looked, and his cunning legs? And now he's grown so big and fierce! But I can't help liking him, either."

"He's a cute critter, that's sartain; but he does too much rootin' to have a pink nose now, I expect: there's consider'ble on't, so I guess it looks as well to have it gray. But I don't know no more'n you do what to do abaout it."

"If I could only get rid of him without knowing what became of him!" exclaimed Miss Lucinda, squeezing her forefinger with great earnestness, and looking both puzzled and pained.

"If Mees Lucinda would pairmit?" said a voice behind her.

She turned round to see Monsieur Leclerc on his crutches, just in the parlor-door.

"I shall, mees, myself dispose of piggee, if it please. I can. I shall have no sound: he shall to go away like a silent snow, to trouble you no more, never!"

"O sir, if you could! But I don't see how."

"If mees was to see, it would not be to save her pain. I shall have him to go by *magique* to fiery land."

Fairy-land probably. But Miss Lucinda did not perceive the *équivoque*.

"Nor yet shall I trouble Meester Israyel. I shall have the aid of myself and one good friend that I have; and some night, when you rise of the morning, he shall not be there."

Miss Lucinda breathed a deep sigh of relief.

"I am greatly obliged,—I shall be, I mean," said she.

"Well, I'm glad enough to wash my hands on't," said Israel. "I shall hanker arter the critter some, but he's a-gettin' too big to be handy; 'n' it's one comfort abaout critters, you ken get rid on 'em somehaow when they're more plague than profit. But folks has got to be let alone, excep' the Lord takes 'em; an' he don't allers see fit."

What added point and weight to these final remarks of old Israel was the well-known fact that he suffered at home from the most pecking and worrying of wives, and had been heard to say, in some moment of unusual frankness, that he "didn't see how 't could be sinful to wish Miss Slater was in heaven, for she'd be lots better off, and other folks too."

Miss Lucinda never knew what befell her pig one fine September night: she did not even guess that a visit paid to monsieur by one of his pupils, a farmer's daughter just out of Dalton, had any thing to do with this *enlèvement*. She was sound asleep in her bed up stairs, when her guest shod his crutches with old gloves, and limped out to the garden-gate by dawn, where he and the farmer tolled the animal out of his sty, and far down the street, by tempting red apples, and then Farmer Steele took possession of him, and he was seen no more. No, the first thing Miss Lucinda knew of her riddance was when Israel put his head into the back-door that same morning, some four hours afterward, and said with a significant nod,—

"He's gone!"

After all his other chores were done, Israel had a conference with

Monsieur Leclerc; and the two sallied into the garden, and in an hour had dismantled the low dwelling, cleared away the wreck, levelled and smoothed its site, and monsieur, having previously provided himself with an Isabella grape-vine, planted it in this forsaken spot, and trained it carefully against the end of the shed: strange to say, though it was against all precedent to transplant a grape in September, it lived and flourished. Miss Lucinda's gratitude to Monsieur Leclerc was altogether disproportioned, as he thought, to his slight service. He could not understand fully her devotion to her pets; but he respected it, and aided it whenever he could, though he never surmised the motive that adorned Miss Lucinda's table with such delicate superabundance after the late departure, and laid bundles of lavender-flowers in his tiny portmanteau till the very leather seemed to gather fragrance.

Before long Monsieur Leclerc was well enough to resume his classes, and return to his boarding-house; but the latter was filled, and only offered a prospect of vacancy in some three weeks after his application: so he returned home somewhat dejected; and as he sat by the little parlor-fire after tea, he said to his hostess in a reluctant tone,—

"Mees Lucinda, you have been of the kindest to the poor alien. I have it in my mind to relieve you of this care very rapidly, but it is not in the Fates that I do. I have gone to my house of lodgings, and they cannot to give me a chamber as yet. I have fear that I must yet rely me on your goodness for some time more, if you can to entertain me so much more of time?"

"Why, I shall like to, sir," replied the kindly, simple-hearted old maid. "I'm sure you are not a mite of trouble, and I never can forget what you did for my pig."

A smile flitted across the Frenchman's thin dark face, and he watched her glittering needles a few minutes in silence before he spoke again.

"But I have other things to say of the most unpleasant to me, Mees Lucinda. I have a great debt for the goodness and care you to me have lavished. To the angels of the good God we must submit to be debtors; but there are also of mortal obligations. I have lodged in your mansion for more of ten weeks, and to you I pay yet no silver; but it is that I have it not at present. I must ask of your goodness to wait."

The old maid's shining black eyes grew soft as she looked at him.

"Why," said she, "I don't think you owe me much of any thing, Mr. Leclerc. I never knew things last as they have since you came. I really think you brought a blessing. I wish you would please to think you don't owe me any thing."

The Frenchman's great brown eyes shone with suspicious dew.

"I cannot to forget that I owe to you far more than any silver of man repays; but I should not think to forget that I also owe to you silver, or I should not be worthy of a man's name. No, mees! I have two hands and legs. I will not let a woman most solitary spend for me her good self."

"Well," said Miss Lucinda, "if you will be uneasy till you pay me, I would rather have another kind of pay than money. I should like to know how to dance. I never did learn when I was a girl, and I think it would be good exercise."

Miss Lucinda supported this pious fiction through with a simplicity that quite deceived the Frenchman. He did not think it so incongruous as it was. He had seen women of sixty, rouged and jewelled and furbelowed, foot it deftly in the halls of the Faubourg St. Germain in his earliest youth; and this cheery, healthy woman, with lingering blooms on either cheek, and uncapped head of curly black hair but slightly strewn with silver, seemed quite as fit a subject for the accomplishment. Besides, he was poor; and this offered so easy a way of paying the debt he had so dreaded! Well said Solomon, "The destruction of the poor is their poverty." For whose moral sense, delicate sensitiveness, generous longings, will not sometimes give way to the stringent need of food and clothing, the gall of indebtedness, and the sinking consciousness of an empty purse and threatening possibilities?

Monsieur Leclerc's face brightened.

"Ah, with what grand pleasure shall I teach you the dance!"

But it fell dark again as he proceeded,—

"Though not one, nor two, nor three, nor four quarters shall be of value sufficient to achieve my payment."

"Then, if that troubles you, why, I should like to take some French lessons in the evening, when you don't have classes. I learned French when I was quite a girl, but not to speak it very easily; and if I could get some practice, and the right way to speak, I should be glad."

"And I shall give you the real *Parisien* tone, Mees Lucinda," said he proudly. "I shall be as if it were no more an exile when I repeat my tongue to you."

And so it was settled. Why Miss Lucinda should learn French any more than dancing was not a question in Monsieur Leclerc's mind. It is true that Chaldaic would, in all probability, be as useful to our friend as French; and the flying over poles, and hanging by toes and fingers, so eloquently described by apostles of the body, would have been as well adapted to her style and capacity as dancing. But his own language, and his own profession!—what man would not have regarded these as indispensable to improvement, particularly when they paid his board?

During the latter three weeks of Monsieur Leclerc's stay with Miss Lucinda, he made himself surprisingly useful. He listed the doors against approaching winter breezes; he weeded in the garden, trimmed, tied, trained, wherever either good office was needed, mended china with an infallible cement, and rickety chairs with the skill of a cabinet-maker; and, whatever hard or dirty work he did, he always presented himself at table in a state of scrupulous neatness. His long brown hands showed no trace of labor; his iron-gray hair was reduced to smoothest order; his coat speckless, if threadbare; and he ate like a gentleman,—an accomplishment not always to be found in the "best society," as the phrase goes: whether the best in fact ever lacks it is another thing. Miss Lucinda appreciated these traits; they set her at ease; and a pleasanter home-life could scarce be painted than now enlivened the little wooden house. But three weeks pass away rapidly; and when the rusty portmanteau was gone from her spare chamber, and the well-worn boots from the kitchen-corner, and the hat from its nail, Miss Lucinda began to find herself wonderfully lonely. She missed the armfuls of wood in her wood-box that she had to fill laboriously, two sticks at a time; she missed the other plate at her tiny round table, the other chair beside her fire; she missed that dark, thin, sensitive face, with its rare and sweet smile; she wanted her story-teller, her yarn-winder, her protector, back again. Good gracious! to think of an old lady of forty-seven entertaining such sentiments for a man.

Presently the dancing-lessons commenced. It was thought advisable that Miss Manners should enter a class, and in the fervency of her good intentions she did not demur. But gratitude and respect had to strangle with persistent hands the little serpents of the ridiculous in Monsieur Leclerc's soul when he beheld his pupil's first appearance. What reason was it, O rose of seventeen! adorning thyself with cloudy films of lace and sparks of jewelry before the mirror that reflects youth and beauty, that made Miss Lucinda array herself in a brand-new dress of yellow muslin-de laine strewed with round green spots, and displace her customary handkerchief for a huge tamboured collar, on this eventful occasion? Why, oh, why! did she tie up the roots of her black hair with an unconcealable scarlet string? And, most of all, why was her dress so short, her slipper-strings so big and broad, her thick slippers so shapeless, by reason of the corns and bunions that pertained to the feet within? The "instantaneous rush of several guardian angels" that once stood dear old Hepzibah Pynchon[5] in good stead was wanting here; or perhaps they stood by all-invisible, their calm eyes softened with love deeper than tears, at this spectacle so ludicrous to man, beholding in the grotesque dress and adornments only the budding of life's divinest blossom, and in the strange skips and hops of her first attempts at dancing only the buoyancy of those inner wings that goodness and generosity and pure self-devotion were shaping for a future strong and stately flight upward. However, men, women, and children do not see with angelic eyes, and the titterings of her fellow-pupils were irrepressible. One bouncing girl nearly choked herself with her handkerchief, trying not to laugh; and two or three did not even try. Monsieur Leclerc could not blame them. At first he could scarce control his own facial muscles; but a sense of remorse smote him, as he saw how unconscious and earnest the little woman was, and remembered how often those knotty hands and knobbed feet had waited on his need or his comfort. Presently he tapped on his violin for a few moments' respite, and approached Miss Lucinda as respectfully as if she had been a queen.

"You are ver' tired, Mees Lucinda?" said he.

"I am a little, sir," said she, out of breath. "I am not used to dancing: it's quite an exertion."

"It is that truly. If you are too much tired, is it better to wait? I shall finish for you the lesson till I come to-night for a French conversation?"

"I guess I will go home," said the simple little lady. "I am some afraid of getting rheumatism. But use makes perfect, and I shall stay through next time, no doubt."

"So I believe," said monsieur, with his best bow, as Miss Lucinda departed and went home, pondering all the way what special delicacy she should provide for tea.

"My dear young friends," said Monsieur Leclerc, pausing with the uplifted bow in his hand, before he recommenced his lesson, "I have observed that my new pupil does make you much to laugh. I am not so surprise; for you do not know all, and the good God does not robe all angels in one manner. But she have taken me to her mansion with a leg broken, and have nursed me like a saint of the blessed, nor with any pay of silver, except that I teach her the dance and the French. They are pay for the meat and the drink; but she will have no more for her good patience and care. I like to teach you the dance; but she could teach you the saints' ways, which are better. I think you will no more to laugh."

"No, I guess we *won't!*" said the bouncing girl with great emphasis; and the color rose over more than one young face.

After that day Miss Lucinda received many a kind smile and hearty welcome, and never did anybody venture even a grimace at her expense. But it must be acknowledged that her dancing was at least peculiar. With a sanitary view of the matter, she meant to make it exercise; and fearful was the skipping that ensued. She *chasséd* on tiptoe, and *balancéd* with an indescribable hopping twirl, that made one think of a chickadee pursuing its quest of food on new-ploughed ground; and some late-awakened feminine instinct of dress, restrained, too, by due economy, endued her with the oddest decorations that woman ever devised. The French lessons went on more smoothly. If Monsieur Leclerc's Parisian ear was tortured by the barbarous accent of Vermont, at least he bore it with heroism, since there was nobody else to hear; and very pleasant, both to our little lady and her master, were these long winter evenings, when they diligently waded through Racine, and even got so far as the golden periods of Chateaubriand. The pets fared badly for petting in these days: they were fed and waited on, but not with the old devotion. It began to dawn on Miss Lucinda's mind that something to talk to was preferable, as a companion, even to Fun, and that there might be a stranger sweetness in receiving care and protection than in giving it.

Spring came at last. Its softer skies were as blue over Dalton as in the wide fields without, and its foot-steps as bloom-bringing in Miss Lucinda's garden as in mead or forest. Now Monsieur Leclerc came to her aid again at odd minutes, and set her flower-beds with mignonette-borders, and her vegetable-garden with salad-herbs of new and flourishing kinds. Yet not even the sweet season seemed to hurry the catastrophe, that we hope, dearest reader, thy tender eyes have long seen impending. No; for this quaint alliance a quainter Cupid waited: the chubby little fellow with a big head and a little arrow, who waits on youth and loveliness, was not wanted here. Lucinda's god of love wore a lank, hard-featured, grizzly shape, no less than that of Israel Slater, who marched into the garden one fine June morning, earlier than usual, to find monsieur in his blouse, hard at work weeding the cauliflower-bed.

"Good-mornin', sir, good-mornin'!" said Israel, in answer to the Frenchman's greeting. "This is a real slick little garden-spot as ever I see, and a pootty house, and a real clever woman too. I'll be skwitched ef it a'n't a fust-rate consarn, the hull on't. Be you ever a-goin' back to France, mister?"

"No, my goot friend. I have nobody there. I stay here. I have friend here; but there,—*oh, non! je ne reviendrai pas! ah, jamais, jamais!*"[6]

"Pa's dead, eh? or shamming? Well, I don't understand your lingo; but, ef you're a-goin' to stay here, I don't see why you don't hitch hosses with Miss Lucindy."

Monsieur Leclerc looked up astonished.

"Horses, my friend? I have no horse."

"Thunder 'n' dry trees! I didn't say you hed, did I? But that comes o' usin' what Parson Hyde calls figgurs, I s'pose. I wish 't he'd use one kind o' figgurin' a leetle more: he'd pay me for that wood-sawin'. I didn't mean nothin' about hosses. I sot out fur to say, Why don't ye marry Miss Lucindy?"

"I?" gasped monsieur,—"I, the foreign, the poor? I could not to presume so!"

"Well, I don't see 's it's sech drefful presumption. Ef you're poor, she's a woman, and real lonesome too: she ha'n't got nuther chick nor child belongin' to her, and you're the only man she ever took any kind of a notion to. I guess 'twould be jest as much for her good as yourn."

"Hush, good Is-ray-el! it is good to stop there. She would not to marry after such years of goodness. She is a saint of the blessed."

"Well, I guess saints sometimes fellerships with sinners; I've heerd tell they did: and, ef I was you, I'd make trial for't. Nothin' ventur', nothin' have."

Whereupon Israel walked off, whistling.

Monsieur Leclerc's soul was perturbed within him by these suggestions. He pulled up two young cauliflowers, and reset their places with pig-weeds; he hoed the nicely sloped border of the bed flat to the path, and then flung the hoe across the walk, and went off to his daily occupation with a new idea in his head. Nor was it an unpleasant one. The idea of a transition from his squalid and pinching boarding-house to the delicate comfort of Miss Lucinda's *ménage*, the prospect of so kind and good a wife to care for his hitherto dreaded future,—all this was pleasant. I cannot honestly say he was in love with our friend: I must even confess that whatever element of that nature existed between the two was now all on Miss Lucinda's side, little as she knew it. Certain it is, that when she appeared that day at the dancing-class in a new green calico flowered with purple, and bows on her slippers big enough for a bonnet, it occurred to Monsieur Leclerc, that, if they were married, she would take no more lessons. However, let us not blame him. He was a man, and a poor one; one must not expect too much from men or from poverty: if they are tolerably good, let us canonize them even, it is so hard for the poor creatures! And, to do Monsieur Leclerc justice, he had a very thorough respect and admiration for Miss Lucinda. Years ago, in his stormy youth-time, there had been a pair of soft-fringed eyes that looked into his as none would ever look again. And they murdered her, those mad wild beasts of Paris, in the chapel where she knelt at her pure prayers,—murdered her because she knelt beside an aristocrat, her best friend, the Duchess of Montmorenci, who had taken the pretty peasant from her own estate to bring her up for her maid. Jean Leclerc had lifted that pale shape from the pavement, and buried it himself: what else he buried with it was invisible. But now he recalled the hour with a long, shuddering sigh, and, hiding his face in his hands, said softly, "The violet is dead: there is no spring for her. I will have now an amaranth: it is good for the tomb."

Whether Miss Lucinda's winter dress suggested this floral metaphor, let us not inquire. Sacred be sentiment, when there is even a shadow of reality about it: when it becomes a profession, and confounds itself with millinery, and shades of mourning, it is "bosh," as the Turkeys say.[7]

So that very evening Monsieur Leclerc arrayed himself in his best to give another lesson to Miss Lucinda. But, somehow or other, the lesson was long in beginning. The little parlor looked so homelike and so pleasant, with its bright lamp and gay bunch of roses on the table, that it was irresistible temptation to lounge and linger. Miss Lucinda had the volume of Florian in her hands, and was wondering why he did not begin, when the book was drawn away, and a hand laid on both of hers.

"Lucinda," he began, "I give you no lesson tonight. I have to ask. Dear mees, will you to marry your poor slave?"

"Oh, dear!" said Miss Lucinda.

Don't laugh at her, Miss Tender-eyes. You will feel just so yourself some day, when Alexander Augustus says, "Will you be mine, loveliest of your sex?" Only you won't feel it half so strongly, for you are young, and love is nature to youth; but it is a heavenly surprise to age.

Monsieur Leclerc said nothing. He had a heart, after all, and it was touched now by the deep emotion that flushed Miss Lucinda's face, and made her tremble so violently; but presently he spoke.

"Do not," said he. "I am wrong. I presume. Forgive the stranger."

"Oh, dear!" said poor Lucinda again. "Oh! you know it isn't that; but how can you like *me*?"

There, mademoiselle, there's humility for you! *you* will never say that to Alexander Augustus.

Monsieur Leclerc soothed this frightened, happy, incredulous little woman into quiet before very long; and, if he really began to feel a true affection for her from the moment he perceived her humble and entire devotion to him, who shall blame him? Not I. If we were all heroes, who would be *valet-de-chambre*? If we were all women, who would be men? He was very good as far as he went; and, if you expect the chivalries of grace out of nature, you "may expect," as old Fuller saith.[8] So it was peacefully settled that they should be married, with a due amount of tears and smiles on Lucinda's part, and a great deal of tender sincerity on monsieur's. She missed her dancing-lesson next day; and, when Monsieur Leclerc came in the evening, he found a shade on her happy face.

"Oh, dear!" said she, as he entered.

"Oh, dear!" was Lucinda's favorite aspiration. Had she thought of it as an Anglicizing of "*O Dieu!*" perhaps she would have dropped it; but this time she went on headlong, with a valorous despair,—

"I have thought of something. I'm afraid I can't! Monsieur, aren't you a Romanist?"

"What is that?" said he, surprised.

"A Papist, a Catholic."

"Ah!" he returned, sighing, "once I was *bon Catholique*,—once in my gone youth; after then I was nothing but the poor man who bats for his life; now I am of the religion that shelters the stranger, and binds up the broken poor."

Monsieur was a diplomatist. This melted Miss Lucinda's orthodoxy right down: she only said,—

"Then you will go to church with me?"

"And to the skies above, I pray," said monsieur, kissing her knotty hand like a lover.

So in the earliest autumn they were married, monsieur having previously presented Miss Lucinda with a delicate plaided gray silk for her wedding attire, in which she looked almost young; and old Israel was present at the ceremony, which was briefly performed by Parson Hyde in Miss Manners's parlor. They did not go to Niagara, nor to Newport; but that afternoon Monsieur Leclerc brought a hired rockaway to the door, and took his bride a drive into the country. They stopped beside a pair of bars, where monsieur hitched his horse, and, taking Lucinda by the hand, led her into Farmer Steele's orchard, to the foot of his biggest apple-tree. There she beheld a little mound, at the head and foot of which stood a daily rose-bush shedding its latest wreaths of bloom, and upon the mound itself was laid a board, on which she read,—

"Here lie the bones of poor piggy."

Mrs. Lucinda burst into tears; and monsieur, picking a bud from the bush, placed it in her hand, and led her tenderly back to the rockaway.

That evening Mrs. Lucinda was telling the affair to old Israel with so much feeling, that she did not perceive at all the odd commotion in his face, till, as she repeated the epitaph to him, he burst out with, "He didn't say what become o' the flesh, did he?" and therewith fled through the kitchen-door. For years afterward Israel would entertain a few favored auditors with his opinion of the matter, screaming till the tears rolled down his cheeks,—

"That was the beateree of all the weddin'-towers I ever heerd tell on. Goodness! it's enough to make the Wanderin' Jew die o' larfin'."

DELY'S COW

I WENT DOWN to the farmyard one day last month, and as I opened the gate I heard Pat Malony say, "Biddy, Biddy!" I thought at first he was calling a hen; but then I remembered the hens were all shut into the poultry-house that day, to be sorted, and numbered, and condemned. So I looked again, thinking perhaps Pat's little lame sister had strayed up from the village, and gone into the barn after Sylvy's kittens, or a pigeon-egg, or to see a new calf; but, to my surprise, I saw a red cow, of no particular beauty or breed, coming out of the stable-door, looking about her as if in search of somebody or something; and when Pat called again, "Biddy, Biddy, Biddy!" the creature walked up to him across the yard, stretched out her awkward neck, sniffed a little, and cropped from his hand the wisp of rowen hay he held, as composedly as if she were a tame kitten, and then followed him all round the yard for more, which I am sorry to say she did not get. Pat had only displayed her accomplishments to astonish me, and then shut her in her stall again. I afterward hunted out Biddy's history, and here it is.

On the Derby turnpike, just before you enter Hanerford, everybody that ever travelled that road will remember Joseph German's bakery. It was a red brick house, with dusty windows toward the street, and just inside the door a little shop, where Mr. German retailed the scalloped cookies, fluted gingerbread, long loaves of bread, and scantily-filled pies in which he dealt, and which were manufactured in the long shop, where in summer you caught glimpses of flour barrels all a-row, and men who might have come out of those barrels, so strewed with flour were all their clothes,—

paper cap and white apron scarcely to be distinguished from the rest of the dress as far as color and dustiness went. Here, too, when her father drove out the cart every afternoon, sitting in front of the counter with her sewing and her knitting, Dely German, the baker's pretty daughter, dealt out the cakes, and rattled the pennies in her apron-pocket, with so good a grace, that not a young farmer came into Hanerford with grain, or potatoes, or live-stock, who did not cast a glance in at the shop-door going toward town, and go in on his return, ostensibly to buy a sheet of gingerbread, or a dozen cookies, for his refreshment on the drive homeward. It was a curious thing to see how much hungrier they were on the way home than coming into town. Though they might have had a good dinner in Hanerford, that never appeased their appetites entirely; while in the morning they had driven their slow teams all the way without so much as thinking of cakes and cheese. So by the time Dely was seventeen, her black eyes and bright cheeks were well known for miles about; and many a youth, going home to the clean kitchen where his old mother sat by the fire, knitting, or his spinster sister scolded and scrubbed over his muddy boot-tracks, thought how pretty it would look to see Dely German sitting on the other side, in her neat calico frock and white apron, her black hair shining smooth, and her fresh, bright face looking a welcome.

But Dely did not think about any one of them in a reciprocal manner. She liked them all pretty well; but she loved nobody except her father and mother, her three cats and all their kittens, the big dog, the old horse, and a wheezy robin that she kept in a cage, because her favorite cat had half killed it one day, and it never could fly any more. For all these dumb things she had a really intense affection. As for her father and mother, she seemed to be a part of them: it never occurred to her that they could leave her, or she them; and when old Joe German died one summer day, just after Dely was seventeen, she was nearly distracted. However, people who must work for their living have to get over their sorrows practically much sooner than those who can afford time to indulge them; and, as Dely knew more about the business and the shop than anybody but the foreman, she had to resume her place at the counter before her father had been buried a week. It was a great source of embarrassment to her rural admirers to see Dely in her black frock, pale and sober, when they went in. They did not know what to say: they felt as if their hands and feet had grown very big all at once, and as if the cents in their pockets never could be got at, at which they turned red and hot, and got choked, and went away, swearing internally at their own blundering shyness, and deeper smitten than ever with Dely, because they wanted to comfort her so very much, and didn't know how.

One, however, had the sense and simplicity to know how; and that was George Adams, a fine, healthy young fellow from Hartland Hollow, who came in at least once a week with a load of produce from the farm on which he was head man. The first time he went after his rations of gingerbread, and found Dely in her mourning, he held out his hand, and shook hers heartily. Dely looked up into his honest blue eyes, and saw them full of pity.

"I'm real sorry for you," said George. "My father died two years ago."

Dely burst into tears; and George couldn't help stroking her bright hair softly, and saying, "Oh, don't!" So she wiped her eyes, and sold him the cookies he wanted; but from that day there was one of Dely's customers that she liked best, one team of white horses she always looked out for, and one voice that hurried the color into her face if it was ever so pale; and the upshot of pity and produce and gingerbread was that George Adams and Dely German were heartily in love with each other, and Dely began to be comforted for her father's loss six months after he died. Not that she knew why, or that George had ever said any thing to her more than was kind and friendly; but she felt a sense of rest, and yet a sweet restlessness, when he was in her thoughts or presence, that beguiled her grief, and made her unintentionally happy. It was the old, old story,—the one eternal novelty that never loses its vitality, its interest, its bewitching power, nor ever will till time shall be no more.

But the year had not elapsed, devoted to double crape and triple quillings, before Dely's mother, too, began to be consoled. She was a pleasant, placid, feeble-natured woman, who liked her husband very well, and fretted at him in a mild, persistent way a good deal. He swore, and chewed tobacco, which annoyed her; he also kept a tight grip of his money, which was not pleasant: but she missed him very much when he died, and cried and rocked, and said how afflicted she was, as much as was necessary, even in the neighbors' opinion. But, as time went on, she found the business very hard to manage: even with Dely and the foreman to help her, the ledger got all astray, and the day-book followed its example. So when old Tom Kenyon, who kept the tavern half a mile farther out, took to coming Sunday nights to see the "Widder German," and finally proposed to share her troubles, and carry on the bakery in a matrimonial partnership, Mrs. German said she "guessed she would," and announced to Dely on Monday morning that she was going to have a step-father. Dely was astonished and indignant, but to no purpose. Mrs. German cried and rocked, and rocked and cried again, rather more saliently than when her husband died. But for all that she did not retract; and in due time she got into the stage with her elderly lover, and went to Meriden, where they got married, and came home next day to carry on the bakery.

Joe German had been foolish enough to leave all his property to his wife; and Dely had no resource but to stay at home, and endure her disagreeable position as well as she could, for Tom Kenyon swore and chewed, and smoked beside: moreover, he drank,—not to real drunkenness, but enough to make him cross and intractable. Worse than all, he had a son, the only child of his first marriage; and it soon became unpleasantly evident to Dely, that Steve Kenyon had a mind to marry her, and his father had a mind he should. Now, it is all very well to marry a person one likes; but to go through that ceremony with one you dislike is more than anybody has a right to require, in my opinion, as well as Dely's: so when her mother urged upon her the various advantages of the match,—Steve Kenyon being the present master and prospective owner of his father's tavern, a great resort for horse-jockeys, cattle-dealers, and frequenters of state and county fairs,—Dely still objected to marry him. But, the more she objected, the more her mother talked; her step-father swore; and the swaggering lover persisted in his attentions at all times; so that the poor girl had scarce a half-hour to herself. She grew thin and pale and unhappy enough; and one day George Adams, stepping in unexpectedly, found her with her apron to her eyes, crying most bitterly. It took some persuasion, and some more daring caresses than he had yet ventured on, to get Dely's secret trouble to light. I am inclined to think George kissed her at least once before she would tell him what she was crying about. But Dely naturally came to the conclusion, that if he loved her enough to kiss her, and she loved him enough to like it, she might as well share her troubles; and the consequence was, George asked her then and there to share his.

Not that either of them thought there would be troubles under that copartnership, for the day was sufficient to them; and it did not daunt Dely in the least to know that George's only possessions were a heifer calf, a suit of clothes, and twenty dollars.

About a month after this eventful day, Dely went into Hanerford on an errand, she said: so did George Adams. They stepped into the minister's together, and were married: so Dely's errand was done, and she rode out on the front-seat of George's empty wagon, stopping at the bakery to tell her mother, and get her trunk; having wisely chosen a day for her errand when her step-father had gone away after a load of flour down to Hanerford wharves. Mrs. Kenyon went at once into wild hysterics, and called Dely a jade-hopper and an ungrateful child. But not understanding the opprobrium of the one term, and not deserving the other, the poor girl only cried a little, and helped George with her trunk, which held all she could call her own in the world,—her clothes, two or three cheap trinkets, and a few books. She kissed the cats all round, hugged the dog, was glad her robin had died, and then said good-by to her mother, who refused to kiss her, and said George Adams was a snake in the grass. This was too much for Dely: she wiped her eyes, and clambered over the wagon-wheel, and took her place beside George with a smile so much like crying, that he began to whistle, and never stopped for two miles. By that time they were in a piece of thick pine-woods, when, looking both before and behind to be certain no one was coming, he put his arm round his wife and kissed her, which seemed to have a consoling effect; and, by the time they reached his mother's little house, Dely was as bright as ever.

A little bit of a house it was to bring a wife to, but it suited Dely. It stood on the edge of a pine-wood, where the fragrance of the resinous boughs kept the air sweet and pure, and their leaves thrilled responsive to every breeze. The house was very small and very red. It had two rooms below, and one above; but it was neater than many a five-story mansion, and far more cheerful. And, when Dely went in at the door, she thought there could be no prettier sight than the exquisitely neat old woman sitting in her arm-chair on one side of the fireplace, and her beautiful cat on the other, purring and winking, while the tea-kettle sang and sputtered over the bright fire of pine-cones, and the tea-table at the other side of the room was spread with such clean linen, and such shining crockery, that it made one hungry even to look at the brown-bread and butter, and pink radishes, that were Dely's wedding-supper.

It is very odd how happy people can be when they are as poor as poverty, and don't know where to look for their living, but to the work of their own hands. Genteel poverty is horrible. It is impossible for one to be poor and elegant, and comfortable; but downright, simple, unblushing poverty may be the most blessed of states. And though it was somewhat of a descent in the social scale for Dely to marry a farm-hand, foreman though he might be, she loved her George so devoutly and healthily, that she was as happy as a woman could be. George's mother, the sweetest and tenderest mother to him, took his wife to a place beside his in her heart; and the two women loved each other the more for this man's sake. He was a bond between them, not a division. Hard work left them no thought of rankling jealousy to make their lives bitter; and Dely was happier than ever she had thought she should be away from her mother. Nor did the hard work hurt her; for she took to her own share all of it that was out of doors, and troublesome to the infirmities of the old lady. She tended the calf in its little log-hut, shook down the coarse hay for its bed, made its gruel till it grew beyond gruel, then drove it daily to the pasture where it fed, gave it extra rations of bread and apple-parings and carrot-tops, till the creature knew her voice, and ran to her call like a pet kitten, rubbing its soft, wet nose against her red cheek, and showing in a dozen blundering, calfish ways that it both knew and loved her.

There are two sorts of people in the world,—those who love animals, and those who do not. I have seen them both, I have known both; and if sick or oppressed, or borne down with dreadful sympathies for a groaning nation in mortal struggle, I should go for aid, for pity, or the relief of kindred feeling, to those I had seen touched with quick tenderness for the lower creation, who remember that the "whole creation travaileth in pain together," and who learn God's own lesson of caring for the fallen sparrow, and the ox that treadeth out the corn. With men or women who despise animals, and treat them as mere beasts and brutes, I never want to trust my weary heart or my aching head. But with Dely I could have trusted both safely; and the calf and the cat agreed with me.

So, in this happy, homely life, the sweet centre of her own bright little world, Dely passed the first year of her wedded life, and then the war came! Dreadful pivot of so many lives!—on it also this rude idyl turned. George enlisted for the war.

It was not in Dely or his mother to stop him. Though tears fell on every round of his blue socks, and sprinkled his flannel shirts plentifully; though the old woman's wan and wrinkled face paled and saddened, and the young one's fair throat quivered with choking sobs when they were alone; still, whenever George appeared, he was greeted with smiles and cheer, strengthened and steadied from this home armory better than with sabre and bayonet,—"with might in the inner man." George was a brave fellow, no doubt, and would do good service to his free country; but it is a question with me, whether, when the Lord calls out his "noble army of martyrs" before the universe of men and angels, that army will not be found officered and led by just such women as these, who fought silently with the flesh and the Devil by their own hearth, quickened by no stinging excitement of battle, no thrill of splendid strength and fury in soul and body, no tempting delight of honor or even recognition from their peers, upheld only by the dull, recurrent necessities of duty and love.

At any rate, George went, and they staid. The town made them an allowance as a volunteer's family; they had George's bounty to begin with; and a friendly boy from the farm near by came and sawed their wood, took care of the garden, and, when Dely could not go to pasture with the heifer, drove her to and fro daily.

After George had been gone three months, Dely had a little baby. Tiny and bright as it was, it seemed like a small star fallen down from some upper sky to lighten their darkness. Dely was almost too happy; and the old grandmother, fast slipping into that other world whence baby seemed to have but newly arrived, stayed her feeble steps a little longer to wait upon her son's child. Yet, for all the baby, Dely never forgot her dumb loves. The cat had still its place on the foot of her bed; and her first walk was to the barn, where the heifer lowed welcome to her mistress, and rubbed her head against the hand that caressed her, with as much feeling as a cow can show, however much she may have. And Biddy the heifer was a good friend to that little household all through that long ensuing winter. It went to Dely's heart to sell her first calf to the butcher; but they could not raise it: and when it was taken away she threw her check apron over her head, and buried her face deep in the pillow, that she might not hear the cries of appeal and grief her favorite uttered. After this, Biddy would let no one milk her but her mistress; and many an inarticulate confidence passed between the two while the sharp streams of milk spun and foamed into the pail below, as Dely's skillful hands coaxed it down.

They heard from George often. He was well, and busy with drill and camp life,—not in active service as yet. Incidentally, too, Dely heard of her mother. Old Kenyon was dead of apoplexy, and Steve like to die of drink. This was a bit of teamster's gossip, but proved to be true. Toward the end of the winter, old Mother Adams slept quietly in the Lord. No pain or sickness grasped her, though she knew she was dying, kissed and blessed Dely, sent a mother's message to George, and took the baby for the last time into her arms; then she laid her head on the pillow, smiled, and drew a long breath—no more.

Poor Dely's life was very lonely. She buried her dead out of her sight, wrote a loving, sobbing letter to George, and began to try to live alone. Hard enough it was. March revenged itself on the past toleration of winter: snow fell in blinding fury; and drifts hid the fences, and fenced the doors, all through Hartland Hollow. Day after day Dely struggled through the path to the barn to feed Biddy, and milk her; and a warm mess of bread and milk often formed her only meal in that bitter weather. It is not credible to those who think no more of animals than of chairs and stones, how much society and solace they afford to those who do love them. Biddy was really Dely's friend. Many a long day passed when no human face but the baby's greeted her from dawn till dusk. But the cow's beautiful purple eyes always turned to welcome her as she entered its shed-door; her wet muzzle touched Dely's cheek with a velvet caress; and, while her mistress drew from the downy bag its white and rich stores, Biddy would turn her head round, and eye her with such mild looks, and breathe such fragrance toward her, that Dely, in her solitary and friendless state, came to regard her as a real sentient being, capable of love and sympathy, and had an affection for her that would seem utter nonsense to half, perhaps three-quarters, of the people in this unsentimental world. Many a time did the lonely little woman lay her head on Biddy's neck, and talk to her about George, with sobs and silences interspersed; and many a piece of dry bread steeped in warm water, or golden carrot, or mess of stewed turnips and bran, flavored the dry hay that was the staple of the cow's diet. The cat was old now, and objected to the baby so strenuously, that Dely regarded her as partly insane from age; and though she was kind to her of course, and fed her faithfully, still a cat that could growl at George's baby was not regarded with the same complacent kindness that had always blessed her before; and, whenever the baby was asleep at milking-time, pussy was locked into the closet,—a proceeding she resented. Biddy, on the contrary, seemed to admire the child,—she certainly did not object to her,—and necessarily obtained thereby a far higher place in Dely's heart than the cat.

As I have already said, Dely had heard of her step-father's death some time before; and one stormy day, the last week in March, a team coming from Hanerford with grain stopped at the door of the little red house, and the driver handed Dely a dirty and ill-written letter from her mother. Just such an epistle it was as might have been expected from Mrs. Kenyon,— full of weak sorrow, and entreaties to Dely to come home and live: she was old and tired; the bakery was coming to trouble for want of a good manager; the foreman was a rogue, and the business failing fast, and she wanted George and Dely there. Evidently she had not heard, when the letter began, of George's departure, or baby's birth; but the latter half said, "Cum anyway. I want to se the baby. Ime an old critur a-sinking into my graiv, and when george cums back from the wars he must liv hear the rest off his life."

Dely's tender heart was greatly stirred by the letter, yet she was undecided what to do. Here she was, alone and poor; there would be her mother,—and she loved her mother, though she could not respect her; there, too, was plenty for all: and, if George should ever come home, the bakery business was just the thing for him; he had energy and courage enough to redeem a sinking affair like that. But then what should she do with the cow? Puss could go home with her; but Biddy?—there was no place for Biddy. Pasture was scarce and dear about Hanerford: Dely's father had given up keeping a cow long before his death for that reason. But how could Dely leave and sell her faithful friend and companion? Her heart sank at the thought: it almost turned the scale, for one pitiful moment, against common sense and filial feeling. But baby coughed, nothing more than a slight cold; yet Dely thought, as she had often thought before, with a quick thrill of terror, What if baby were ever sick? Seven miles between her and the nearest doctor; nobody to send, nobody to leave baby with, and she herself utterly inexperienced in the care of children. The matter was decided at once; and, before the driver who brought her mother's letter had come on his next journey for the answer he had offered to carry, Dely's letter was written, sealed, and put on the shelf, and she was busy contriving and piecing out a warm hood and cloak for baby to ride in.

But every time she went to the barn to milk Biddy, or feed her, the tears sprang to her eyes, and her mind misgave her. Never before had the dainty bits of food been so plentiful for her pet, or her neck so tenderly stroked. Dely had written to her mother that she would come to her as soon as her affairs were settled, and she had spoken to Orrin Nye, who brought the letter, to find a purchaser for her cow. Grandfather Hollis, who bought Biddy, and in whose farmyard I made her acquaintance, gave me the drover's account of the matter, which will be better in his words than mine. It seems he brought quite a herd of milch cows down to Avondale, which is twenty miles from Hanerford, and, hearing that grandfather wanted a couple of cows, he came to "trade with him," as he expressed it. He had two beautiful Ayrshires in the lot,—clean heads, shining skins, and good milkers,—that mightily pleased the old gentleman's fancy; for he had long brooded over his favorite scheme of a pure-blooded herd, and the red-and-white-clouded Ayrshires showed beautifully on his green hillside pastures, and were good stock besides. But Aaron Stow insisted so pertinaciously that he should buy this red cow, that the squire shoved his hat back, and put both his hands in his pockets, a symptom of determination with him, and began to question him. They fenced a while in true Yankee fashion, till at last grandfather became exasperated.

"Look, here, Aaron Stow!" said he, "what in thunder do you pester me so about that cow for? She's a good enough beast, I see, for a native; but those Ayrshires are better cows and better blood, and you know it. What are you navigating round me for so glib?"

"Well, now, squire," returned Aaron, whittling at the gate with sudden vehemence, "fact is, I've set my mind on your buyin' that critter, an' you jes' set down on that 'ere milkin'-stool, an' I'll tell ye the rights on't, though I feel kinder meechin' myself, to be so soft about it as I be."

Dely's Cow

"Leave off shaving my new gate, then, and don't think I'm going to trust a hundred and eighty-five solid flesh to a three-legged stool. I'm too old for that. I'll sit on the step here. Now go ahead, man."

So grandfather sat down on the step, and Aaron turned his back against the gate, and kicked one boot on the other. He was not used to narration.

"Well, you know we had a dreadful spell o' weather a month ago, squire. There ha'n't never been such a March in my day as this last; an' 'twas worse up our way'n 'twas here; an' down to Hartland Holler was the beat of all. Why, it snowed, an' it blowed, an' it friz, till all natur' couldn't stan' it no more. Well, about them days I was down to Hartland Centre a-buyin' some fat cattle for Hanerford market; an' I met Orrin Nye drivin' his team pretty spry, for he see it was comin' on to snow; but, when he catched sight o' me, he stopped the horses, an' hollered out to me: so I stepped along, an' asked what he wanted. An' he said there was a woman down to the Holler that had a cow to sell, an' he knowed I was apt to buy cow-critters along in the spring, so he'd spoke about it, for she was kinder in a hurry to sell, for she was goin' to move. So I said I'd see to't, an' he driv along. I thought likely I should git it cheap, ef she was in a hurry to sell, an' I concluded I'd go along next day: 'twa'n't more'n seven mile from the Centre, down by a piece o' piny woods, an' the woman was Miss Adams. I used ter know George Adams quite a spell ago, an' he was a likely feller. Well, it come on to snow jest as fine an' dry as sand, an' the wind blew like needles; an' come next day, when I started to foot it down there, I didn't feel as though I could ha' gone ef I hadn't been sure of a good bargain. The snow hadn't driv much, but the weather had settled down dreadful cold: 'twas dead still, an' the air sorter cut ye to breathe it; but I'm naterally hardy, an' I kep' along till I got there. I didn't feel so all-fired cold as I hev sometimes; but when I stepped in to the door, an' she asked me to hev a cheer by the fire, fust I knew I didn't know nothin': I come to the floor like a felled ox. I expect I must ha' been nigh on to dead with clear cold, for she was the best part o' ten minutes bringin' on me to. She rubbed my hands an' face with camphire, an' gin me some hot tea. She hadn't got no sperits in the house; but she did every thing a little woman could do, an' I was warmed through an' through afore long, an' we stepped out into the shed to look at the cow.

"Well, squire, I ha'n't got much natur' into me noway, an' it's well I ha'n't; but that cow beat all, I declare for't! She put her head round the minute Miss Adams come in; an', if ever you see a dumb beast pleased, that 'ere cow was tickled to pieces. She put her nose down to the woman's cheek, an' she licked her hands, an' she moved up agin' her, an' rubbed her ear on her: she all but talked. An' when I looked round, an' see them black eyes o' Miss Adams's with wet in 'em, I 'most wished I had a pocket-handkerchief myself.

"'You won't sell her to a hard master, will you?' says she. 'I want her to go where she'll be well cared for, an' I shall know where she is; for, if ever things comes right agin, I want to hev her back. She's been half my livin' an' all my company for quite a spell, an' I shall miss her dreadfully.'

"'Well,' says I, 'I'll take her down to Squire Hollis's in Avondale: he's got a cow-barn good enough for a representative to set in, an' clean water, an' chains to halter 'em up with, an' a dry yard where the water all dreens off as slick as can be; an' there a'n't such a piece o' land nowhere round for root-crops; an' the squire he sets such store by his cows an' things, I've heerd tell he turned off two Irishmen for abusin' on 'em; an' they has their bags washed, an' their tails combed, every day in the year, an' I don't know but what they ties 'em up with a blew ribbin.'"

"Get out!" growled grandfather.

"Can't, jest yet, squire, not till I've done. Anyway, I figgered it off to her, an' she was kinder consoled up to think on't; for I told her I thought likely you'd buy her cow. An' when we come to do the tradin' part, why, con-found it! she wa'n't no more fit to buy an' sell a critter than my three-year-old Hepsy. I said a piece back I ha'n't got much natur', an' a man that trades dumb beasts the biggest part o' the time hedn't oughter hev; but I swan to man! natur' was too much for me this time. I couldn't no more ha' bought that cow cheap than I could ha' sold my old gran'ther to a tin-peddler. Somehow, she was so innocent, an' she felt so to part with the critter, an' then she let me know't George was in the army; an' thinks I, I guess I'll help the gov'ment along some: I can't fight, 'cause I'm subject to rheumatiz in my back, but I can look out for them that can: so, take the hull on't, long an' broad, why, I up an' gin her seventy-five dollars for that cow, an' I'd ha' gin twenty more not to ha' seen Miss Adams's face a-lookin' arter me an' her when we went away from the door.

"So now, squire, you can take her, or leave her."

Aaron Stow knew his man. Squire Hollis pulled out his pocket-book, and paid seventy-five dollars on the spot for a native cow called Biddy.

"Now clear out with your Ayrshires!" said he irascibly. "I'm a fool, but I won't buy them too."

"Well, squire, good-day," said Aaron with a grin.

But I am credibly informed that the next week he did come back with the two Ayrshires, and sold them to grandfather, remarking to the farmer, that he "should ha' been a darned fool to take the old gentleman at his word; for he never knowed a man hanker arter harnsome stock, but what he bought it fust or last."

Now I also discovered that the regiment George enlisted in was one whose colonel I knew well: so I wrote, and asked about Sergeant Adams. My report was highly honorable to George, but had some bad news in it: he had been severely wounded in the right leg, and, though recovering, would be disabled from further service. A fortnight after, I drove into Hanerford with Grandfather Hollis, and we stopped at the old bakery. It looked exquisitely neat in the shop, as well as prosperous externally, and Dely stood behind the counter with a lovely child in her arms. Grandfather bought about half a bushel of crackers and cookies, while I played with the baby. As he paid for them, he said in his kind old voice, that nobody can hear without pleasure,—

"I believe I have a pet of yours in my barn at Avondale, Mrs. Adams."

Dely's eyes lighted up, and a quick flush of feeling glowed on her pretty face.

"O sir! you did buy Biddy, then? And you are Squire Hollis?"

"Yes, ma'am; and Biddy is well, and well cared for,—as fat and sleek as a mole, and still comes to her name."

"Thank you kindly, sir!" said Dely, with an emphasis that gave the simple phrase most earnest meaning.

"And how is your husband, Mrs. Adams?" said I.

A deeper glow displaced the fading blush grandfather had called out, and her beautiful eyes flashed at me.

"Quite well, I thank you, and not so very lame. And he's coming home next week."

She took the baby from me as she spoke, and, looking in its bright little face, said,—

"Call him, baby."

"Pa-pa!" said the child.

"If ever you come to Avondale, Mrs. Adams, come and see my cows," said grandfather as he gathered up the reins. "You may be sure I won't sell Biddy to anybody but you."

Dely smiled from the steps where she stood; and we drove away.

MISS BEULAH'S BONNET

"*I DON'T WANT* to be too fine, ye know, Mary Jane,—somethin' tasty and kind of suitable. It's an old bunnit; but my! them Leghorns'll last a generation if you favor 'em.¹ That was mother's weddin' bunnit."

"You don't say so! Well, it has kept remarkable well; but a good Leghorn will last, that's a fact, though they get real brittle after a spell: and you'll have to be awful careful of this, Miss Beulah; it's brittle now, I see."

"Yes, I expect it is; but it'll carry me through this summer, I guess. But I want you to make it real tasty, Mary Jane; for my niece Miss Smith, she that was 'Liza Barber, is coming to stay a while to our house this summer, and she lives in the city, you know."

"'Liza Barber! Do tell! Why, I haven't seen her sence she was knee-high to a hop-toad, as you may say. He ain't livin', is he?"

"No: he died two years ago, leavin' her with three children. Sarah is a grown girl; and then there's Jack, he's eight, and Janey, she's three. There was four died between Jack and Sarah. I guess she's full eighteen."

"Mercy to me! time flies, don't it? But about the bunnit: what should you say to this lavender ribbin?"

"Ain't I kind of dark for lavender? I had an idee to have brown, or mabbe dark green."

"Land! for spring? Why, that ain't the right thing. This lavender is real han'some; and I'll set it oft with a little black lace, and put a bow on't in the front. It'll be real dressy and seemly for you."

"Well, you can try it, Mary Jane; but I give you fair warnin', if I think it's too dressy, you'll have to take it all off."

Miss Beulah's Bonnet

"I'm willin'," laughed Miss Mary Jane Beers, a good old soul, and a contemporary of her customer, Miss Beulah Larkin, who was an old maid living in Dorset on a small amount of money carefully invested, and owning the great red house which her grandfather had built for a large family on one corner of his farm. Farm and family were both gone now, save and except Miss Beulah and her niece; but the old lady and a little maid she had taken to bring up dwelt in one end of the wide house, and contrived to draw more than half their subsistence from the garden and orchard attached to it. Here they spun out an innocent existence, whose chief dissipations were evening meetings, sewing-societies, funerals, and the regular Sunday services, to which all the village faithfully repaired, and any absence from which was commented on, investigated, and reprobated, if without good excuse, in the most unsparing manner. Miss Beulah Larkin was tall, gaunt, hard-featured, and good. Everybody respected her, some feared, and a few loved her: but she was not that sort of soul which thirsts to be loved; her whole desire and design was to do her duty and be respectable. Into this latter clause came the matter of a bonnet, over which she had held such anxious discourse. If she had any feminine vanity,—and she was a woman,—it took this virtuous aspect of a desire to be "respectit like the lave," for decency of dress as well as demeanor. This spring she had received a letter from her niece, the widowed Mrs. Smith, asking if she could come to visit her; and, sending back a pleased assent, Miss Beulah and her little handmaid Nanny Starks bestirred themselves to sweep and garnish the house, already fresh and spotless from its recent annual cleaning. Windows were opened, beds put out to sun, blankets aired, spreads unfolded, sheets taken from the old chests, and long-disused dimity curtains washed, ironed, and tacked up against the small-paned sashes, and tied back with scraps of flowered ribbon, exhumed from hidden shelves, that might well have trimmed that Leghorn bonnet in its first youth.

Mrs. Eliza Smith was a poor woman, but a woman of resource. Her visit was not purely of affection, or of family respect. Her daughter Sarah—a pretty, slight, graceful girl, with gold-brown hair, dark straight brows above a pair of limpid gray eyes, red lips, and a clear pale skin—had been intended by her mother to blossom into beauty in due season, and "marry well," as the phrase goes; but Sarah and a certain Fred Wilson, telegraph-operator in Dartford, had set all the thrifty mother's plans at defiance, and fallen head over heels in love, regardless of Mrs. Smith or anybody else. Sarah's brows were not black and straight, or her chin firm and cleft with a dimple, for nothing: she meant to marry Fred Wilson as soon as was convenient; and Mrs. Smith, having unusual common sense, as well as previous experience of Sarah's capacity of resistance, ceased to oppose that young lady's resolute intention. Master Wilson had already gone West, to a more lucrative situation than Dartford afforded; and Sarah was only waiting to get ready as to her outfit, and amass enough money for the cost of travelling, to follow him, since he was unable to return for her, both from lack of money and time. In this condition of things it occurred to Mrs. Smith that it would save a good deal of money if she could spend the summer with Aunt Beulah, and so be spared the expense of board and lodging for her family. Accordingly she looked about for a tenant for her little house; and, finding one ready to come in sooner than she had anticipated, she answered aunt Beulah's friendly letter of invitation with an immediate acceptance, and followed her own epistle at once, arriving just as the last towel had been hung on the various wash-stands, and while yet the great batch of sweet home-made bread was hot from the oven, and, alas for Miss Beulah! before that Leghorn bonnet had come home from Miss Beers's front-parlor, in which she carried on her flourishing millinery business.

Miss Larkin was unfeignedly glad to see Eliza again, though her eyes grew a little dim, perceiving how time had transformed the fresh, gay girl she remembered into this sad and sallow woman; but she said nothing of these changes, and, giving the rest an equal welcome, established them in the clean, large, cool chambers that were such a contrast to the hot rooms, small and dingy, of their city home.

Jack was a veritable little pickle, tall of his age, and light of foot and hand; nature had framed him in body and mind for mischief: while Sarah was a pleasant, handy young girl, as long as nothing opposed her; and Janey a round and rosy poppet, who adored Jack, and rebelled against her mother and Sarah hourly. Jack was a born nuisance: Miss Beulah could hardly endure him, he did so controvert all the orders and manners of her neat house. He hunted the hens to the brink of distraction, and broke up their nests till eggs were scarce to find,—a state of things never before known in that old barn, where the hens had dwelt and done their duty, till that duty had consigned them to the stew-pan, for years and years. He made the cat's life a burden to her in a hundred ways; and poor Nanny Starks had never any rest or peace till her tormentor was safe in bed.

Mrs. Smith began to fear her visit would be prematurely shortened on Jack's account: and Sarah, who had wisely confided her love-affair to aunt Beulah, and stirred that hardened heart to its core by her pathetic tale of poverty and separation, began to dread the failure of her hopes also; for her aunt had more than hinted that she would give something toward that travelling money which was now the girl's great object in life, since by diligent sewing she had almost finished her bridal outfit. As for Janey, she was already, in spite of her naughtiness, mistress of aunt Beulah's very soul. Round, fat, rosy, bewitching as a child and only a child can be, the poor spinster's repressed affection, her denied maternity, her love of beauty,—a secret to herself,—and her protecting instinct, all blossomed for this baby, who stormed or smiled at her according to the caprice of the hour, but was equally lovely in the old lady's eyes whether she smiled or stormed. If Janey said "Tum!" in her imperative way, Miss Beulah came, whether her hands were in the wash-tub or the bread-tray. Janey ran riot over her most cherished customs; and, while she did not hesitate to scold or even slap Jack harshly for his derelictions, she had an excuse always ready for Janey's worst sins, and a kiss instead of a blow for her wildest exploits of mischief. Jack hated the old aunty as much as he feared her tongue and hand: and this only made matters worse; for he felt a certain right to torment her that would not have been considered a right, had he felt instead any shame for abusing her kindness. But a soft answer from her never turned away his wrath, or this tale of woe about her bonnet had never been told.

There had been long delay concerning that article. The bleacher had been slow, and the presser impracticable: it had been sent back once to be reshaped, and then the lavender ribbon had proved of scant measure, and had to be matched. But at last, one hot day in May, Nanny brought the queer old bandbox home from Miss Beers's, and aunt Beulah held up her head-gear to be commented on. It was really a very good-looking bonnet. The firm satin ribbon was a pleasant tint, and contrasted well with the pale color of the Leghorn; and a judicious use of black lace gave it an air of sobriety and elegance combined, which pleased Miss Beulah's eye, and even moved Mrs. Smith to express approbation.

"Well, I'm free to own it suits me," said the old lady, eying the glass with her head a little on one side, as a bird eyes a worm. "It's neat, and it's becomin', as fur as a bunnit can be said to be becomin' to an old woman, though I ain't really to call old. Mary Jane Beers is older than me; and she ain't but seventy-three,—jest as spry as a lark too. Yes, I like the bunnit; but it doos—sort of—seem—as though that there bow wa'n't really in the middle of it. What do you think, 'Lizy?"

"I don't see but what it's straight, aunt Beulah."

" 'Tain't," said the spinster firmly. "Sary, you look at it."

Sarah's eye was truer than her mother's. " 'Tis a mite too far to the left, aunt Beulah; but I guess I can fix it."

"You let her take it," said Mrs. Smith. "She's a real good hand at millinery: she made her own hat, and Janey's too. I should hate to have her put her hand to that bunnit if she wa'n't; for it's real pretty—'specially for a place like Dorset to get up."

"Lay it off on the table, aunt Beulah. I'm going up stairs to make my bed, and I'll fetch my work-basket down, and fix that bow straight in a jiffy."

"Well, I must go up too," said Mrs. Smith, and followed Sarah out of the room; but Miss Beulah, though duty called her too, in the imperative shape of a batch of bread waiting to be moulded up, lingered a little longer, poising the bonnet on her hand, holding it off to get a distant view, turning it from side to side, and, in short, behaving exactly as younger and prettier women do over a new hat, even when it is a miracle of art from Paris, instead of a revamped Leghorn from a country shop.

She laid it down with a long breath of content, for taste and economy had done their best for her; and then she, too, left the room, never perceiving that Jack and Janey had been all the time deeply engaged under the great old-fashioned breakfast-table, silently ripping up a new doll to see what was inside it,—silently, because they had an inward consciousness that it was mischief they were about; and Jack, at least, did not want to be interrupted till he was through. But he had not been too busy to hear and understand that aunt Beulah was pleased; and, still smarting from the switch with which she had whipped his shoulders that very morning for putting the cat into the cistern, he saw an opportunity for revenge before his eyes: he would hide this precious bonnet so aunt Beulah could never find it again. How to do this, and not be found out, was a problem to be considered; but mischief is quick-witted. There stood in the window a large rocking-chair, well stuffed under its chintz cover, and holding a plump soft feather cushion so big it fairly overflowed the seat. Under this cushion he was sure nobody would think of looking; and, to save himself from consequences, he resolved to make Janey a cat's-paw: so he led her up to the table, made her lift the precious hat and deposit it under the cushion, which he raised for the purpose; then, carefully dropping the frill, he tugged Janey, unwilling but scared and silent, out into the yard, and, impressing on her infant mind with wild threats of bears and guns that she must never tell where the bonnet was, he contrived to interest her in a new play so intensely, that the bonnet went utterly into oblivion, as far as she was concerned; and when they were called in to dinner, and she had taken her daily nap, Janey had become as innocent of mischief in her own memory as the dolly who lay all disemboweled and forlorn under the table.

When Sarah came down and did not find the bonnet, she concluded aunt Beulah had put it away in her own room, for fear a sacrilegious fly or heedless speck of dust might do it harm: so she took up a bit of lace she was knitting, and went out into the porch, glad to get into a cool place, the day was so warm.

And when the bread was moulded up, aunt Beulah came back, and, not seeing her bonnet, supposed Sarah had taken it up stairs to change the bow. She was not an impatient woman, and the matter was not pressing: so she said nothing about the bonnet at dinner, but hurried over that meal in order to finish her baking. Mrs. Smith had not come down again, for a morning headache had so increased upon her, she had lain down: so that no one disturbed the rocking-chair in which that bonnet lay hid till Mrs. Blake, the minister's wife, came in to make a call about four o'clock. She was a stout woman, and the walk had tired her. Aunt Beulah's hospitable instincts were roused by that red, weary face.

"You're dreadful warm, ain't you, Miss Blake?" said she. "It's an amazin' warm day for this time of year, and it's consider'ble more'n a hen-hop from your house up here. Lay your bunnit off, do, and set down in the rocker. I'll tell Nanny to fetch some shrub and water. Our ras'berry shrub is good, if I do say it; and it's kep' over as good as new."

So Mrs. Blake removed her bonnet, and sank down on that inviting cushion with all her weight, glad enough to rest, and ignorant of the momentous consequences. Her call was somewhat protracted. Had there been any pins in that flattened Leghorn beneath her, she might have shortened her stay. But Miss Mary Jane Beers was conscientiously opposed to pins; and every lavender bow was sewed on with silk to match, and scrupulous care. After the whole village news had been discussed, the state of religion lamented, and the short-comings of certain sisters who failed in attending prayer-meetings talked over,—with the charitable admission, to be sure, that one had a young baby, and another a sprained ankle,—Mrs. Blake rose to go, tied on her bonnet, and said good-by all round, quite as ignorant as her hosts of the remediless ruin she had done.

It was tea-time now; and, as they sat about the table, Sarah said, "I guess I'll fix your bonnet after tea, aunty: 'twon't take but a minute, and I'd rather do it while I recollect just where that bow goes."

"Why, I thought you had fixed it!" returned Miss Beulah.

"Well, I came right back to ; but it wa'n't here. I thought you'd took it into your bedroom."

"I hain't touched it sence it lay right here on the table."

"I'll run up and ask ma: maybe she laid it by."

But Mrs. Smith had not been down stairs since she left aunt Beulah with the bonnet in her hands. And now the old lady turned on Jack. "Have you ben and carried off my bunnit, you little besom?"

"I hain't touched your old bonnet!" retorted Jack with grand scorn.

"I don't believe he has," said Sarah; "for, when I come down stairs and found it wa'n't here, I went out and set on the bench to the front-door, and I heard him and Janey away off the other side of the yard, playin'; and you know they wa'n't in here when the bonnet come."

"Well, of course Janey hasn't seen it, if Jack hasn't; and, if she had, the blessed child wouldn't have touched old aunty's bonnet for a dollar— would she, precious lamb?" And aunt Beulah stroked the bright curls of her darling, who looked up into her face, and laughed; while Jack grinned broadly between his bites of bread and butter, master of the situation, and full of sweet revenge. "And Nanny hain't seen it, I know," went on aunt Beulah; "for she was along of me the whole enduring time. She set right to a-parin' them Roxbury russets the minnit she fetched home the bunnit; and I kep' her on the tight jump ever sence, because it's bakin'-day, and there was a sight to do. But I'll ask her: 'tain't lost breath to ask, my mother used to say, and mabbe it's a gain."

The old lady strode out into the kitchen with knit brows, but came back without any increased knowledge. "She hain't ben in here once sence she set down the bandbox; and, come to think on't, I know she hain't, for I cleared the table myself to-day, and, besides, the bunnit wa'n't here at dinner-time. Now let's hunt for it. Things don't gener'lly vanish away without hands; but, if we can't find no hands, why, it's as good as the next thing to look for the bunnit."

So they went to work and searched the house, as they thought, most thoroughly. No nook or corner but was investigated, if it was large enough to hold that bonnet; but nobody once thought of looking under the chair-cushion. If it had been as plump and fluffy as when Jack first had Janey put the lost structure under it, there might have been a suspicion of its hiding-place; but Mrs. Blake's two hundred pounds of solid flesh had reduced bonnet and cushion alike to unusual flatness. Or, if it had been any other day but Saturday, the chair might have been dusted and shaken up, and revealed its mystery; but early that very morning the house below stairs had been swept, and the furniture dusted, the cushions shaken out, the brasses polished, and all the weekly order and purity restored everywhere. The bonnet was evidently lost; and Jack, who had followed the domestic detectives up stairs and down, retired behind the wood-pile, and executed a joyful dance to relieve his suppressed feelings, snapping his fingers, and slapping his knees, and shouting scraps of all the expletives he knew, in the joy of his heart. How tragic would this mirth have seemed to a spectator aware of its cause, contrasted with the portentous gloom on aunt Beulah's forehead, and the abstracted glare of her eye! For several days this deluded spinster mused and mazed over her bonnet, going to church on Sunday in her shabby old velvet hat, which had scarcely been respectable before, but now, in the glare of a hot May sun, not only showed all its rubbed and worn places, its shiny streaks and traces of eaves-drops in the depressed and tangled nap, but also made her head so hot that she fairly went to bed at last with sick-headache, unable to attend evening service,—a most unheard-of thing for her.

Before the week was half done, she had settled into a profound belief that some tramp had passed while they were all out of the room, and, charmed by that lavender satin ribbon and black lace, stolen the bonnet, and carried it off to sell; and many a time did Miss Beulah sit rocking to and fro on top of her precious Leghorn, wondering and bemoaning at its loss. But murder will out—sometimes, and would certainly have come out in the weekly cleaning the next Saturday, if, on the Friday morning, Miss Beulah had not set down a pitcher of milk, just brought in by a neighbor, on the end of the table nearest to that rocking-chair—set it down only for a moment, to get the neighbor a recipe for sugar gingerbread peculiar to the Larkin family. Janey happened to be thirsty, and reached after the pitcher, but was just tall enough to grasp the handle so low down, that when she pulled at it, steadying herself against the chair, it tipped sideways, and poured a copious stream of fresh milk on the cushion. The chintz was old, and had lost its glaze, and the feathers were light; so the rich fluid soaked in at once; and before the two women, recalled from the cupboard by Janey's scream, could reach the pitcher, there was only a very soppy and wet cushion in the chair.

"For mercy's sakes!" said the neighbor. But Miss Beulah, with great presence of mind, snatched up the dripping mass and flung it out of the open window, lest her carpet should suffer. She reverted to the chair in a second, and stood transfixed.

"What under the everlastin' canopy!" broke from her dismayed lips; for there, flattened out almost beyond recognition, and broken wherever it was bent, its lavender ribbons soaked with milk, the cheap lace limp and draggled, lay the remains of the Leghorn bonnet.

"Of all things!" exclaimed the neighbor; but there was an echo of irrepressible amusement in her tones. Aunt Beulah glared at her, and lifted the damp bonnet as tenderly as if it had been Janey's curls, regarding it with an expression pen or pencil fails to depict,—a mixture of grief, pity, indignation, and amazement, that, together with the curious look of the bonnet, was too much for the neighbor; and, to use her own after-expression in describing the scene, she "snickered right out."

"Laugh, do," said aunt Beulah witheringly.—"do laugh! I guess, if your best bunnit had ben set on and drownded, you'd laugh the other side o' your mouth, Miss Jackson. This is too much."

"Well, I be sorry," said the placable female; "but it doos look so dreadful ridiculous like, I couldn't noways help myself. But how on earth did it git there, I admire to know?"

"I dono myself as I know; but I hain't a doubt in my own mind that it was that besom of a Jack. He is *the* fullest of 'riginal sin and actual transgression of any boy I ever see. He did say, now I call to mind, that he hadn't never touched it; but I mistrust he did. He beats all for mischief that I ever see. I'm free to say I never did like boys. I suppose divine Providence ordained 'em to some good end; but it takes a sight o' grace to believe it: and, of all the boys that ever was sent into this world for any purpose, I do believe he is the hatefulest. I'd jest got my bunnit to my mind, calc'latin' to wear it all summer; and I am a mite pernickity, I'll allow that, about my bunnits. Well, 'tain't no use to cry over spilt milk."

"I'll fetch ye some more to-morrow," said the literal neighbor.

"You're real good, Miss Jackson; but I'm more exercised a lot about my bunnit that I be about the milk.—Sary, look a-here!"

Sarah, just coming in at the door, did look, and, like Mrs. Jackson, felt a strong desire to smile, but with native tact controlled it.

"Why, where on earth did you find it, aunt Beulah?"

"Right under the rocker-cushion. It must have ben there when Miss Blake come in that day and set down there; for I remember thinkin' Nanny must ha' shook that cushion up more'n usual, it looked so comfortable and high."

"I don't wonder it's flat, if Miss Blake set on't," giggled Mrs. Jackson, at which aunt Beulah's face darkened so perceptibly that the good neighbor took her leave. Comedy to her was tragedy to the unhappy owner of the bonnet; and she had the sense to know she was alien to the spirit of the hour, and go home.

"But how did it get there?" asked Sarah.

"You tell," replied Miss Beulah, "for I can't. I do mistrust Jack."

"Jack said he hadn't touched it, though; and it couldn't get there without hands."

"Well, mabbe Jack don't always say the thing that is. 'Foolishness is bound up in the heart of a child,' Scriptur says; and I guess he hain't had enough of the rod o'correction to drive it out of him yet. He's the behavin'est youngster *I* ever see; and I'm quite along in years, if I be spry."

"I'll call him, aunty, and see what he'll say this time."

"'Twon't be no use: if he's lied once, he'll lie twice. Scriptur says the Devil was a liar from the beginnin'; and I expect that means that lyin' is ingrain. I never knowed it to be fairly knocked out of anybody yet, even when amazin' grace wrastled with it. There's Deacon Shubael Morse: why, he's as good as gold; but them Morses is a proverb, you may say, and always hes ben, time out o' mind,—born liars, so to speak. I've heerd Grandsir Larkin say, that, as fur back as he could call to mind, folks would say,—

> 'Steal a horse,
> An' b'lieve a Morse.'

But the deacon he's a hero at prayer, and gives heaps to the s'cieties; but he ain't reely to be relied on. He's sharper'n a needle to bargain with; and, if his word ain't writ down in black and white, why, 'taint nowhere. He don't read no novils, nor play no cards: he'd jest as lives swear outright as do one or t'other. But I do say for't, I'd ruther myself see him real honest than any o' them things. I don't believe in no sort o' professin' that falls short in practisin'; but I can't somehow feel so real spry to blame the deacon as though he wa'n't a Morse. But you call Jack anyhow."

So Jack was called.

He came in, with Janey, flushed, lovely, and dirty, trotting behind him, and was confronted with the bonnet.

"Jack, did you hide it?"

"I hain't touched your old bonnet. I said so before."

An idea struck Sarah.

"Janey," she said sharply, "did you put aunty's bonnet under the cushion?"

"Janey don't 'member," said the child, smiling as innocently as the conventional cherub of art.

"Well, you must remember!" said Sarah, picking her up from the floor, and setting her down with emphasis on the table.

Janey began to cry.

"Naughty Salah hurt Janey!" and the piteous tears coursed down her rosy, dust-smeared cheeks from those big blue eyes that looked like dew-drowned forget-me-nots.

Aunt Beulah could not stand this. "You let that baby alone, Sarah! She don't know enough to be naughty, bless her dear little soul!—There, there, don't you cry a mite more, Janey. Aunty'll give you ginger-cooky this very minute!"

And Janey was comforted with kisses and smiles and gingerbread, her face washed, and her curls softly turned on tender fingers; while Jack, longing for gingerbread with the preternatural appetite of a growing boy, was sent off in disgrace.

"I make no doubt you done it, you little rascal, and lied it out too. But I don't b'lieve you no more for your lyin': so don't look for no extries from me. Fellers like you don't get gingerbread nor turnovers, now I tell you!"

How Jack hated her! How glad he was he had spoiled her bonnet! Shall I draw a moral here to adorn my tale? No, dear reader: this is not a treatise on education. Miss Beulah was a good woman; and if she made mistakes, like the rest of us, she took the consequences as the rest of us do; and the consequences of this spoiled bonnet were not yet ended.

She felt as if she must have a new one for Sunday. She really did not know how to afford it; for she had promised to help Sarah, and in her eyes a promise was as sacred as an oath. And, as for giving up her subscriptions to home missions, that would be a wilful sin. But, without a bonnet, she could not go to meeting; and that was a sin too. So she put on her sun-bonnet; and taking the wreck of the Leghorn, carefully concealed in a paper, she set out after tea that same evening for a conference with Miss Beers, stopping at the post-office as she went along. She found one letter awaiting her, and knew by the superscription that it was from a second-cousin of hers in Dartford, who had charge of such money of hers as was not in the savings bank or Dartford and Oldbay Railroad stock—a road paying steady dividends. But, besides the three or four thousands in these safe investments that Miss Beulah owned, she had two shares in a manufacturing company, and one in Dartford Bridge stock, from which her cousin duly remitted the annual dividends: so, knowing what was in the letter, for the tool company's payment was just due, she did not open it till she sat down in Miss Beer's shop, and first opened the Leghorn to view.

"Of all things!" said Miss Beers, lifting up hands and eyes during Miss Beulah's explanations. "And you can't do nothing with it—never. Why, it's flatter'n a pancake. Well, you couldn't expect nothing else, with Miss

Blake on top on't: she'd squash a baby out as thin as a tin plate if she happened to set on't, which I do hope she won't. See! the Leghorn's all broke up. I told you 'twas dreadful brittle. And the ribbin is spoiled entire. You can't never clean lavender, nor yet satin, it frays so. And the lace is all gum: anyway, that's gone. Might as well chuck the hull into the fire."

"So do, Mary Jane, so do. I never want to set eyes on't again. I haven't no patience with that boy now, and the bunnit riles me to look at. I do want to do right by the boy, but it goes against the grain dreadful. I mistrust I shall have to watch and pray real hard before I can anyway have patience with him. I tell you he's a cross to 'Liza as well as to me. But don't let's talk about him. What have you got that'll do for a bunnit for me?"

Then the merits of the various bonnets in Miss Beers's small stock were canvassed. A nice black chip suited aunt Beulah well; and a gray corded ribbon, with a cluster of dark pansies, seemed just the thing for trimming. In fact, she liked it, and with good reason, better than the Leghorn; but it was expensive. All the materials, though simple, were good and rich. Try as she would, Miss Beers could not get it up for less than six dollars, and that only allowed twenty-five cents for her own work. The alternative was a heavy coarse straw, which she proposed to deck with a yellow-edged black ribbon, and put some gold-eyed black daisies inside. But Miss Beulah did want the chip.

"Let's see," said she. "Mabbe this year's dividend is seven per cent: 'tis once in a while. I'll see what cousin Joseph says. If 'tain't more than usual, I must take the straw."

But cousin Joseph had to tell her, that owing to damage by flood and fire, as well as a general disturbance of business all over the county, the C.A. Company paid *no* dividend this year.

"Then I sha'n't have no bunnit," said Miss Larkin firmly.

"Why, you've got to have some kind of a bunnit," said the amazed Miss Beers.

"I hain't got to if I can't."

"But why can't ye, Beulah? All your money and all your dividends ain't in that comp'ny."

"Well, there's other uses for money this year besides bunnits."

"You can't go to meetin'."

"I can stay to home."

"Why, Beulah Larkin, I'll trust you, and welcome."

"But I won't be trusted. I never was, and I never will be. What if I should up and die?"

"I'd sue the estate," practically remarked Miss Beers.

"No: 'out of debt, out of danger,' mother always said, and I believe in't. I shall hate to stay to home Sundays, but I can go to prayer-meetin' in my slat bunnit well enough."

"Why, the church'll deal with ye, Beulah, if ye neglect stated means of grace."

"Let 'em deal," was the undaunted answer. Miss Beulah had faced the situation, arranged it logically, and accepted it. She had promised Sarah fifteen dollars in June. She had lost a dividend of twelve dollars on which she had reckoned with certainty; five dollars was due to home missions; and, with her increased family, there would be no margin for daily expenses. There were twenty dollars in the savings bank over and above the five hundred she had laid up for a rainy day, and left in her will, made and signed but last week, to little Janey. On this she would not trench, come what might, except in case of absolute distress; and the twenty dollars were sacred to Sarah and home missions. But this was her private affair: she would not make the poverty of her niece known abroad, or the nature of her will. If the church chose to deal with her, it might; but her lips should never open to explain,—a commonplace martyrdom enough, and less than saintly because so much of human pride and self-will mingled in its suffering; yet honesty and uprightness are so scarce in these days as to make even such a sturdy witness for them respectable, and many a woman who counts herself a model of sanctity might shrink from a like daily ordeal. But aunt Beulah set her face as a flint, and pursued her way in silence. June came and went; and with it went Sarah to her expectant bridegroom in Chicago, from whence a paper with due notice of her marriage presently returned. Aunt Beulah strove hard to make both ends meet in her housekeeping, and, being a close manager, succeeded. There was no margin, not even twenty-five spare cents to take Janey to the circus; though she cut aunt Beulah's heart with entreaties to be taken to see "lions an' el'phants," and said, "P'ease take Janey," in a way to melt a stone. For to get food enough to satisfy Jack was in itself a problem. Often and often the vexed spinster declared to Nanny, her sympathizing handmaid,—

" 'Tain't no use a-tryin' to fill him. He's holler down to his boots, I know. He eat six b'iled eggs for breakfast, and heaps of johnny-cake, besides a pint o' milk, and was as sharp-set for dinner as though he'd ben a-mowin' all the forenoon. 'Lizy says he's growin'. If he grows anyways accordin' to what he eats, he'll be as big as Goliath of Gath, as sure as you're born. I don't begrudge the boy reasonable vittles, but I can't buy butcher's-meat enough to satisfy him noway. And as to garden sass, he won't eat none. That would be real fillin' if he would. Thanks be to praise! he likes Indian. Pudding and johnny-cake do help a sight."

But while aunt Beulah toiled and moiled, and filled her wide measure of charity toward these widowed and fatherless with generous hand, the church, mightily scandalized at her absence from its services, was preparing to throw a shell into her premises. It was all very well to say to Miss Beers that she was not afraid of such a visitation; but a trouble at hand is of quite another aspect than a trouble afar off. Her heart quailed and fluttered, when, one July afternoon, Nanny ushered into the dark, cool parlor Deacon Morse and Deacon Flint, come to ask her why she had not attended church since the middle of last May, when she was in usual health and exercise of her faculties. Miss Beulah, however, was equal to the occasion. She faced the deacons sternly, but calmly.

"It is so," she said, when they had finished their accusation. "I hain't ben to meetin' for good cause. You can't say I've did any thing that's give occasion to the enemy more'n this. I've attended reg'lar to prayer-meetin's and sewin'-circle. I've give as usual to home missions. You can't say I've made any scandal, or done nothin' out o' rule, save an' except stayin' at home sabbath days; and my family has attended punctooally."

But this did not satisfy the deacons: they pressed for a reason.

"If you would free your mind, sister Larkin, it would be for the good of the church," said Deacon Morse.

"Mabbe 'twouldn't be altogether to your likin' deacon, if I did free my mind. Seems as though stayin' at home from meetin' wa'n't no worse'n sandin' sugar an' waterin' rum; and I never heerd you was dealt with for them things."

Deacon Morse was dumb, but Deacon Flint took up the discourse.

"Well, sister Larkin, we didn't know but what you was troubled in your mind."

"I ain't!" snapped Miss Beulah.

"Or perhaps was gettin' a mite doubtful about doctrines, or suthin'."

"No, I ain't. I go by the 'Sembly's Catechism, and believe in every word on't, questions and all."

"Well, you seem to be a leetle contumacious, sister Larkin, so to speak: if you had a good reason, why, of course, you'd be willin' to tell it."

This little syllogism caught Miss Beulah.

"Well, if you must know, I hain't got no bunnit."

The deacons stared mutually; and Deacon Morse, forgetful of his defeat, and curious, as men naturally are, asked abruptly, "Why not?"

"Cause Miss Blake sot on it."

The two men looked at each other in blank amazement, and shook their heads. Here was a pitfall. Was it proper, dignified, possible, to investigate this truly feminine tangle? They were dying to enter into particulars, but ashamed to do so: nothing was left but retreat. Miss Beulah perceived the emergency, and chuckled grimly. This was the last straw. The deacons rose as one man, and said, "Good-day," with an accent of reprobation, going their ways in deep doubt as to what they should report to the church, which certainly would not receive with proper gravity the announcement that Miss Beulah Larkin could not come to church because the minister's wife had sat on her Sunday bonnet. The strife of tongues, however, did not spare aunt Beulah, if the deacons did; and for a long time Miss Beers, who had the key to the situation, did not hear any of the gossip, partly because she had been ill of low fever, and then gone to her sister's in Dartford for change of air, and partly, that, during July and August, the sewing-circle was temporarily suspended. But it renewed its sessions in September; and Miss Beers was an active member, sure to be at the first meeting. It was then and there she heard the scorn and jeers and un-founded stories come on like a tidal wave to overwhelm her friend's character. She listened a few minutes in silence, growing more and more indignant. Then, for she was a little woman as far as stature went, she mounted into a chair, and demanded the floor in her own fashion.

"Look, a-here!" said she, her shrill voice soaring above the busy clapper of tongues below. "It's a burnin' shame to say a hard word about Beulah Larkin. She's as good a woman as breathes the breath of life, and I know the hull why and wherefore she hain't ben to meetin'. She hain't had no bunnit. I made her as tasty a bunnit as ever you see last spring; and that jackanapes of a boy he chucked it under the rocker-cushion jest to plague her, and Miss Blake she come in and sot right down on it, not knowin', of course, that 'twas there; and, as if that wa'n't enough to spile it" (an involuntary titter seemed to express the sense of the audience that it was), "that other sprig, she took and upsot a pitcher of milk onto the cushion, and you'd better believe that bunnit was a sight!"

"Why didn't she get another?" severely asked Deacon Morse's wife.

"Why? Why, becos she's a-most a saint. Her dividends some on 'em didn't come in, and she'd promised that biggest girl fifteen dollars to help her get out to her feller at Chicago, for Sary told me on't herself; and then she gives five dollars to hum missions every year, and she done it this year jest the same; and she's took that widder and them orphans home all summer, and nigh about worked her head off for 'em, and never charged a cent o' board; and therefor and thereby she hain't had no money to buy no bunnit, and goes to prayer-meetin' in her calico slat."

A rustle of wonder and respect went through the room as the women moved uneasily in their chairs, exchanged glances, and said, "My!" which inspired Miss Beers to go on.

"And here everybody's ben a-talkin' bad about her, while she's ben a real home-made kind of a saint. I know she don't look it; but she doos it, and that's a sight better. I don't b'lieve there's one woman in forty could ha' had the grit and the perseverance to do what she done, and hold her tongue about it too. I know I couldn't for one."

"She shouldn't ha' let her good be evil spoken of," said Mrs. Morse with an air of authority.

"I dono as anybody had oughter have spoken evil of her good," was Miss Beers's dry answer; and Mrs. Morse said no more.

But such a warm and generous vindication touched many a feminine heart, which could appreciate Miss Beulah's self-sacrifice better than the deacons could. There was an immediate clustering and chattering among the good women, who, if they did love a bit of gossip, were none the less kindly and well-meaning; and presently a spokeswoman approached Miss Beers with the proposition, that, if she would make Miss Beulah a handsome bonnet, a dozen or more had volunteered to buy the materials.

Miss Beulah's Bonnet

"Well," said Miss Mary Jane, wiping her spectacles, "this is real kind; and I make no doubt but what Beulah'd think the same, though she's a master-hand to be independent, and some folks say proud. Mabbe she is; but I know she couldn't but take it kind of friends and neighbors to feel for her. However, there ain't no need on't. It seems that Sary's husband ain't very forehanded, and she's got a dreadful taste for the millinery business: so she's gone to work in one of the fust shops there, and is gettin' great wages, for her; and only yesterday there come a box by *express* for Miss Beulah, with the tastiest bunnit in it I ever see in my life,—good black velvet, with black satin kinder puffed into the brim, and a dark-green wing to one side of the band, and a big bow in under a jet buckle behind. I tell *you* it was everlastin' pretty. Sary she sent a note to say she hoped aunt Beulah'd give her the pleasure to accept it; for she'd knowed all along how that she was the cause of her goin' without a bunnit all summer (I expect her ma had writ to her), and she felt real bad about it. You'd better b'lieve Beulah was pleased."

And Miss Beulah was pleased again when the women from the village began to call on her even more frequently than before, and express cordial and friendly interest in a way that surprised her, all unaware as she was of Miss Beers's enthusiastic vindication of her character before the sewing-circle. Yet, poor, dear, silly old woman,—only a woman, after all,—nothing so thrilled and touched her late-awakened heart as little Janey's soft caresses and dimpled patting hands on that sallow old face, when she climbed into her lap the next Sunday, and, surveying Miss Beulah's new bonnet exclaimed, with her silvery baby voice, "Pitty, pitty bonnet!"

Jack did not say any thing about it, nor did the congregation, though on more than one female face beamed a furtive congratulatory smile; and Deacon Flint looked at Deacon Morse across the aisle.

If there is any moral to this story, as no doubt there should be, it lies in the fact that Mrs. Blake never again sat down in a chair without first lifting the cushion.

TOO LATE

❧❧❧❧❧❧

" 'Tis true 'tis pity! pity 'tis 'tis true!"[1]

IN ONE OF THOSE scanty New England towns that fill a stranger with the acutest sense of desolation, more desolate than the desert itself, because there are human inhabitants to suffer from its solitude and listlessness, there stood, and still stands, a large red farm-house, with sloping roof, and great chimney in the middle, where David Blair lived. Perhaps Wingfield was not so forlorn to him as to another, for he had Scotch blood in his veins, and his shrewd thrift found full exercise in redeeming the earth from thorns and briers, and eating his bread under the full force of the primeval curse. He was a "dour" man, with a long, grim visage that would have become any Covenanter's conventicle in his native land; and his prayers were as long and grim as his face. Of life's graces and amenities he had no idea; they would have been scouted as profane vanities had they blossomed inside his threshold. Existence to him was a heavy and dreadful responsibility; a drear and doubtful working out of his own salvation; a perpetual fleeing from the wrath to come, that seemed to dog his heels and rear threatening heads at every turn. A cowardly man, with these ever-present terrors, would have taken refuge in some sweet and lulling sin or creed, some belief of a universal salvation, some epicurean "let us eat and drink, for to-morrow we die," or some idea in nothing beyond the grave.

But David Blair was full of courage. Like some knotty, twisted oak, that offers scant solace to the eye, he endured, oak-like, all storms, and bent not an atom to any fierce blast of nature or Providence; for he made a distinction between them. His wife was a neat, quiet, subdued woman, who held her house and her husband in as much reverence as a Feejee holds his idols. Like most women, she had an instinctive love for grace and beauty, but from long repression it was only a blind and groping instinct. Her house was kept in a state of spotless purity, but was bald as any vineless rock within. Flies never intruded there; spiders still less. The windows of the "best room" were veiled and double-veiled with green paper shades and snow-white cotton curtains, and the ghastly light that strayed in through these obstructions revealed a speckless, but hideous, homespun carpet, four straight-backed chairs, with horse-hair seats, an equally black and shining sofa, and a round mahogany table with a great Bible in the midst. No vases, no shells, no ornament of useless fashion stood on the white wooden mantel-piece over the open fireplace; no stencil border broke the monotonous whitewash of the walls. You could see your face in a state of distortion and jaundice anywhere in the andirons, so brilliant were their brassy columns; and the very bricks of the chimney were scraped and washed from the soot of the rare fire. You could hardly imagine that even the leaping, laughing wood-fire could impart any cheer to the funereal order of that chill and musty apartment. Bedroom, kitchen, shed, wood-house,—all shared this scrupulous array. The processes that in other households are wont to give cheery tokens of life, and bounty, and natural appetites and passions, seemed here to be carried on under protest. No flour was spilled when Thankful Blair made bread; no milk ever slopped from an overfull pail; no shoe ever brought in mud or sand across the mats that lay inside and outside of every door. The very garret preserved an aspect of serenity, since all its bundles of herbs hung evenly side by side, and the stores of nuts had each their separate boundaries, lest some jarring door or intrusive mouse should scatter them.

In the midst of all this order there was yet a child, if little Hannah Blair ever was a child in more than name. From her babyhood she was the model of all Wingfield babies: a child that never fretted; that slept nights through all the pangs and perils of teething; that had every childish disease with perfect decency and patience; was a child to be held up to every mother's admiration. Poor little soul! the mother love that crushed those other babies with kisses; that romped and laughed with them, when she was left straight and solemn in her cradle; that petted, and slapped, and spoiled, and scolded all those common children, Thankful Blair kept under lock and key in her inmost heart.

"Beware of idols!" was the stern warning that had fallen on her first outburst of joy at the birth of one living child at last, and from that time the whole tenor of her husband's speech and prayer had been that they both might be saved from the awful sin of idolatry, and be enabled to bring up their child in the fear of the Lord, a hater of sin and a follower of the Law: the gospel that a baby brought to light was not yet theirs! So Hannah grew to girlhood, a feminine reproduction of her father. Keen, practical insight is not the most softening trait for a woman to possess. It is iron and steel in the soul that does not burn with love mighty and outflowing enough to fuse all other elements in its own glow, and as Hannah grew older and read her mother's repressed nature through and through, the tender heart, the timid conscience, the longing after better and brighter things than life offered to her, only moved her child to an unavowed contempt for a soul so weak and so childish. In a certain way Hannah Blair loved her mother, but it was more as if she had been her child than her parent. Toward her father her feelings were far different. She respected him; he was her model. She alone knew, from a like experience, what reserved depth of feeling lay unawakened under his rigid exterior; she knew, for there were times when her own granite nature shuddered through and through with volcanic forces; when her only refuge against generous indignation or mighty anger was in solitary prayer and grievous wrestlings of the flesh against the spirit as well as the spirit against the flesh. So Hannah grew up to womanhood. Tall and slight as any woodland sapling, but without the native grace of a free growth, her erect and alert figure pleased only by its alacrity and spotless clothing. She was "dredful spry," as old Moll Thunder, the half-breed Indian woman used to say,—"dredful spry; most like squaw—so still, so straight; blue eyes, most like ice. Ho! Moll better walk a chalk 'fore Miss Hanner!"

And Moll spoke from bitter experience, for old Deacon Campbell himself never gave her severer lectures on her ungodly life and conversation than dropped with cutting distinctness from those prim, thin, red lips. Yet Hannah Blair was not without charms for the youth of Wingfield. Spare as she was, her face had the fresh bloom of youth upon its high, straight features; her eyes were blue and bright; her hair, smoothed about her small head, glittered like fresh flax, and made a heavy coil, that her slender white throat seemed over-small to sustain. She was cool, serene, rather unapproachable to lovers or love-makers; but she was David Blair's only child, and his farm lay fair and wide on the high plains of Wingfield. She was well-to-do and pious,—charms which hold to this day potent sway over the youth of her native soil,—and after she was eighteen no Sunday night passed in solitude in the Blair keeping-room; for young men of all sorts and sizes ranged themselves against the wall, sometimes four at once, tilted their chairs, twirled their thumbs, crossed one foot and then the other over their alternate knees, dropping sparse remarks about the corn, or the weather, or the sermon, sometimes even the village politics; but one and all stared at Hannah, as she sat upright by the fireplace or the window, arrayed in a blue-stuff gown or a flowered chintz, as the season might be, and sitting as serene, as cool, as uninteresting as any cherub on a tombstone, till the old Dutch clock struck nine, the meeting-house bell tolled, and the young men, one and all, made their awkward farewells and went home, uttering, no doubt, a sigh of relief when the painful pleasure was over.

By and by the Wingfield store, long kept by Uncle Gid Mayhew, began to have a look of new life, for the old man's only son, Charley Mayhew, had come home from Boston, where he had been ten years in a dry-goods shop, to take the business off his father's hands. Just in time, too, for the store was scarce set to rights in symmetrical fashion when Uncle Gid was struck with paralysis and put to bed for the rest of his life,—a brief one at that. Wingfield gossips shook their heads and muttered that the new order of things was enough to kill him. After so many years of dust and confusion, to see the pepper-corns, candy, and beeswax sorted out into fresh, clean jars; the shoes and ribbons, cut nails and bar-soap, neatly disentangled and arranged; the ploughs, harrows, cheeses, hoes and bales of cotton and calico divorced and placed at different ends of the store; the grimy windows washed, and the dirty floor cleaned and swept,—was perhaps a shock to the old man, but not enough to kill him. His eighty years of vegetation sufficed for that; but he left behind him this son, so full of life, and spirit, and fun, so earnest at work, so abounding in energy, but withal so given over to frolic in its time, that it seemed as if even Wingfield stagnation never could give him a proper dulness or paralyze his handsome face and manly figure. Of course Charley Mayhew fell in love with Hannah Blair.

A mischievous desire at first to wake up those cold blue eyes and flush that clear, set face with blushes soon deepened into a very devoted affection. The ranks of Sunday-night lovers began to look at him with evil eyes, for not even the formality of the best parlor restrained his fun, or the impassive visage of David Blair awed him into silence. Even Hannah began to glow and vivify in his presence; a warmer color flushed her cheeks, her thin lips relaxed in real smiles; her eyes shone with deeper and keener gleams than the firelight lent them, and, worst of all, the sheepish suitors themselves could not help an occasional giggle, a broad grin, or even a decided horse-laugh, at his sallies; and when at last David Blair himself relaxed into an audible laugh, and declared to Charley he was "a master hand at telling stories," the vexed ranks gave it up, allowed that the conquering hero had come, and left Charley Mayhew a free field thereafter, which of course he improved. But even after Hannah Blair had promised in good, set terms to be his wife, and David had given his slow consent, it was doubtful to Charley if this treasure was his merely out of his own determined persistence or with any genuine feeling of her own, any real response of heart; for the maiden was so inaccessible, so chill, so proper, that his warm, impulsive nature dashed against hers and recoiled as the wild sea from a rocky coast. Yet after many days the rock does show signs of yielding; there are traces on its surface, though it needs years to soften and disentegrate its nature. They were a handsome couple, these two, and admiring eyes followed them in their walks. Never had Hannah's face mantled with so rich a color, or her eyes shone with so deep and soft a blue; the stern, red lips relaxed into a serene content, and here and there a tint of gayety about her dress—a fresh ribbon, a flower at her throat, a new frill—told of her shy blossom-time. She was one of those prim, old-fashioned pinks, whose cold color, formal shape, stiff growth, and dagger-shaped gray-green leaves, stamp them the quaint old-maid sisterhood of flowers, yet which hold in their hearts a breath of passionate spice, an odor of the glowing Orient or the sweet and ardent South, that seems fitter for the open-breasted roses, looking frankly and fervently up to the sun.

No, not even her lover knew the madness of Hannah Blair's hungry heart, now for the first time fed,—a madness that filled her with sweet delirium, that she regarded as nothing less than a direct Satanic impulse, against which she fought and prayed, all in vain; for God was greater than her heart, and he had filled it with that love which every wife and mother needs, strong enough to endure all things, to be forever faithful and forever fresh. But no vine-planted and grass-strewn volcano ever showed more placidly than Hannah Blair. Her daily duties were done with such exactness and patience, her lover's demands so coolly set aside till those duties were attended to, her face kept so calm even when the blood thrilled to her finger-tips at the sound of his voice, that, long as her mother had known her, she looked on with wonder, and admired afar off the self-control she never could have exhibited. For Hannah's wooing was carried on in no such style as her mother's had been. Thankful Parsons had accepted David Blair from a simple sense of duty, and he had asked her because she was meek and pious, had a good farm, and understood cows; no troublesome sentiment, no turbulent passion, disturbed their rather dull courtship. A very different wooer was this handsome, merry young fellow, with his dark curls and keen, pleasant eyes, who came into the house like a fresh, dancing breeze, and stirred its dusty stagnation into absolute sparkle. Mrs. Blair loved him dearly already; her repressed heart opened to him all its motherly instincts. She cooked for him whatever she observed he liked, with simple zeal and pleasure. She unconsciously smiled to hear his voice. Deeply she wondered at Hannah, who, day by day, stitched on her quilts, her sheets, her pillow-cases, and her napery, with as diligent sternness as ever she applied to more irksome tasks, and never once blushed or smiled over the buying or shaping of her personal bridal gear, only showing, if possible, a keener eye for business, a more infallible judgment of goods and prices, wear and tear, use and fitness, than ever before.

So the long winter wore away. Hannah's goods lay piled in the "spare chamber,"—heaps of immaculate linen, homespun flannel, patchwork of gayest hues, and towels woven and hemmed by her own hands; and in the clothes-press, whose deep drawers were filled with her own garments in neat array, hung the very wedding dress of dove-colored paduasoy, the great Leghorn bonnet, with white satin ribbons, and the black silk cardinal. Hannah had foregone all the amusements of the past months, at no time consonant to her taste, in order to construct these treasures for her new life. In vain had Charley coaxed her to share in the sleighing frolics, the huskings, the quilting-bees of the neighborhood. It did not once enter into his mind that Hannah had rather be alone with the fulness of her great joy than to have its sacred rapture intermeddled with by the kindly or unkindly jokes and jeers of other people. He never knew that her delight was full even to oppression, when she sat by herself and sewed like an automaton, setting with every stitch a hope or a thought of her love and life.

It was spring now. The long, cold winter had passed at last; the woods began to bud, the pastures grew green even in Wingfield, and brave little blossoms sprung up in the very moisture of the just melted snow-drifts. May had brought the robins and the swallows back; here and there an oriole darted like a flake of fire from one drooping elm to another; the stiff larches put out little crimson cones; the gracious elm boughs grew dusk and dense with swelling buds, and the maple hung out its dancing yellow tassels high in air. The swamps were transfigured with vivid verdure and lit with rank yellow blossoms, where

"The wild marsh marigold shone like fire,"—[2]

the quaint, sad-colored trillium made its protest in fence corners and by the low buttresses of granite on the hills far and near, and the rough-leaved arbutus nestled its baby faces of sweetest bloom deep in the gray grass and stiff moss beds. The day drew near for the wedding. It was to be the last Wednesday in May.

"Darned unlucky!" muttered Moll Thunder, drying her ragged shoes before Mrs. Blair's kitchen fire, having just brought a fagot of herbs and roots for the brewing of root-beer,—even then a favorite beverage in New England, as it is to-day. "Darned unlucky! Married in May, repent alway. Guess Hanner pretty good like ter set up 'ginst ole debbil heself. No good, no good; debbil pretty good strong. Moll knows! He! he! he!"

Mrs. Blair shivered. She was superstitious, like all women, and old Moll was a born witch, everybody knew. But then her daughter's pure, fair, and resolute face rose up before her, and the superstitious fear flickered and went out. She thought Hannah altogether beyond the power of "ole debbil." At last the last Wednesday came,—a day as serene and lovely as if new created; flying masses of white cloud chased each other through the azure sky, and cast quick shadows on the long, green range of hills that shut in Wingfield on the west. Shine and shadow added an exquisite grace of expression to the shades of tender green veiling those cruel granite rocks; a like flitting grace at last transfigured Hannah Blair's cold-featured face. The apple-trees blossomed everywhere with festive garlands of faint pink bloom, and filled the air with their bitter-sweet, subtle odor, clean and delicate, yet the parent of that luscious, vinous, oppressive perfume that autumn should bring from the heaps of gold and crimson fruit, as yet unformed below those waxen petals.

To-day at last Hannah had resolved to give her beating heart one day of freedom,—one long day of unrestrained joy,—if she could bear the freedom of that ardent rapture, so long, so conscientiously repressed. For once in her life she sung about her work; psalm-tunes, indeed, but one can put a deal of vitality into Mear and Bethesda; and Cambridge,[3] with its glad, exultant repeat, has all the capacity of a love-song. Mrs. Blair heard it from the kitchen where she was watching the last pan of cake come to crisp perfection in the brick oven. The old words had a curious adaptation to the sweet, intense triumph of the air, and Hannah carried the three parts of the tune as they came in with a flexibility of voice new to her as to her sole hearer:—

> "'Twas in the watches of the night
> I thought upon thy power;
> I kept thy lovely face in sight
> Amid the darkest hour!"

What a subdued ecstasy rose and fell in her voice as she swept and garnished the old house.

"Amid the darkest hour!"

Oh, there could never be a dark hour for her again, she thought,—never a doubt, or fear, or trouble.

"My beloved is mine and I am his,"

rose to her lips from the oldest of all love-songs. Half profane she seemed to herself; but to-day her deeper nature got the better of her deep prejudices; she was at heart, for once, a simple, love-smitten girl.

The quiet wedding was to be after tea. Nobody was asked, for the few relatives David Blair possessed were almost strangers to him, and lived far away. His wife had been an only child, and Hannah had made no girl friends in the village. The minister was to come at eight o'clock, and the orthodox cake and wine handed round after the ceremony. The young couple were to go to their own house, and settle down at once to the duties and cares of life. Charley had been ordered not to appear till tea-time, and after the dinner was eaten and everything put to rights Mrs. Blair went to her room to plait a cap-ruffle, and Hannah sat down in the spare room by herself, to rest, she said; really to dream, to hope, to bury her face in her trembling hand, and let a mighty wave of rapture overflow her whole entranced soul. The cap-ruffle troubled Mrs. Blair much. Twice it had to be taken from the prim plaits and relaid, then to be sprinkled and ironed out. This involved making a fresh fire to heat the flat-iron, and it got to be well on in the afternoon, and Mrs. Blair was tired. There was nobody to reflect on her waste of time, so she lay down a moment on the bed. David had gone to plough a lot on the furthest part of the farm. He neglected work for no emergency. As a godless neighbor said once, "Dave Blair would sow rye on the edge of hell if he thought he could get the cattle there to plough it up!" A daughter's wedding-day was no excuse for idleness in him. So Mrs. Blair was safe in her nap.

Meantime, as Hannah sat a little withdrawn from the open window, where for once the afternoon sun streamed in unguardedly, and the passionate warble of the song-sparrows, and the indescribable odor of spring followed too, she was suddenly half aware of an outside shadow, and a letter skimmed through the window, and fell at her feet. Scarce roused from her dream, she looked at it fixedly a moment before she stooped to pick it up. Its coming was so sudden, so startling, it did not once occur to her to look out and see who brought it. She hesitated before she broke the broad, red seal, and swept her hand across her eyes as if to brush away the dreams that had filled and clouded them. But the first few words brought back to those eyes their native steely glint, and, as she read on, life, light, love, withdrew their tender glories from her face. It settled into stone, into flint. Her mouth set in lines of dreadful implacable portent, her cheek paled to the whiteness of a marble monument, and the red lips faded to pale, cold purple. What she read in that letter neither man nor woman save the writer and the reader ever knew, for when it was read Hannah Blair walked like an unrepentant conspirator to the stake, fearless, careless, hopeless, out into the small, silent kitchen, and laying that missive of evil on the smouldering coals, stood by stark and stiff till every ash was burned or floated up the chimney. Then she turned, and said in the voice of one who calls from his grave:—

"Mother!"

Mrs. Blair sprung from her doze at the sound. Her mother instinct was keen as the hen's who hears the hawk scream in the sky, and knows her brood in danger. She was on the threshold of the kitchen door almost as soon as Hannah spoke; and her heart sank to its furthest depth when she saw the face before her. Death would have left no such traces—given her no such shock. This was death in life, and it spoke, slowly, deliberately, with an awful distinctness.

"Mother, when Charles Mayhew comes here to-night, you must tell him I will not marry him."

"What?" half screamed the terrified woman, doubtful of her own hearing. Again the cold, relentless tones, in accents as clear and certain as the voice of fate itself:—

"When Charles Mayhew comes here to-night you must see him, and tell him I will not marry him."

"Hanner, I can't! I can't! What for? What do you mean? What is it?"

The words syllabled themselves again out of the thin, rigid lips:—

"I will not marry him."

"Oh, I can't tell him! he will die! I *cannot*, Hanner. You must tell him yourself—you must! you must!"

Still the same answer, only the words lessening each time:—

"I will not!"

"But, Hanner, child, stop and think—do. All your things made; you're published; the minister's spoke to. Why do you act so? You can't, Hanner. Oh, I never can tell him! What shall I say? What will he do? Oh, dear! You must tell him yourself; I can't—I won't! I ain't goin' to; you must!"

A shade of mortal weariness stole across the gray, still face, most like the relaxation of the features after death; but that was all the shrill tirade produced, except the dull, cold repetition:—

"I will not!"

And then Hannah Blair turned and crept up the narrow stairway to her bedroom; her mother, stunned with terror and amazement, still with a mother's alert ear, heard the key grate in the lock, the window shut quietly down, and heard no more. The house was silent even to breathlessness. In her desperation Mrs. Blair began to wish that David would come; and then the unconscious spur of life-long habit stung her into action. It was five o'clock, and she must get tea; for tea must be prepared though the crack of doom were impending. So she built the fire, filled the kettle, hung it on the crane, laid the table, all with the accuracy of habit, her ear strained to its utmost to hear some voice, some sigh, some movement from that bolted chamber above. All in vain. There might have been a corpse there for any sound of life, and Mrs. Blair felt the awe of death creep over her as she listened. For once it was glad relief to hear David coming with the oxen; to see them driven to their shed; to watch his gaunt, erect figure come up the path to the back door; but how hard it was to tell him. He asked no question, he made no comment, but the cold, gray eye quickened into fire like the sudden glitter of lightning, and without a word he strode up the stair to Hannah's room.

"Hannah!"

There was no answer. David Blair was ill-used to disobedience. His voice was sterner than ever as he repeated the call:—

"Hannah, open your door!"

Slowly the key turned, slowly the door opened, and the two faced each other. The strong man recoiled. Was this his child,—this gray, rigid masque, this old woman? But he had a duty to do.

"Hannah, why is this?"

"I cannot tell you, father."

"But you must see Charles Mayhew."

"I will not!"

Still calm, but inexpressibly bitter and determined, like one repeating a dreadful lesson after some tyrant's torture. David Blair could not speak. He stood still on that threshold, without speech or motion, and softly as it had opened, the door closed in his face, the key turned, he was shut out,—not merely from the chamber, but forever from the deepest recess of Hannah's heart and life, if indeed he had ever, even in imagination, entered there. He stood a moment in silent amazement, and then went down into the kitchen utterly speechless. He swallowed his supper mechanically, reached down his hat, but on the door-step turned and said:—

"Thankful, you must tell Charles Mayhew: Hannah will not; I cannot. It is women's work—yea, it was a woman that first time in Paradise!"

And with this scriptural sneer he left his frightened wife to do the thing he dared not. Not the first man who has done so, nor the last. An hour later the joyful bridegroom came in, his dark eyes full of happy light, his handsome figure set off by a new suit of clothes, the like of which Wingfield never had seen, much less originated; his face fairly radiant; but it clouded quickly as a storm-reflecting lake when he saw the cold, wet face of Mrs. Blair, the reddened eyes, the quivering lips, and felt the close, yet trembling pressure of the kind old arms, for the first time clasped round his neck as he stooped toward her. How Thankful Blair contrived to tell him what she had to tell she never knew. It was forced from her lips in incoherent snatches; it was received at first with total incredulity, and she needed to repeat it again and again; to recall Hannah's words, to describe, as she best might, her ghastly aspect, her hollow, hoarse voice, her reply to her father. At last Charles Mayhew began to believe—to rave, to give way to such passionate, angry grief that Thankful Blair trembled, and longed for Parson Day to come, or for David to return. But neither thing happened, for David had warned the parson, and then hidden his own distress and dismay as far as he could get from the house in his own woodland, sitting on a log for hours, lest in coming back to the house he should face the man he could not but pity and fear both; for what reason or shadow of excuse could he offer to him for his daughter's cruel and mysterious conduct? So Mrs. Blair had to bear the scene alone. At last the maddened man insisted on going upstairs to Hannah's door; but that her mother withstood. He should not harass Hannah; she would keep her from one more anguish, if she stood in the door-way and resisted physically.

"But I will see her! I will speak to her! I will know myself what this means! I am not a fool or a dog, to be thrown aside for nothing!"

And with this he rushed out of the kitchen door, round the end of the house, to the grass-plot below Hannah's window. Well he knew that little window, with its white curtain, where he had so often watched the light go out from the hill-side, where he always lingered in his homeward walks.

The curtain was down now, and no ray of light quivered from behind it.

"Hannah! Hannah! *my* Hannah!" he called, with anguish in every tone. "Hannah, look at me! only just look at me! tell me one word!" And then came the fondest pleadings, the most passionate remonstrances—all in vain. He might as well have agonized by her coffin side—by her grass-grown grave. Now a different mood inspired him, and he poured out threats and commands till the cool moonlight air seemed quivering with passion and rage. Still there was no voice nor answer, nor any that replied. The calmness of immortal repose lay upon this quiet dwelling, though the torment and tumult without stormed like a tempest. Was there, then, neither tumult nor torment within? At last, when hours—ages it seemed to the desperate man—had passed by, nature could endure no more. The apathy of exhaustion stole over him; he felt a despair, that was partly bodily weariness, take entire possession of him; he ceased to adjure, to remonstrate, to cry out.

"Good-by, Hannah; good-by!" he called at length. The weak, sad accents beat like storm-weary birds vainly against that blank, deaf window. Nothing spoke to him, not even the worn-out and helpless woman who sat on the kitchen door-step with her apron over her head, veiling her hopeless distress, nor lifting that homely screen to see a ruined man creep away from his own grave,—the grave of all his better nature, to be seen there no more; for from that hour no creature in Wingfield ever saw or heard of him again.

There was a mighty stir among the gossips of the village for once. Not often did so piquant and mysterious a bit of scandal regale them at sewing societies, at tea-fights, even at prayer-meetings, for it became a matter of certain religious interest, since all the parties therein were church-members. But in vain did all the gossips lay their heads together. Nothing was known beyond the bare facts that at the last minute Hannah Blair had "gi'n the mitten" to Charley Mayhew, and he had then and there disappeared. His store was sold to a new-comer from Grenville Centre, who was not communicative,—perhaps because he had nothing to tell,—and Charley dropped out of daily talk before long, as one who is dead and buried far away; as we all do, after how brief a time, how vanishing a grief. As for the Blairs, they endured in stoical silence, and made no sign. Sunday saw both the old people in their places early; nobody looked for Hannah, but before the bell ceased its melancholy toll, just before Parson Day ambled up the broad aisle, her slender figure, straight and still as ever, came up to her seat in the square pew. True her face was colorless; the shadow of death lingered there yet; and though her eyes shone with keener glitter than ever, and her lips burned like a scarlet streak, an acute observer would have seen upon her face traces of a dreadful conflict: lines around the mouth that years of suffering might have grown; a relaxation of the muscles about the eye and temple; a look as of one who sees only something afar off, who is absent from the body as far as consciousness goes. There she sat,—through short prayer and long prayer, hymn, psalm, and sermon, and the battery of looks, both direct and furtive, that assailed her,—all unmoved. And at home it was the same,—utterly listless, cold, silent, she took up her life again; day by day did her weary round of household duties with the same punctilious neatness and despatch; spun and knit, and turned cheeses; for her mother had been broken down visibly for a time by this strange and sad catastrophe, and was more incapable than ever in her life before of earnest work, so Hannah had her place to supply in part as well as her own. We hear of martyrs of the stake, the fagot, the arena, the hunger-maddened beasts, the rising tide, the rack, and our souls shudder, our flesh creeps; we wonder and adore. I think the gladdest look of her life would have illuminated Hannah Blair's face had it been possible now to exchange her endurance for any of these deaths; but it is women who must endure; for them are those secret agonies no enthusiasm gilds, no hope assuages, no sympathy consoles. God alone stoops to this anguish, and he not always; for there is a stubborn pride that will not lift its eyes to heaven lest it should be a tacit acknowledgment that they were fixed once upon poor earth. For these remains only the outlook daily lessening to all of us,—the outlook whose vista ends in a grave.

But the unrelenting days stole on; their dead march, with monotonous tramp, left traces on even Hannah's wretched, haughty soul. They trampled down the past in thick dust; it became ashes under their feet. Her life from torture subsided into pain; then into bitterness, stoicism, contempt,—at last into a certain treadmill of indifference; only not indifference from the strong, cruel grasp she still found it needful to keep upon thought and memory: once let that iron hand relax its pressure, and chaos threatened her again; she dared not. Lovers came no more to Hannah; a certain instinct of their sure fate kept them away; the store of linen and cotton she had gathered, her mother's careful hands had packed away directly in the great garret. The lavender silk, the cardinal, the big bonnet, had been worn to church, year after year, in the same spirit in which a Hindoo woman puts on her gorgeous garments and her golden ornaments for suttee. Mrs. Blair looked on in solemn wonder, but said not a word. Nor were these bridal robes worn threadbare ten years after, when another change came to Hannah's life; when Josiah Maxwell, a well-to-do bachelor from Newfield, the next village, was "recommended" to her, and came over to try his chance. Josiah was a personable, hale, florid man of forty; generous, warm-hearted, a little blustering perhaps, but thoroughly good, and a rich man for those days. He had a tannery, a foundry, and a flourishing farm. Newfield was a place of great water-privileges, sure to grow; it was pretty, bright, and successful; the sleepy, mullein-growing farms of Wingfield had in them no such cheer or life. Hannah was thirty years old; the matter was set before her purely as a matter of business. Josiah wanted a pious, capable wife. He had been too busy to fall in love all his life; now he was too sensible (he thought); so he looked about him calmly, after royal fashion, and, hearing good report of Hannah Blair, proceeded to make her acquaintance and visit her. She, too, was a rational woman; feeling she had long set aside as a weak indulgence of the flesh; all these long and lonely years had taught her a lesson—more than one. She had learned, that a nature as strong, as dominant, as full of power and pride as hers must have some outlet or burn itself out, and here was a prospect offered that appealed to her native instincts, save and except that one so long trodden under foot. She accepted Mr. Maxwell; listened to his desire for a short engagement favorably; took down the stores prepared for a past occasion from the chests in the garret, washed and bleached them with her own hands; and purchased once more her bridal attire, somewhat graver, much more costly than before,—a plum-colored satin dress, a white merino shawl, a hat of chip with rich white ribbons. Moll Thunder, who served as chorus to this homely tragedy, was at hand with her quaint, shrewd comment, as she brought Mrs. Blair her yearly tribute of hickory nuts the week before the wedding.

"He! he! She look pretty much fine; same as cedar tree out dere, all red vine all ober; nobody tink him ole cedar been lightnin'-struck las' year. He! he! Haint got no heart in him—pretty much holler."

One bright October day Hannah was married. Parson Day's successor performed the ceremony in the afternoon, and the "happy couple" went home to Newfield in a gig directly. Never was a calmer bride, a more matter-of-fact wedding. Sentiment was at a discount in the Blair family; if David felt anything at parting with his only child, he repressed its expression; and since that day her mother never could forget, Hannah had wrought in poor Mrs. Blair's mind a sort of terror toward her that actually made her absence a relief, and the company of the little "bound girl" she had taken to bring up a pleasant substitute for Hannah's stern, quiet activity. Everybody was suited; it was almost a pleasure to Mrs. Maxwell to rule over her sunny farm-house and become a model to all back-sliding house-keepers about her. Her butter always "came;" her bread never soured; her hens laid and set, her chickens hatched, in the most exemplary manner; nobody had such a garden, such a loom and wheel, such spotless linen, such shiny mahogany; there was never a hole in her husband's garments or a button off his shirt; the one thing that troubled her was that her husband—good, honest, tender man—had during their first year of married life fallen thoroughly in love with her; it was not in his genial nature to live in the house a year with even a cat and not love it. Hannah was a handsome woman, and his wife; what could one expect? But she did not expect it; she was bored and put out by his demonstrations; almost felt a cold contempt for the love he lavished on her, icy and irresponsive as she was, though all the time ostensibly submissive. Josiah felt after a time that he had made a mistake; but he had the sense to adapt himself to it, and to be content, like many another idolater, with worship instead of response. Not even the little daughter born in the second year of their marriage thawed the heart so long frost-sealed in Hannah's breast; she had once worshipped a false god, and endured the penalty; henceforward she would be warned. Baby was baptized Dorothy, after her father's dead mother, and by every one but Hannah that quaint style was softened into Dolly. Never was a child better brought up, everybody said,—a rosy, sturdy, saucy little creature, doing credit to fresh air and plain food; a very romp in the barn and fields with her father, whom she loved with all her warm, wayward heart; but, alas! a child whose strong impulses, ardent feeling, violent temper, and stormy will were never to know the softening, tempering sweetness of real mother love. She knew none of those tender hours of caressing and confidence that even a very little child enjoys in the warmth of any mother-heart, if not its own mother's; no loving arms clasped her to a mother's bosom to soothe her baby-griefs, to rest her childish weariness. There were even times when Hannah Maxwell seemed to resent her existence; to repel her affection, though her duty kept her inexorably just to the child. Dolly was never punished for what she had not done, but always for nearly everything she did do, and services were exacted from her that made her childhood a painful memory to all her later life. Were there butter or eggs wanted from Wingfield on any emergency, at five years old Dolly would be mounted on the steady old horse that Josiah had owned fifteen years, and, with saddle-bags swinging on either side, sent over to her grandfather's at Wingfield to bring home the supplies,—a long and lonely road of five full-measured miles for the tiny creature to traverse; and one could scarce believe the story did it not come direct to these pages from her own ·lips. In vain was Josiah's remonstrance; for by this time Hannah was fully the head of the house, and the first principle of her rule was silent obedience. All her husband could do was to indulge and spoil Dolly in private, persistently and bravely. Alas for her, there was one day in the week when even father could not interfere to help his darling. Sunday was a sound of terror in her ears: first the grim and silent breakfast, where nobody dared smile, and where even a fixed routine of food, not in itself enticing, became at last tasteless by mere habit; codfish-cakes and tea, of these, "as of all carnal pleasure, cometh satiety at the last," according to the monk in "Hypatia;"[4] then, fixed in a high, stiff-backed chair, the pretty little vagrant must be still; and read her Bible till it was time to ride to church; till she was taken down and arrayed in spotlessness and starch, and set bodkinwise into the gig beside her silent mother and subdued father.

Once at meeting, began the weariest routine of all. Through all the long services, her little fat legs swinging from the high seat, Dolly was expected to sit perfectly quiet; not a motion was allowed, not a whisper permitted; she dared not turn her head to watch a profane butterfly or a jolly bumblebee wandering about that great roof or tall window. Of course she did do it instinctively, recovering herself with a start of terror and a glance at her mother's cold blue eyes, always fixed on Parson Buck, but always aware of all going on beside her, as Dolly knew too well. At noon, after a hurried lunch of gingerbread and cheese, the child was taken to the nearest house, there to sit through the noon prayer-meeting, her weary legs swinging this time off the edge of the high bed, and her wearier ears dinned with long prayers. Then, as soon as the bell tolled, off to the meeting-house to undergo another long sermon, till, worn out mentally and physically, the last hour of the *séance* became a struggle with sleep, painful in the extreme, as well in present resistance as in certainty of results; for, soon as poor Dolly reached home, after another silent drive, she was invariably taken into the spare bedroom, and soundly whipped for being restless in meeting. And, adding insult to injury, after dinner, enjoyed with the eager appetite of a healthy child used to three meals on a week-day, she was required to repeat that theological torture,—the Assembly's Catechism,[5]—from end to end. But in spite of this, partly because Sunday came only once a week, partly because of her father's genial nature and devoted affection for his girl, which grew deeper and stronger constantly, Dolly did not miss of her life as many a morbid character might have in her place. She grew up a rosy, sunny, practical young woman, with a dominant temper toward everybody but her mother. Plump, healthy, and pretty, her cheeriness and usefulness would have made her popular had she been a poor man's daughter,—and by this time Josiah Maxwell was the richest man in the town; so Dolly had plenty of lovers, and in due time married a fine young fellow, and settled down at home with her parents, who were almost as much pleased with Mr. Henderson as was their daughter. But all this time Mrs. Maxwell preserved the calm austerity of her manner, even to her child. She did her duty by Dolly. She prepared for her marriage with liberal hand and unerring judgment; but no caress, no sympathetic word, no slightest expression of affection, soothed the girl's agitated heart or offered her support in this tender, yet exciting, crisis of her life.

Hannah Maxwell made her life a matter of business,—it had been nothing else to her for years; it was an old habit at sixty; and she was well over that age when one day Dolly, rocking her first baby to sleep, was startled to see her mother, who sat in her upright chair reading the county paper, fall quietly to the floor and lie there. Baby was left to fret while her mother ran to the old lady and lifted her spare, thin shape to the sofa; but she did not need to do more, for Mrs. Maxwell's eyes opened and her hand clasped tight on Dolly's.

"Do not call any one," she whispered faintly, and, leaning on her daughter's shoulder, her whole body shook with agonized sobs. At last that heart of granite had broken in her breast; lightning-struck so long ago, now it crumbled. With her head still on Dolly's kind arms, she told her then and there the whole story of her one love, her solitary passion, and its fatal ending. She still kept to herself the contents of that anonymous letter, only declaring that she knew, and the writer must have been aware she would know, from the handwriting as well as the circumstances detailed, who wrote it, and that the information it conveyed of certain lapses from virtue on the part of Charles Mayhew must be genuine.

"O Dolly!" groaned the smitten woman, "when he stood under my window and called me I was wrung to my heart's core. The pains of hell gat hold upon me. I was upon the floor, with my arms wound about the bed-rail and my teeth shut like a vice, lest I should listen to the voice of nature, and, going to the window to answer him, behold his face. Had I seen him I must have gone down and done what I thought a sin; so I steeled myself to resist, although I thought flesh would fail in the end; but it did not. I conquered then and after. Oh, how long it has been! I meant to do right, Dolly; but to-day, when I saw in the paper that he died last week in a barn over Goshen way, a lonely, drunken pauper—Dolly, my heart came out of its grave and smote me. Had I been a meeker woman, having mercy instead of judgment, I might have helped him to right ways. I might have saved him—I loved him so."

The last words struck upon her hearer with the force of a blow, so burning, so eager, so intense was the emphasis: "I loved him *so!*"

Ah, who could ever know the depths out of which that regretful utterance sprang!

"Dear mother, dear mother," sobbed Dolly, altogether overcome by this sudden revelation of gulfs she had never dreamed of,—a heart which, long repressed, convulsively burst at last, and revealed its bleeding arteries.

"Dear, good mother, don't feel so—don't! You meant right. Try to forgive yourself. If you made a mistake then, try to forget it now. Try to believe it was all for the best—do, dear."

But all she got for answer was—"Dolly, it is too late!"

SOME ACCOUNT OF THOMAS TUCKER

❦❦❦❦❦

"Whom now seekinge, O Diogenes! have I found: ye Sunne's shine Beinge more Discoverable untoe that whiche is Sunne-like, than Thy poore Blinkinge Lanthorne."

—*Marriages of Ye Deade*

AMASA TUCKER and his wife lived on a lonely farm in Vermont, remote from villages or neighbors. Amasa's work was that hardest of all work, forcing from rocky and reluctant fields enough produce to feed and clothe his family; to do more, with the most strenuous exertion, was impossible, and he did not expect it. To him life was a brief and bitter pilgrimage toward heaven. If it had amenities, they were snares; its pleasures were unknown to him. Rugged, stern, hard as the granite rocks beneath the sward he tilled, he found no consolations in the outer world, on which he walked as they that have eyes and see not, ears and hear not, nor even human interests to cloud their awed and reverent look into the world which is to come. Alone in his arid fields, Amasa Tucker revolved within himself the vast problems of theology,—free-will, election, infant damnation, the origin of evil, and like dogmas; for to such thoughts had he been trained from childhood by the widowed mother who owned and inhabited this solitary mountain farm. Duty was ground into the very bone and sinew of his life. He walked always between a dreadful hell and an awful heaven, set aside from the ordinary temptations of life, and taught to believe that every leaning toward transgression was the whisper of an omnipresent devil, eager to enlist him in his own service; and learning to feel that untruth, disobedience, a thought he could not utter to his mother, or a wish that could not be uplifted to God, were crimes of fatal and total depravity.

He ploughed the brown sod of the sad New England hills under the full force of the primeval curse; uncomplaining, because Adam had sinned for him, and he must bear the doom; and unquestioning, because Job, under a worse pressure of suffering, had taught him that he who challenges the will of God does so in vain.

He saw the sun rise above the purple mountains, and wheel its splendid way through the sky, life-giving and wonderful, with only a sombre thought of that impending day when the sun shall be turned into darkness and the moon into blood, for which it behooved him to be ready and waiting. The melancholy glory of the moon and the keen sparkle of the starry heavens gave him no joy: their story was alone of that creative and judging Lord who should roll them away as a scroll. To him the fear of God was not only the beginning of wisdom, but its course and end; the perfect love that casteth out fear was strange to him as heaven; he knew not its soft steppings about him, nor its clear shining in the beauty that beset his path. He lived only to prepare for death, and to see that his kindred followed in that straight way.

Philura, whom he had married from a sense of the fitness of things, was a meek, spiritless creature, with no sentiment and little feeling; always conscious that she was an unprofitable servant, afraid to love her children lest it should be idolatry, and struck with as keen a pang as her slender nature could know, if her butter was streaky or her cheese crumbled.

She considered her husband lord and head, after the old-fashioned Scriptural order, and listened to his daily prayers with deep reverence for such striking piety, though she knew very well that Amasa was a hard man, gathering where he had not strewed, and reaping where he had not sown, and a tyrant where a man can be tyrannical in safety,—in his own home.

Two children out of ten survived to this pair. Abundant dosing, insufficient food, and a neglected sink-drain had killed all the others who outlived their earliest infancy; but these two evaded the doom that had fallen on their brothers and sisters, by the fate which modern science calls the survival of the fittest, and spindled up among the mullein-stalks of their stone-strewn pastures as gray, lank, dry, and forlorn as the mulleins themselves; with pale eyes, straight white hair, sallow faces, and the shy aspect of creatures who live in the woods, and are startled at a strange footstep.

They were taught to work as soon as they could walk, to consider sin and holiness the only things worth consideration, to attend meeting as a necessity, and take deserved punishment in silence. To obedience and endurance their physical training, or want of training, conduced also; alternate pie and pork are not an enlivening diet to soul or body, and play was an unknown factor in their dreary existence. Keziah grew up a repetition of her mother,—dull, simple, and dutiful; but Thomas, from the moment he entered the little red school-house, two miles away, to complete the education which his father had begun by the evening fire at home, showed a hunger for books and knowledge that amounted to a passion.

Not a particle did he care for the girls who laughed at him, or the boys who tried to torment him. His soul was filled with the joy of the born student, to whom every fresh study is a rapture that never palls, every new book a possession outvaluing gold; to whom the daily needs and pangs of life are as a tale that is told.

It was but a very little while before Thomas knew all his teacher could impart, far better than the teacher herself knew it; but his thirst was scarcely appeased. He longed for ampler opportunity, for better instruction, as earnestly as Amasa longed for the kingdom of heaven, and at last plucked up shamefaced courage enough to beg his father that he might go to the academy at Bantam, ten miles down the valley.

If one of his oxen had made a like request Amasa Tucker could not have been more astounded. What his boy could want with more education than sufficed himself was past his imagining. To farm an upland in Vermont, after the hereditary fashion of those lonely hills, did not seem to him to require any special science. Hard work, perpetual battle with the elements and the soil, primarily doomed to bear thorns and thistles,— surely this could be carried on with no higher education!

Yet, though he neither answered the boy's request nor the entreating look in his eyes, his inmost heart softened with pride in his son. No genuine New Englander ever despises a desire for knowledge, or sneers at learning without an inward feeling of having been profane; and Amasa Tucker was a typical New Englander of the old sort, now so fast passing away.

When Thomas turned back to his work, in that habit of dumb obedience which is stronger than nature, he did not know that he had dropped into his father's mind a seed that would take root and grow as surely as the corn he had just dropped into the furrow, or that the harvest of its planting would be for him; and it was not till that corn had sprouted, grown to rustling, glittering blades, tasselled out, ripened, been husked, and heaped in shining golden ears in the corn-house, till the apples were brought in to their long bins, and purple-streaked turnips and yellow carrots stored in the barn-cellar, that the boy knew how this other grain had at last come to the full ear.

One Saturday night, as they put the last cow into the stanchions after milking was done, his father said grimly:—

"Thomas, ef you want more edication than what you have had, and can pay your way to go to Bantam 'cademy this winter, why, I'll give ye your time."

Thomas was not demonstrative; the dark blood rushed up to his face, and it seemed to him as if the sudden joy seized him by the throat; but he only answered, "I'll try."

So the next week he walked down to Bantam, applied at once to Parson Lathrop for advice, and, arriving at the nick of time, when Semanthy Pratt, the parson's old house-keeper, was threatened with her annual attack of "rheumatiz," he was taken at once into the minister's house to "do chores" for his board. His schooling was free, since he lived in the county of which Bantam was the shire town; for Parsons Academy was an endowed school, and only pupils from other counties paid for instruction; and there were many such, for the school had a wide reputation.

Perhaps Thomas was not the best chore-boy in the world. Absorbed in pure mathematics, Greek roots, or the proportions and problems of chemistry, he too often forgot the kindlings, or neglected to comb and curry the old white horse. But then he never went out nights; no husking, or apple-bee, or quilting frolic, no sleigh-ride or turkey-shoot, tempted him from his beloved books.

If anybody complained of him it was Semanthy, who declared to her cronies, "Well, he's good enough, for't I know. He don't find fault with his vittles, nor yet he don't set by 'em no great. He's as big a dreamer as Joseph in the Bible. I don't more'n half believe he knows what he doos eat. But land! he aint no company; you might as well set down along of a rake-tail, an' try to visit with it; he's dumber'n a dumb critter, for they do make a sound. I say, mabbe, 'Come, Thomas, you fetch me in a pail o' water, real spry; and take that air squash off'n the hooks, and get me a piggin o' soft soap down sullar.' Well, he'll lay down his book, and fetch them things slow as molasses,—not a peep nor mutter,—and smack right to ag'in at that book o' hisn, and peg away at it till bed-time. I do mistrust he takes it to bed along with him; he would ef I'd let him have a taller dip! I'd jest as lives have ol Bose around, as fur as talkin' goes; p'r'aps ruther, for he does wag his tail real knowin', jest as though he'd speak ef he could; but Thomas, he wouldn't ef he could, now I tell ye!"

Parson Lathrop grew interested in the lad, because he was such a student, for there was nothing lovable about Thomas. His aspect was more ungainly than ever, since age had added to his height without rounding or filling out his lank and angular figure; and by long study in imperfect light—for Semanthy's "taller dips" served for little more than to show the darkness—he had become very near-sighted, winking and blinking like an owl when he looked away from his book, and wearing the perpetual anxious frown of imperfect vision. In the summer he returned to his work on the farm, more dull than ever to the outer world's beauty and joy. One thing alone possessed his soul,—an eager longing for winter and his return to the precious opportunities of Bantam; regardless entirely of Semanthy's scorn, the laughter of his companions, or any lack or discomfort in his daily existence, if he could resume the study that was his delight and life. Before the second winter was over, Parson Lathrop, observing the boy as he had done from day to day, made up his mind as to Thomas's vocation, and determined to come up to his aid in fulfilling so marked and earnest a call. So one day he had the old white horse put into the high-backed sleigh, bundled himself up in his fox-skin coat, put in a hot brick to set his feet upon, tied his otter cap close about his ears, drew on his double-knit mittens, and, tucking a big buffalo robe closely about him, set off for the Tucker farm.

It is a great strain on a man's benevolence to drive an old horse ten miles of an uphill country road, with the thermometer below zero; but Parson Lathrop was one of the uncanonized saints who used to glorify the waste places of New England, and of whom the world was not worthy. It was enough for him that he was about his Master's work; in that, he did not consider himself or his inconveniences.

It was "borne in upon his mind," as he phrased it, that Thomas Tucker's devotion to study was an open indication of Providence concerning his future career, and therefore he must talk with his father about it. Amasa had met the parson now and then, when business took him to Bantam, so they were not strangers. He laid down the axe with which he was chopping wood when the parson drove into the yard, and went out to meet him. A man of softer nature and less faith might have feared that this visit meant some harm had happened to his boy, but Amasa's soul was firm in a confidence that was half nature and half grace; he was not afraid.

"'Mazin' cold weather, Parson Lathrop," was his greeting; and after hospitably stabling the old horse he followed the minister into the house, where, before the blazing kitchen fire, and over a mighty mug of steaming flip, still hissing from its hot guest the poker, the two "reasoned high" as the recalcitrant spirits of hell, and on the same themes, until the parson, at last, wearied of mystic theological doctrine, and came to the point of his errand. He set down the blue and yellow mug, and opened the subject abruptly: "Well, Brother Tucker, I came up especially to say to you that I believe your son Thomas hath a call to minister in divine things."

"I dono!" said Amasa. Thomas was as yet his boy; he could not look upon him in any other light without further experience.

"I think it is even so," went on the parson. "He is like Samuel of old in that he was early called; I have found him a close walker, strict in attention to ordinances, well grounded in Scripture; not given to foolishness, such as youths are too apt to seek after, but one that studies to be quiet. And such a lover of knowledge, such a hungerer after learning, I have scarce ever met with."

"Well, Parson Lathrop, I should as lieves take your judgment as any man's. I had calc'lated on Thomas's keepin' right along here, and cultivatin' the airth in the sweat of his brow, same as I do, and his grandsir' did afore me. I don't wan't to stand in the way ef he's got a call to the ministry, though. I wouldn't hold him back from the Lord's work, no way; but yet I aint clear in my mind, I'm free to confess, how to fetch it. This farm has gi'n me and mine a livin', no more; it's 'sows, an' grows, and goes,' as the sayin' is; but I have striv' always, havin' food and raiment, therewith to be content, but I haint laid up a cent, nor I aint in debt nuther. I didn't rightly know how to spare Thomas to the 'cademy; I couldn't, only that he paid his way; and I don't know how he can get through college. Seems as though there was a lion in the path, don't there?"

"I foresaw this, Brother Tucker," answered the parson, gently. "It has been a trial to me that in that day I cannot say to the Master, 'Lo, here am I, and the children that thou gavest me.' I have a silent house. My beloved wife was under a weary dispensation of bodily ailment all her days, and it pleased the Lord to deny us offspring. It was the last drop in her bitter cup of suffering that she had to leave me, humanly speaking, alone; and I have always purposed to use the small portion of earthly riches she left behind her for the good of those who had the blessing I wanted, and needed the gifts I had. If so be you can spare Thomas, I will help him to his desired education; not so that he shall cease from self-help,—I would not have him weighted with a sense of utter dependence. I propose to have him teach a school when his academic course is over, and remain with me till I can fit him for college myself. He will have laid up something then, and can further teach in vacations. I will see that his funds do not come short. All this if you consent."

Amasa pushed back his chair with a sharp, creaking scrape, his face set, his eyes cold and stern as ever. The most acute observer could not have seen one softening quiver, one tremulous line, to indicate gratitude or assent; yet the heart within him glowed, chill and rayless as it seemed. "I'm obleeged to ye," he said at last, in the dryest fashion, tilting his chair back against the wall and clearing his throat, as if that said all. But Parson Lathrop knew the man and the race; nor was he himself one of those uneasy souls who exact their pound of effusive gratitude for every ounce of good expended on their fellows. His left hand did not know nor inquire what his right hand did, nor even shake that comrade palm in self-congratulation. He had obtained the father's consent to take care of Thomas; now he would go home and do it. So, with a kindly farewell, the good man replaced his wraps, and took his way down the mountain, meditating on heavenly things, an unconscious saint, if indeed saints ever are conscious!

Thomas Tucker's school-teaching, however, did not prove efficient. Wrapped up in his studies, he was so absent-minded that he lacked that modified omniscience which is the *sine qua non* of a country school-teacher. The boys played marbles under his very nose, and he did not see them; they told him the most audacious lies, and he believed them, because he had never told a lie himself; they filched his pens and spilt his ink; they put burrs in the crown of his hat, and smeared his mittens with pitch scraped from the pine-logs in the open fireplace; they ate his dinner, and tied his comforter into knots. But he endured it all with amazement and patience, never thinking his pupils could or would be hard at heart. Then they began to serenade him with the old nursery rhymes of Little Tommy Tucker; to draw pictures of him on the slate, with that vivacious legend attached; and in short to learn so little and misbehave so much that after one term Thomas was "advised to resign," and Parson Lathrop saw that his *protégé* would never earn even the clothes needful to his college course. But the good man had counted the cost when he set out to build this tower of learning, and he sent Thomas at once to the nearest college; becoming answerable for all his expenses, which were somewhat lessened by the fact that a brother clergyman at Deerford gave Thomas his board on condition that he did the "chores" of the family and took care of the horse.

During his first year in this institution the mountain farm where he was born, always, heretofore, considered beyond the reach of fevers such as haunted the lowlands, was suddenly stricken. Amasa Tucker and his wife both fell ill with one of those malignant diseases that were once regarded with a mystical horror as "visitations of God," but are now referred to contaminated wells and neglected drainage. Amasa came in from the woods where he was chopping, one afternoon, livid and ghastly with pain, exclaiming, like the child of the Shunammite woman, "My head! my head!" [1] and fell upon the bed senseless. He lay there unconscious all night, and the next morning Keziah set out at dawn to walk two miles to the nearest neighbor, and send him to Bantam for a doctor. He went at once, but when she got home her father was still senseless, and her mother sat by his side, with both hands clasped about her own head, and her face scarcely less changed than her husband's. Amasa was dead when Dr. Knight arrived, and in twenty-four hours Philura had followed him; both dying speechless, without one parting word or look for their bereft daughter, and before Thomas could come from Deerford. It was a strange, sad funeral at which Parson Lathrop officiated, early on a sweet spring day, the air fragrant with the new buds and fresh scent of the upturned earth, birds twittering among the lofty pine-trees, that set the north winds at defiance on two sides of that quiet graveyard, and the tiny lake below repeating the fair blue heaven above. A divine peace seemed to fill that solitude among the sheltering mountains, and as the good man looked about him he reverently removed his hat, and, before the dead were laid among their kindred dust, he burst involuntarily into the sublime cadences of that psalm so fitted for the time and place:—

> "Lord! Thou hast been our dwelling-place in all generations.
> Before the mountains were brought forth,
> Or ever Thou hadst formed the earth and the world,
> Even from everlasting to everlasting,
> Thou art God."

But the triumphant submission, the lofty ascription, awoke no thrill in Thomas's heart. He stood by the double grave like one in a dream; no tear dimmed his eye, no quiver moved his set lips. He knew well that these deaths were no real loss to him, and he was too vitally and thoroughly honest to put on any outward aspect of mourning. Neither father nor mother had ever tried to awaken in their children one spark of affection. Duty, grim, hard duty, had been the spring of Amasa Tucker's life toward God and man. He had toiled, and prayed, and striven to fulfil his tale of debt toward One whom he knew only as an exacting Master, and to "set loose by the things of this world," as he expressed it, lest he might not be ready for the summons to another; and from him Keziah had learned to dread the indulgence of natural affection as idolatry and a weakness of the carnal heart, which was always "at enmity with God." Consequently the children had grown up unloving, because they were unloved. There were no tender recollections to wring their souls to-day; no unspeakable longings for the hand that had been ever ready to guide, or the voice always eager to cheer. Even Parson Lathrop was astonished and grieved to see that prim composure of the one and dreamy indifference of the other, and forbore to pray that God would bind up the broken in heart, being too honest to be conventional.

Happily for Keziah, Parson Lathrop's widowed sister had come to Bantam to "make it home with him," as the country phrase is; and, never weary in well-doing, the good man took Keziah home, and sent her to Parsons Academy; and in due time she became a school-teacher, more successful than Thomas, for she only attempted to teach little children, whom her dull, quiet nature enabled her to drill in their earliest education with unwearied patience and smiling endurance.

Thomas himself went on in his college course utterly unmoved by the tricks of sophomores or the contempt of seniors. He was called "Little Tommy Tucker" through the recurring terms in every tone of scorn, amusement, and disgust, without seeming to know that it was not his proper title. Nothing interested him but his books. Society was a meaningless waste of time in his eyes, and he respected holidays only because he could spend them undisturbed in the college library, without need to stir for any purpose save the necessities of food and rest, always at their minimum with him. He went to the end of the career here with absolute success as far as learning goes, graduated with the highest honors, and passed on into the theological seminary in Hartland, an epitome of learning, but without a single friend.

Here he revelled in Greek and Hebrew; became still more lank, bent, pale, and introverted than ever; and when he was at last through with his divinity course knew more of his studies and less of his fellow creatures than any other man of his class. He was temporarily placed in charge of the college chapel when he returned to Deerford, its pulpit being vacant for the time; and he preached to the students before him such discourses as might have edified a body of old Puritan divines,—erudite, doctrinal, logical, orthodox, but without one spark of human sympathy or divine love. The eager crowd refused such husks, and expressed their disgust, as a crowd of boys will; but Thomas Tucker took no more notice of their scuffling feet, their laughter, their feigned sleep, or their simultaneous attacks of cold in the head or distressing cough than he took of the wintry winds without that dashed the elm-tree boughs against the lofty chapel windows, or the streaming rain that pattered on its roof. He was there to preach, and preach he did; gladly, however, retiring from the office when the clergyman for whom he had been *locum tenens* arrived. It was evident to those who knew him best in the city that it was not his vocation to preach; and as he was respected among those learned men for his devotion to study and his vast acquisition of knowledge for so young a man, and as the professor of ancient languages was about to resign his position, and his life too, it was brought about that Thomas Tucker should be offered his place.

It was true, he was comparatively young; but there was no real youth about him. He went his way with the absorption of a sexagenarian, only that his were the cares of learning and meditation rather than of this world and declining years.

Soon after his acceptance of the professorship he was sent for to say good-by to Parson Lathrop. For this good man, who had been a real father to him in the best fatherly sense, Thomas felt all the affection in his power; and as he stood by his death-bed, the dreamy, deep-set eyes sparkled with unshed tears, and the melancholy lips trembled. He could not speak; he could only grasp the emaciated and burning hand held out to him, and see through a dim haze the faint, sweet smile on the old man's face.

"I am going home, my son," whispered the parson. "I sent for you to say it is best now that you should take Keziah to be with you. Sister Keery has gone before me, having had an abundant entrance into the kingdom." Here he paused, and Keziah gave him a sip of restorative. "My tongue is parched, even as the tongue of Dives, but I am not afraid of his fate. I know in whom I have believed. Thomas, as I said, take Keziah home with you. Well sayeth the Apocrypha, though it be not with inspiration, 'Without women cannot men live.' It is better for you, in this new honor that hath come to you, to have the dignity of a home, and it is best that she should have its comfort. 'He setteth the solitary in families,' and what better earthly thing could he do for them?"

"I will!" said Thomas, as solemnly as if this were a marriage ceremony.

The parson smiled, but the wandering of death was on him. It seemed as if his will had controlled the fluttering of the spirit, eager to break its chrysalis and soar, until he had finished his good work on earth; now he ceased from his labors, but his heart yet beat, and his disordered mind babbled on those clay-cold lips.

"They're all in the yard, Celia," he said; "and the sun isn't down yet; it's above Saltash;[2] and I cocked all the hay on the lower meadow. Tell Semanthy to fetch the milk-pails." Then he muttered something they could not hear. Celia was his wife's name, and that recurred audibly over and over. Suddenly his looked changed, his eyes opened, a radiant gleam broke across the pallid face, and, lifting one hand upward, he said, "Why, Celia! Come! rise! let us be going; the Master calleth for thee;" so he went as bidden.

Some Account of Thomas Tucker

Thomas and Keziah walked behind the coffin, when Parson Lathrop's funeral train wound its way along the shore of the tranquil lake to the same lonely graveyard where their parents lay, feeling in their hearts that here and now they buried a nearer and dearer friend than either father or mother had been; and the silent crowd who followed them were all alike mourners, for the parson had been a power and a presence of goodness in their midst for many a long year. They stayed, too, after they had lain the worn-out body to sleep in the tender shadow of the hills he loved, to hear his funeral sermon, preached by a neighboring brother, who was in such pathetic earnest that his misuse of speech could not stir a smile in the attentive audience, even when he said, in describing the good man's last hours, that "a heavenly smile eradicated his countenance."

Then the brother and sister went back to Deerford, and, hiring a small house, began their life together. Parson Lathrop had left his little property to Keziah, and these few thousands, added to the yearly rental of the old farm and the house in Bantam, kept her independent soul from feeling that she was a burden upon Thomas, and his salary was more than sufficient for their daily needs. So for a year or two they lived in peace, until Satan, or some lesser minion of evil, put it into the head of a student, whose mischief always over-rode his manners, to play a joke upon "Old Tommy."

Professor Tucker, throughout his college life, had never been known to address the least attention, scarcely the least civility, to any woman; he avoided all society but that of his books, refused all invitations, and lived in his room like a hermit in his cell. But when his sister arrived, and he became a householder, the maids and matrons collateral to the faculty of which he was a member at once felt it their duty to call on Keziah, and welcome her to their social enjoyments. But she was as shy as her brother, and proved impracticable to almost every one. Her nearest neighbor alone, a maiden lady of good family and fine, cheerful presence, well-to-do, and having the courageous *aplomb* that all these gifts bestow on a woman, made some headway in the good graces of the quiet rustic spinster. Miss Eleanor Yale would, welcomed or not, invade Keziah's solitude now and then, insist on driving her out to show her the beautiful environs of Hartland, send her flowers from her own elaborate garden and fruit from her peach and pear trees, all out of the most frank and free benevolence; for she pitied the solitary creature, knowing in her own heart how forlorn loneliness is to any woman, though all the other good things of life be poured out abundantly into her hands. Miss Keziah had a heart,—somewhat torpid for want of exercise, perhaps, but still a heart,—and she felt Miss Yale's kindness, without finding words to express it to that lady; but she spoke of her so often to the professor that he learned to know her name, and thereby precipitated a certain impending catastrophe, set in motion by Jack Mason, the aforesaid student. On Valentine's day—a day of which Thomas Tucker was no more conscious and no better informed than Confucius or Aristotle—he received by mail a flowing ditty, of the most tender sort, written in a woman's hand, and signed "Eleanor." The professor stood aghast. Poetry had no charms for him; he had not the remotest idea of its figurative speech, its license, or its "tricks and manners;" to him it was merely curiously arranged prose, and this devoted and tender valentine seemed neither more nor less than an offer of marriage. His hair fairly stood on end, and his forehead was knit with perplexity. Who could have done this thing? Suddenly he remembered that Eleanor was the name of his sister's friend, and even on his learned and abstracted soul dawned a glimmer of the man's instinctive contempt for women, as he bethought himself how this woman had sought his sister's friendship and done her such kindnesses all for his sake. Still, being an exceptional man, he was moved rather to pity than scorn, on further reflection, thinking of all this wasted trouble and useless feeling on the lady's part. There was but one thing to be done. He did not want to marry any one; he had not planned or intended any such thing; his life and love were all centred in his studies, his books, his profession. And was not Keziah able and willing to do for him all those services which some men had no sisters to attend to, and therefore were obliged to marry?

But this poor woman,—she must not be deluded with so futile a hope. It was unpleasant to contemplate, but Thomas Tucker never shrank from duty; he must be honest or die. So he put on his hat and coat, and, presenting himself at Miss Yale's door, asked to see that lady. Miss Yale was astonished, but she received the professor a little more kindly because she was astonished, and afraid she should not put him entirely at ease. But he was more formal, more awkward, more stiff than ever before. He sat down on the highest chair in the room, and, drawing the luckless missive from his breast-pocket, plunged at once into the middle of things.

"Madam!" he began, sternly, "I have received this epistle, bearing your name in superscription, which doubtless you recognize. I thank you for the regard herein expressed; but as an honest man, and one who is in bonds to the truth, I come to say to you that marriage has not entered into my plans at any time, nor is there any likelihood that it will."

Miss Yale looked at him with wide eyes. "What?" she cried, in amazement.

"I refer to this letter you have sent me, couched in the mode of verse," replied the professor, grim as a lion on a sign-post of old time, and full as wooden.

"Give me the letter, if you please," said Miss Yale, her color rising, and her eyes full of a dangerous glow. But the professor knew nothing of the sex and its ways, except theoretically; he handed her the document, without any fear of its explosive tendencies. Miss Yale read it through, and looked up at him. He was already lost in some problem, or evolving some theory; but her voice roused him.

"Do you think I sent you this?" she asked, in a very quiet voice,— altogether too quiet to be reassuring.

"Is not that your given name by which it is signed?" returned the professor.

"Yes. But I want to understand what you considered this letter to mean," she went on, with the same ominous quietness of manner, holding herself in leash, as it were, till the time for a spring.

"I think it has but one meaning, which he that runs may read: that you are desirous of entering the state of matrimony."

"With you?"

"With me," responded Thomas Tucker, with curt and ghastly honesty.

Miss Yale rose to her feet, and her clear eyes flashed. The professor felt danger; he shrank visibly into himself, yet fixed an undaunted gaze upon her. She looked at him a moment, and, with the vivid speed of thought, remembered herself, her position, his nature and his habits. Her anger died; she threw herself back on the sofa, and laughed till the tears rolled down her fair face.

The professor was entirely speechless; he knew not what to say, but at last, in honest indignation, opened his mouth, much like his Scriptural prototype, to the angel in the path:—

"It seems, madam, unsavory subject for mirth. I am in earnest."

"And so am I," said Miss Yale, drying her bedewed cheeks, and trying to be sober. "Professor Tucker, I did not write that letter. Some silly and impertinent boy sent it to you to deceive and disturb you. If I wished to marry you I should not take that method of obtaining my wish. I am a woman and a lady: good women and true ladies do not do such things."

She looked directly at him as she said this, and her eyes sparkled. Some manly shame stirred in the professor's bosom; he extracted a great red and yellow handkerchief, with much contortion, from his coat-tail pocket, and used it sonorously.

Miss Yale's lips quivered a little, and a sudden dimple flashed in her cheek; but she went on, certain, with her own perfect tact, that this man must be treated with absolute truth, like his own: "Moreover, in order to show you convincingly that I had no such intention, beside not having written that letter, I will tell you, in confidence,—a trust I feel will be safe in your hands,—that I have promised to marry President Winthrop some time next summer."

As Professor Tucker looked at the warm flush that covered the fine face of Eleanor Yale, and perceived the soft glow of her eyes, he thought that the widowed president was a happy man, but he did not say so. "Madam, I ask your pardon," he said, humbly. "And for that son of Belial, who hath made me his music, I trust due punishment is somewhere reserved," he gloomily added, and departed in a shambling fashion, that once more provoked Miss Yale's dimples and set her eyes dancing. And—alas for the feminine malice, of which a grain lurks in the best woman's heart!—that very night President Winthrop was entertained with a *résumé* of her afternoon's experience; and that genial gentleman roared and rolled with laughter, for he knew Thomas Tucker far better than Miss Yale did, and could more thoroughly enjoy the situation.

After this occurrence, which Hebrew points and crabbed Syriac idioms soon drove from the professor's mind, he went his way for a while quite undisturbed; but he was so unsuccessful as a teacher that, on some excellent pretext, it pleased the trustees of the college to remove him from his position. They recommended him to a church in the city, seeking for a clergyman to fill its pulpit, and then advised him to accept the call. It was at first an irksome employment for the professor, but he did not love teaching; it was far easier for him to produce two sermons a week, in the seclusion of his study, than to face daily a class of youths, more or less refractory, if they were students, and try to beat into them the beauties and intricacies of the dead languages.

The social duties of a settled clergyman might have pressed on him onerously; but, as if Providence saw that he was best fitted for a life of solitude, just as the Green Street church had listened to their learned and pious pastor for the first time after his installation in their pulpit, Keziah, his sister, was seized with a sudden and dangerous illness. The kind women of the church rallied around Thomas Tucker in this hour of his need, and nursed Keziah with unremitting kindness; but all in vain. She dropped out of life as silently and patiently as she had endured living, and it remained only to say that the place which knew her should now know her no more; for she left behind her no dear friend but her brother, and not an enemy. Even Thomas missed her rather as a convenience than a companion; profiting in a certain sense by her death, as it aroused keenly the sympathy of the church for his loss and loneliness, and attached them to him by those links of pity that are proverbially almost as strong as love. In any other circumstances the Green Street church would no doubt have discovered, early in their relation, that Mr. Tucker was as unfit for any pastoral position as he had been for that post in the college chapel; but much was forgiven him out of his people's abundant kindness; and their respect for his learning, his simplicity, and his sincere piety forbade their objecting at first to his great deficiencies in those things considered quite as needful to pulpit success as the power of preaching and the abundance of knowledge. It happened, soon after Keziah's death, that Mr. Tucker was called to officiate at the funeral of one of his wealthiest parishioners, a man who had just come back from Europe, and been killed in a railroad accident on the way to his home in Deerford. He was personally unknown to Thomas Tucker, but his character was notorious. He went to church, and bought an expensive pew there, merely as a business speculation; it gave him weight in the eyes of his fellows to be outwardly respectable as well as rich; but he was niggardly to his family, ostentatious, overreaching, and cruel as death to the poor and struggling who crossed his path or came into his employ.

The Reverend Mr. Tucker improved the occasion. He took for the text of that funeral address, "What shall it profit a man if he gain the whole world, and lose his own soul?" and after a pungent comparison between the goods of this world and the tortures of a future state he laid down his spectacles, and wound up with, "And now, beloved, I have laid before you the two conditions. Think ye that to-day he whose mortal part lieth before you would not utter a loud Amen to my statement? Yea, if there be truth in the word of God, he who hath left behind him the gain of life and greed is now crying aloud for a drop of water to cool his parched tongue, and longing for an hour of probation wherein to cast off the fetters of ill-gotten gold and sit with Lazarus gathering crumbs in the company of dogs. Wherefore, seeing that God hath spoken sharply to you all in the sudden requirement of this rich man's soul, let his admonition sink into your souls; seek ye first the kingdom of God, and cast in your lot with the poor of this world, rich in faith, and be ready to answer joyfully when the Master calls."

Of course the community was outraged; but for a few kindly souls, who stood by the poor parson, and insisted that Keziah's death had unsettled his mind, and not a few who felt that he had manfully told the truth, without fear or favor, and could not help feeling a certain respect for him, he would have been asked, forcibly, to resign, that very week. As it was, the indignant widow went over to another denomination without delay. "I will never set foot in that church again!" she said. "How can one be safe where a man is allowed to say whatever he chooses in the pulpit? A ritual never can be personal or insulting. I shall abide by the Prayer-Book hereafter."

In due time this matter faded out of the popular mind, as all things do in course of time, and nothing came between pastor and people, except a gradual sense on their part that Solomon was right when he said, "Much study is a weariness to the flesh;" not only the student's flesh, but also theirs who have to hear reiterated all the dry outcome of such study.

But Parson Tucker's career was not to be monotonous. His next astonishing performance was at a wedding. A very pretty young girl, an orphan, living in the house of a relative, equally poor but grasping and ambitious, was about to marry a young man of great wealth and thoroughly bad character: a man whom all men knew to be a drunkard, a gambler, and a dissolute fellow, though the only son of a cultivated and very aristocratic family. Poor Emily Manning had suffered all those deprivations and mortifications which result from living in a dependent condition, aware that her presence was irksome and unwelcome, while her delicate organization was overtaxed with work whose limits were as indefinite as the food and clothing which were its only reward. She had entered into this engagement in a sort of desperation, goaded on by the widowed sister-in-law with whom she lived, and feeling that nothing could be much worse than her present position. Parson Tucker knew nothing of this, but he did know the character of Royal Van Wyck; and when he saw the pallid, delicate, shrinking girl beside this already worn-out, debased, bestial creature, ready to put herself into his hands for life, the "daimon" laid hold upon him, and spake again. He opened the service, as was customary in Hartland, with a short address; but surely never did such a bridal exhortation enter the ears of man and woman before.

"My friends," he began, "matrimony is not to be lightly undertaken, as the matter of a day; it is an awful compact for life and death that ye enter into here. Young man, if thou hast not within thyself the full purpose to treat this woman with pure respect, loyal service, and tender care; to guard her soul's innocence as well as her bodily welfare; to cleave to her only, and keep thyself from evil thoughts and base indulgences for her sake,—if thou art not fit, as well as willing, to be priest and king of a clean household, standing unto her in character and act in God's stead so far as man may, draw back even now from thine intent; for a lesser purpose is sacrilege here, and will be damnable infamy hereafter."

Royal Van Wyck opened his sallow green eyes with an insolent stare. He would have sworn roundly had not some poor instinct of propriety restrained him; as it was, he did not speak, but looked away. He could not bear the keen, deep-set eyes fixed upon him; and a certain gaunt majesty in the parson's outstretched arm and severe countenance daunted him for the moment. But Thomas Tucker saw that he had no intention of accepting this good advice, so he turned to Emily.

"Daughter," he said, "if thou art about to enter into this solemn relation, pause and consider. If thou hast not such confidence in this man that thy heart faileth not an iota at the prospect of a life-long companionship with him; if thou canst not trust him utterly, respect him as thy lord and head, yield him an obedience joyful and secure next to that thou givest to God; if thou hast a thought so free of him that it is possible for thee to imagine another man in his place without a shudder; if thou art not willing to give thyself to him in the bonds of a life-long, inevitable covenant of love and service; if it is not the best and sweetest thing earth can offer thee to be his wife and the mother of his children,—stop now; stop at the very horns of the altar, lest thou commit the worst sin of woman, sell thy birthright for a mess of pottage, and find no place for repentance, though thou seek it carefully and with tears."

Carried away with his zeal for truth and righteousness, speaking as with the sudden inspiration of a prophet, Parson Tucker did not see the terror and the paleness deepening, as he spoke, on the bride's fair countenance. As he extended his hand toward her she fell in a dead faint at his feet. All was confusion in an instant. The bridegroom swore and Mrs. Manning screamed, while the relations crowded about the insensible girl, and tried to revive her. She was taken at once upstairs to her room, and the wedding put off till the next day, as Mrs. Manning announced.

"And you won't officiate at it, old fellow! I'll swear to that!" roared the baffled bridegroom, with a volley of profane epithets, shaking his fist in the parson's calm face.

"Having taken the sword, I am content to perish thereby, even as Scripture saith," answered Thomas Tucker, stalking out of the door.

That night, as he sat in his study, the doop opened softy, and Emily Manning came in and knelt at the side of the parson's chair. "I have no place to go to, sir," she whispered, with trembling lips. "You saved me to-day; will you help me now? I was going to sin, but I didn't know it till you told me."

"Then it was not sin, my child," said Parson Tucker, gently. "Sin is conscious transgression, and from that thou hast instantly departed."

"But what could I do?" she asked, her eyes full of tears. "I have no home. Marcia is tired of me, and I have no other friends. I wanted a home so much. Oh, I was wrong, for I did not love him. And now I have run away from Marcia,—she was so dreadful,—and what shall I do?"

"Poor child!" he said, tenderly. "Sit here. I will help. My old woman, in the kitchen below, shall fetch thee to a chamber. Keziah brought her with us; she is kind, and will care for thee, while I go to bring a friend." So saying, the parson rung his bell for old Jane, gave the girl over to her care, and set out himself for President Winthrop's house.

"I have brought you a good work," he said abruptly to Mrs. Winthrop. "Come with me; there is a soul in need at my house."

Mrs. Winthrop was used to this sort of summons from the parson. They had been good friends ever since the eccentric interview brought about by Jack Mason's valentine, and when charity was needed Eleanor Winthrop's heart and hand were always ready for service. She put on hat and shawl, and went with the parson to his house, hearing on the way all the story.

"Mr. Tucker," she said, as he finished the recital, "aren't you going to make much trouble for yourself by your aggressive honesty?"

Thomas looked at her, bewildered.

"But the truth is to be spoken!" he replied, as if that were the end of the controversy. And she was silent, recognizing the fact that here conventions were useless, and self-preservation not the first law of grace, if it is of nature.

All Mrs. Winthrop's kindliness was aroused by the pitiful condition of Emily Manning. She consoled and counselled her like a mother, and soon after took her into her household as governess to the little girls whom Mr. Winthrop's first wife had left him; making for the grateful girl a happy home, which in after years she left to become the wife of a good man, toward whom she felt all that Parson Tucker had required of her on that painful day which she hated now to remember. And as the parson performed this ceremony he turned, after the benediction, to Eleanor Winthrop, and said, with a beam of noble triumph on his hollow visage, "Blessed be the Lord! I have saved a soul alive!"

But long before this happy sequel came about he had other opportunities to distinguish himself. There came a Sunday when the service of infant baptism was to be performed; and when the fair, sweet babes, who had behaved with unusual decorum, were returned to their mothers' arms, and the parson, according to order, said, "Let us pray," he certainly offered the most peculiar petition ever heard in the Green Street church. After expressing the usual desire that the baptized children might grow up in the nurture and admonition of the Lord, he went on: "But if it please thee, O Father, to recall these little ones to thyself in the innocence of their infancy, we will rejoice and give thanks, and sound thy praises upon the harp and timbrel. Yea! with the whole heart we will praise thee; for we know the tribulations and snares, the evil and folly and anguish, of this life below; and we know that not one child of Adam, coming to man's estate, is spared that bitter and woful cup that is pressed out from the fruit of the knowledge of good and evil, which our progenitors ate of in thy garden of Paradise, and thereby sinned and fell, and bequeathed to us their evil longings and habitual transgression. They are the blessed who are taken away in their infancy, and lie forever by green pastures and still waters in the fields of heaven. We ask of thee no greater or better gift for these lambs than early to be folded where none shall hurt or destroy in all thy holy mountain, and the love that is above all mother's love shall cradle them throughout eternity. Amen!"

Not a mother in that congregation failed to shiver and tremble at this prayer, and tears fell fast and thick on the babes who slumbered softly in the tender arms that had gathered them home, after consecrating them to that God whom yet they were so unwilling should literally accept their offering. Fifty pairs of eyes were turned on Parson Tucker with the look of a bear robbed of its cubs; but far more were drowned in tears of memory and regret, poignant still, but strangely soothed by this vivid presentation of the blessedness wherein their loved and lost were safely abiding.

Much comment was exchanged in the church porch, after service, on the parson's prayer.

"We ought to hold a special meeting to pray that the Lord will not answer such a petition!" cried one indignant mother, whose little flock were clinging about her skirts, and who had left twin babies, yet unbaptized, at home.

"It *is* rather hard on you, aunty!" said graceless Jack Mason, the speaker's nephew, now transformed into an unpromising young lawyer in Hartland. "You'd rather have your babies sin and suffer with you than have 'em safe in their little graves, hadn't you? I don't go with the parson myself. I didn't so much mind his funeral gymnastic over old Baker, and his disposition of that party's soul in Hades, because I never before supposed Roosevelt Baker had a soul, and it was quite reassuring to be certain he met with his dues somewhere; but he's worse than Herod about the babies!"

However, the parson did not hear or know what was said of him, and in an ignorance that was indeed bliss continued to preach and minister to his people in strict accordance with his own views of duty. His next essay was a pastoral visit to one of his flock, recently a widow, a woman weak in body and mind both; desirous above all things to be proper and like other people, to weep where she must, smile when she ought, wear clothes like the advance-guard of fashion, and do "the thing" to be done always, whether it was the right and true thing or not.

Her husband had spent all her fortune in speculation, taken to drink as a refuge from folly and reproach at home, and, under the influence of the consoling fluid, had turned his wife out-of-doors whenever he felt in the mood; kicked her, beaten her, and forced her, in fear of her life, over and over to steal from her own house, and take refuge with the neighbors, and ask from them the food she was not allowed at home. At last the end came. Parson Tucker was sent for to see the widow and arrange for funeral services. She had not been present at the Baker funeral, or indeed been in Deerford for some years after that occasion, so she adhered to the conventions; and when Parson Tucker reached the house he was shown into a darkened room, where the disconsolate woman sat posed already in deep mourning, a widow's cap perched upon her small head. A woman would have inferred at once that Mrs. Spring had anticipated the end of Joe's last attack of *mania à potu*,[3] and prepared these funeral garments beforehand; but Thomas Tucker drew no such conclusions. He sat down silently and grimly, after shaking hands with Mrs. Spring, and said nothing. She began the conversation:—

"This is a dreadful affliction, Mr. Tucker. I don't know how I shall live through it."

"It is terrible, indeed," said the parson. "I do not wonder, madam, that you mourn to see your partner cut off in his sins, without time for repentance; but no doubt you feel with gratitude the goodness which hath delivered you from so sore a burden."

"What!" screamed the widow.

"I speak of God's mercy in removing from your house one who made your life a terror, and your days full of fear and suffering; you might have been as others, bereaved and desolate, and mourning to your life's end."

"I don't know what you mean, Parson Tucker," said Mrs. Spring, sharply, removing a dry handkerchief from unwet eyes. "Poor, dear Joseph is taken away from me, and I'm left a desolate widow, and you talk in this way! I'm sure he had the best of hearts that ever was; it was only, as you may say, accidental to him to be a little overcome at times, and I'm— I'm—O–h!"

Here she gave a little hysterical scream, and did some well-executed sobbing; but the parson did not mind it. He rose up before her, gaunt and gray. "Madam, did not this man beat, and abuse, and insult, and starve you, when he was living? Or have I been misinformed?"

"Well—Oh, dear, what dreadful questions!"

"Did he?" thundered the parson.

"He didn't mean to; he was excited, Mr. Tucker. He"—

"He was drunk. And is that excuse? Not so, madam. You know, and I know, that his death is a relief and a release to you. I cannot condole with you on that which is not a sorrow;" and he walked rigidly out of the door.

Is it necessary to say that Mr. Spring's funeral did not take place in Deerford? His widow suddenly remembered that he had been born in a small town among the hills of West Massachusetts, and she took his body thither, to be "laid beside his dear payrents," as she expressed it.

Things had now come to a bad pass for Parson Tucker. The church committee had held more than one conference over their duty toward him. It was obvious that they had no real reason for dismissing him but his ghastly honesty, and that hardly offers a decent excuse to depose a minister of the gospel. They hardly knew how to face the matter, and were in this state of perplexity when Mr. Tucker announced, one Sunday, after the sermon, that he would like to see the church committee in his study on Tuesday night; and accordingly they assembled there, and found President Winthrop with the parson.

"Brethren," said Thomas Tucker, after the preliminary welcome had passed, "I have sent for you to-night to say, that having now been settled over your church eight years, I have found the salary you pay me so much more than was needed for my bodily support that I have laid by each year as the surplus came to hand, that I might restore to you your goods. The sum is now something over eight thousand dollars, and is placed to the credit of your chairman, in the First Deerford Bank." The committee stared at each other as if each one were trying to arouse himself from sleep. The chairman at last spoke:—

"But, Mr. Tucker, this is unheard of! The salary is yours; we do not desire to take it back; we can't do it."

"That which I have not earned, Brother Street, is not mine. I am a solitary man; my expenses are light. It must be as I said. Moreover, I have to say that I hereby withdraw from your pulpit, of necessity. I have dealt with our best physicians concerning a certain anguish of the breast, which seizes me at times unawares, and they all concur that an evil disease lieth upon me. I have not much time to live, and I would fain withdraw from activities and duties that are external, and prepare for the day that is at hand."

The committee were pained as well as shocked. They felt guilty to think how they had plotted this very thing among themselves; and they felt, too, a certain awe and deep respect for this simple, unworldly nature, this supernatural integrity. Mr. Street spoke again; his voice was husky:—

"If this is so, Mr. Tucker, we must of course accept your resignation; but, my dear pastor, keep the money! You will need care and comforts, now this trouble has come on you. We can't take it back."

Parson Tucker looked at him with a grave, sweet smile. "I thank you, brother, but I have a private store. My sister left her worldly goods to me, and there is enough and to spare for my short sojourn," he answered.

"But it isn't according to the fitness of things that we should take your salary back, Parson Tucker," put in bustling Mr. Taylor. "What upon earth should we do with it?"

"Friend," said the parson, "the eternal fitness of things is but the outcome of their eternal verity. I have not, as I said, earned that wage, and I must restore it: it is for you to decide what end it shall serve in the church."

A few more words passed between them, and then each wrung the parson's hand and left him, not all with unmoved hearts or dry eyes.

"I don't wonder he's going to die!" exclaimed Mr. Street, as the committee separated at the street corner. "He's altogether too honest to live!"

From that day Thomas Tucker sank quietly toward his grave. Friends swarmed about him, and if delicacies of food could have saved him the dainty stores poured in upon him would have renewed his youth; but all was in vain.

President Winthrop sat by him, one summer day, and, seeing a sad gleam in his sunken eye, asked gently, "You are ready and willing to go, Brother Tucker?" nothing doubting a glad assent.

But the parson was honest to the last. "No," he said, "I do not want to die; I am afraid. I do not like strange and new things. I do not want to leave my books and my study."

"But, dear brother," broke in the astonished president, "it is a going home, to your Father's house!"

"I know not what a home is, friend, in the sense of regret or longing for one. My early home was but as the egg to the bird, a prison wherein I was born, from which I fled; nor was my knowledge of a father one that commends itself as a type of good. I trust, indeed, that the Master will take me by the hand, even as he did Peter upon the water; but the utterance of my secret soul is even that of the apostle with the keys: 'Lord, save, or I perish!'"

"But you have been a power for good, and a close follower of Peter's Lord," said Mr. Winthrop, altogether at a loss for the proper thing to say to this peculiar man.

"One thing alone have I been enabled to do, Brother Winthrop, for which I can with heart and soul thank God, even at this hour. Yea, I thank him that I have been enabled to speak the truth even in the face of lies and deceptions, through his upholding." A smile of unearthly triumph filled every line of the wasted face, and lit his eyes with a flash of divine light as he said this. He grasped close the friendly hand he was holding, turning his cheek to the pillow, and closed his eyes, passing into that life of truth and love that awaited him, even as a child that lies down in the darkness, trembling, fearful, and weary, but awakes, in the dawn of a new day, in the heart of home.

"Still," said President Winthrop to his wife, as they walked home after the funeral, "I believe in the good old proverb, Eleanor, that 'the truth is not to be spoken at all times.'"

"And I never believed in it so little!" she cried, indignantly. "Think what a record he has left; what respect hangs about his memory! Do we know how many weak souls have relied on his example, and held to the truth when it was hard, because he did and could? It is something to be heroic in these days, even if it is unpopular!"

The president shrugged his shoulders.

EXPLANATORY NOTES

MAYA, THE PRINCESS

1. Maya, a prominent term in Hindu philosophy, means illusion or unreality; it carries with it suggestions of supernatural power, the force that creates the world, and the concept of the world as a cosmic illusion.

2. Scrip in the nineteenth century referred to a small bag commonly carried by a pilgrim or beggar.

MY VISITATION

1. These lines come from *The Princess* (1847) by Alfred, Lord Tennyson (6.232–33, 235–37), a long narrative poem about the new woman in which the heroine, Ida, founds a university for women.

2. *Shirley* (1849), *Jane Eyre* (1847), and *Villette* (1853) are novels by Charlotte Brontë (1816–55). *Shirley* treats the political turmoil caused by shifting relations between workers and owners in rural England; its title character is based on the author's sister, Emily Brontë (1818–48), author of *Wuthering Heights* (1847). *Jane Eyre* is a Gothic novel about a repressed governess, an autocratic absentee gentleman-landowner, and an insane wife hidden from the world. *Villette* is an intense study of female sensibility, experienced through the mind and passions of Lucy Stone, an Englishwoman teaching in France.

3. *"Evoe"* is a cry of joy said to be associated with pagan Bacchic rites. Athena is the Greek goddess of wisdom, a figure both powerful and virginal. (She is called Pallas a few lines above, a traditional title for this goddess referring to her victory over a Titan or giant of that name.) The expression *"Evoe Athena"* thus suggests a joyful invocation of female strength.

4. This quotation, as well as any others that are not glossed, I have not been able to identify.

5. These lines come from Wordsworth's "Lines Composed a Few Miles above Tintern Abbey" (1798), a poem about returning to a place in nature particularly significant to the poet and his sister, Dorothy.

THE RING FETTER

1. *The Spectator*, an influential English periodical published by Joseph Addison and Richard Steele between March 1711 and December 1712, was supposedly written by the members of a small male club, fictional characters of the English middle class who provided social commentary on the manners, morals, and literature of the time.

2. A *roué* is a rake, a profligate, cunning, or unscrupulous person.

FREEDOM WHEELER'S CONTROVERSY WITH PROVIDENCE

1. The Assembly's Catechism was a declaration of faith created in 1643–44 by the Westminster Assembly, a gathering of learned ministers appointed by the Puritan government of England under Oliver Cromwell. The *Shorter Catechism*, very popular in the United States, is considered a classic of Calvinism and begins with the famous words, "Man's chief end is to glorify God and to enjoy Him forever."

2. In the fable by Aesop (c. 620–560 B.C.) a group of frogs object to the Log that Jupiter has given them as a ruler, and instead are given a Stork, who proceeds to eat them up. Cooke suggests by this allusion that Freedom Wheeler may find his energetic new wife (Queen Stork) more dangerous than his subdued first mate (Queen Log).

3. Rights Women were advocates of legal and civil rights for women, such as the vote. They were especially visible and active following the historic first Women's Rights Convention held in Seneca Falls, New York, in 1848; they

persevered and grew in strength and numbers throughout the nineteenth century. Their work culminated, though did not end, in 1920 with the passage of the Nineteenth Amendment to the United States Constitution, which gave the vote to women.

MRS. FLINT'S MARRIED EXPERIENCE

1. This line comes from Tennyson's "The Poet" (1830) and describes its subject, the poet: "The poet in a golden clime was born, / With golden stars above; / Dower'd with the hate of hate, the scorn of scorn, / The love of love."

HOW CELIA CHANGED HER MIND

1. *Experto crede* means "believe the experienced." It comes from Virgil's *Aeneid* 11.283.

2. The Syrophenician woman appears in the Bible (Mark 6.25–30). She convinces a reluctant Jesus to cast the devil out of her daughter by comparing her daughter to the dogs that are allowed to eat the crumbs under the children's table. The idea expressed by the image is that even the least worthy hope and perhaps deserve to get something.

MISS LUCINDA

1. Tricopherous appears to be a patent hair oil popular in the nineteenth century.

2. Alexis Soyer (1809–58) was the most famous cook of his time. Originally French, he became well known as chef at the Reform Club in London. He was a reformer himself and went to Ireland during the famine in 1847 and to the Crimea during the war in 1855, producing such books as *Culinary Campaign in the Crimea* (1857).

3. First position in ballet is a standing posture in which the backs of the heels are touching and the toes are turned out.

4. "Rareyfaction" (rarefaction) is given a French usage here in its application to the "refinement" of the manners of a dog.

5. Hepzibah Pyncheon, from Nathaniel Hawthorne's novel *The House of Seven*

Gables (1851), is an old maid whose gallant attempt to support herself by opening a shop in her ancestral home sets the plot into motion.

6. "Ah, no! I will not go back! Oh, never, never!"

7. The "Turkeys" are the Turks. "Bosh" meaning empty or worthless is indeed of Turkish origin, popularized in England by Morier's novel *Ayesha* (1834), where those parts of the Koran not from the Bible are pronounced "bosh."

8. Probably Andrew Fuller, an English preacher of the early nineteenth century, who wrote books about Calvinism published in both England and the United States. It could also refer to Thomas Fuller (1608–1661), a popular English preacher, chaplain to Charles II and noted for his common sense.

MISS BEULAH'S BONNET

1. Leghorn refers to a hat or bonnet of straw plaiting made from a particular kind of wheat, cut green and bleached, imported from Leghorn (Livorno) in the Italian province of Tuscany.

TOO LATE

1. The lines come from Shakespeare's *Hamlet* (II.2.97–98), a tragedy that deals in part with parent-child relationships.

2. This quotation is from Tennyson's "The May Queen," in which a maiden rejects her lover in order to be queen of the May.

3. Mear, Bethesda, and Cambridge are the names of tunes found in the early New England hymnals. The words which Hannah sings were set to the tune of Cambridge. "My beloved is mine and I am his" comes from the Song of Solomon (2.16).

4. *Hypatia* (1853), a novel by Charles Kingsley, deals with the fifth-century conflict between pagan and Christian values as seen through the eyes of the monk Philammon.

5. See the first note to "Freedom Wheeler's Controversy with Providence."

Explanatory Notes

SOME ACCOUNT OF THOMAS TUCKER

1. In the biblical story (2 Kings 4.8–27), the son of the Shunammite woman calls out, "My head, my head," and dies. Elisha, who had predicted the son's birth, returns to raise the child from the dead.

2. The reference here is probably to the geographical location of the New England village of Saltash, no longer existing, named after a town in Cornwall, England.

3. *mania à potu*, madness for drink. (This appears to be a cross between Latin and Spanish.)